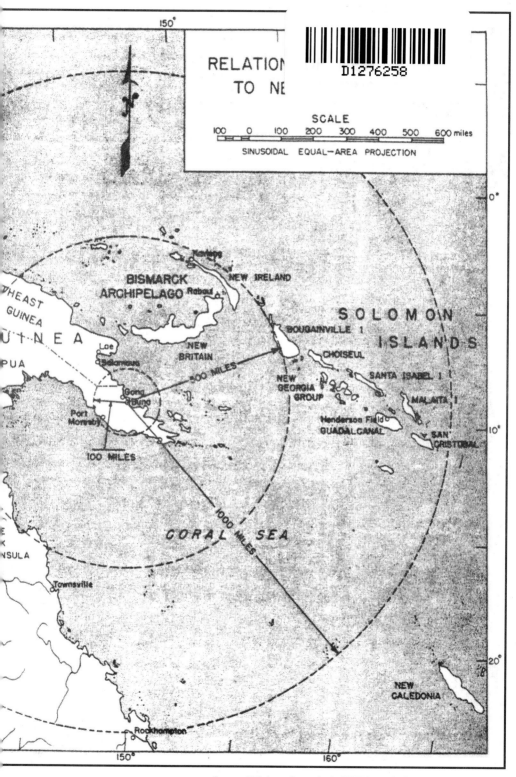

RELATION...
TO N...

D1276258

SCALE

100   0   100   200   300   400   500   600 miles

SINUSOIDAL EQUAL-AREA PROJECTION

150°

0°

THEAST
GUINEA

UINEA

PUA

NEW IRELAND

BISMARCK
ARCHIPELAGO Rabaul

NEW
BRITAIN

SOLOMON

ISLANDS

BOUGAINVILLE I

CHOISEUL

SANTA ISABEL I

Loe

Salomua

Gona

Buna

NEW
GEORGIA
GROUP

MALAITA I

Port
Moresby

Henderson Field
GUADALCANAL

SAN
CRISTOBAL

10°

100 MILES

500 MILES

100 MILES

1000 MILES

CORAL SEA

Townsville

NSULA

20°

NEW
CALEDONIA

Rockhampton

150°

160°

Papuan, U.S. Army Campaign in WWII Series, U.S. Army, Washington, D.C.

The Good Soldier

*The Story of a Southwest Pacific
Signal Corps WAC*

by

Selene H. C. Weise

Burd Street Press

This Burd Street Press publication
was printed by
Beidel Printing House, Inc.
63 West Burd Street
Shippensburg, PA 17257-0152 USA

In respect for the scholarship contained herein, the acid-free paper used in this book meets the guidelines for permanence and durability of the Committee on Production Guidelines for Book Longevity of the Council on Library Resources.

For a complete list of available publications
please write
Burd Street Press
Division of White Mane Publishing Company, Inc.
P.O. Box 152
Shippensburg, PA 17257-0152 USA

Library of Congress Cataloging-in-Publication Data

Weise, Selene H. C., 1921-
    The good soldier : a story of a Southwest Pacific Signal Corps WAC
/ Selene H. C. Weise.
        p.   cm.
    Includes bibliographical references and index.
    ISBN 1-57249-169-8 (alk. paper)
    1. Weise, Selene H. C., 1921-   . 2. World War, 1939-1945-
-Personal narratives, American. 3. World War, 1939-1945--Pacific
Area. 4. United States. Army. Women's Army Corps--Biography.
5. Women soldiers--United States--Biography. 6. Pacific Area-
-History, Military. I. Title.
D811.W4228   1999
940.54'8173--dc21   98-53765
                                                                     CIP

PRINTED IN THE UNITED STATES OF AMERICA

Dedicated to:

Roland,
Haakon,
Niels Christian

"The WACs were my best soldiers. They worked harder than men, complained less, and were better disciplined."

General Douglas MacArthur,
in an interview with Colonel Westray Battle Boyce in Tokyo

Contents

Illustrations

Maps

Acknowledgments

Thanks to the staff at the Women in Military Services for America Memorial for their early encouragement and care of the original letters and documents now in their archives.

Thanks to the commanding general of Fort Gordon, Georgia, for his wonderful hospitality when I was his honored guest. Very special thanks to Carol Stokes, Ph.D., command historian, United States Army Signal Corps, Fort Gordon, Georgia, for her intercession in obtaining the grant that paid for the transcription of the original book from audiotape to paper. Without Dr. Stokes there would be no book. She and her staff, especially Mark Dunn, have searched their archives for historical material, have taken books from their shelves, and given them to me. And they rolled out the red carpet when I was a guest at Fort Gordon. Thanks also to the curator of the Signal Corps Museum at Fort Gordon, who generously pulled material out of boxes and off shelves to refresh fifty-year-old memories.

It was WAC historian, Lt. Col. Ret. Bettie J. Morden's, timely reading of the manuscript, as a matter of fact two readings, and her generous and enthusiastic letter of praise that kept the project from dying on the vine.

My grateful thanks also go to Diane Gordon, Ph.D. for her careful and insightful reading and suggestions. It was at her suggestion that the book has become much more than just a memoir.

Thanks to Linda and Tom Fowler, my dear friends of Dry Fork, Virginia, who put the original manuscript into the computer in a form that I could use. Thanks too for their unfailing and enthusiastic support of this project.

Thanks to Carol and Mike Walton, also Donald New, for keeping my house and grounds under control during the many months that this book has been a work-in-progress, and for their love, friendship, and enthusiastic support. Many thanks to the members of Mt. Tabor

Baptist Church, Keeling, Virginia, for their loving support and help with the many tasks that are part of any major project.

My gratitude and thanks to Dottie Van Haaften for her early reading of the manuscript, her perceptive criticisms, and her sharp pencil. It was she who got the book into its final organizational form and put on that essential polish. And thanks again for her generous willingness to put aside her other concerns when I shouted for help in getting the book camera-ready for the publisher. My computer skills are simply not up to the job. Finally, I would like to acknowledge the advice and assistance of White Mane Publishing's editors Diane and Martin Gordon and of the expert staff of Beidel Printing House.

Introduction

Some years ago, my middle son asked me, "Mother, when did you become the person I know now?" I thought a long time, and said, "Haakon, I don't know, but let me give it some thought. It's a good question." I got back to him later, and said, "Haakon, the answer to your question is, during my army service."

In order to join the army, I flew in the face of tremendous prejudice against women in uniform. This prejudice was shared by my family, who were embarrassed to have me in uniform when I returned home on my first furlough. My letters, which form the skeleton of this book, lay unread and bundled until 1981, when I applied to the Veterans Administration for service connection for the damage done to my lungs during service in the South Pacific. The memories of my war service lay suppressed all those years. Why? I don't know, but, I think now is the time to bring them all out.

I have written this book to tell the story of a small select group of Women's Army Corps enlisted women who served with the Signal Corps during the Second World War in the Asia Pacific Theatre. But mostly, it is a labor of love for my sons, about their mother's development.

The book is based on eighty-five documents pertaining to my service in the Women's Army Corps from February 11, 1944, to December 6, 1945, most of which are my letters to my mother. (The originals are now part of the archives of the Women in Military Service for America Foundation in Washington, D.C.) All of the letters are as I wrote them. None have been edited. Because the other half of the correspondence with my mother did not survive the rigors of overseas service, I have interlarded the letters with comments explaining reference to family and other personal matters. A limitation on letters to my mother was the censor who was usually also my commanding officer, and so the commentary contains much material that is not referenced in my letters. We were not permitted to tell anything at all about what we did, where we were going, or when we left or arrived. Consequently, I have had trouble dating our movements.

I tell about my trip to the recruiting office in Galveston, Texas, and cover the process of being taken into the army, the trip to Fort Oglethorpe, Georgia, for basic training, and the training itself. From Fort Oglethorpe I went to Fort Monmouth, New Jersey, for training as a cryptographer. I was one of only 150 Signal Corps WACs in the South Pacific.

After leaving Fort Monmouth, I went home for an overseas furlough where I received a chilly reception from some of my family who did not approve of my soldiering. I was relieved to go back to Fort Oglethorpe for overseas training. From there I went to the port of embarkation and the troopship, *Monterey*, formerly a luxury liner. After twenty-seven days at sea, we went ashore at Oro Bay, Papua, New Guinea, via a cargo net and landing craft to wade ashore on the beach.

From Oro Bay, we flew to Hollandia, Netherlands New Guinea, via C-47. We took enemy fire on the way, but made it safely. We spent seven months in Hollandia working in a theatre headquarters. My letters in this period talk about the incessant rain and the strange blowing mud of New Guinea. I tell about the seven-day weeks, and the rotating shift work. I was glad I was there, despite the rigors, and enjoyed my friends. We had no supplies for women but had been well equipped to go to Greenland. However, we were infinitely resourceful in scrounging and midnight requisitioning.

My commentary includes the ways we enlisted women managed to circumvent the many restrictions on our activities, including a swim out to an anchored Landing Ship Tanker (LST).

In late March or early April 1945, I left alone by ship for Manila, after losing a friend and fellow Signal Corps WAC to leukemia. Manila was a shock. The enemy had destroyed the city house by house with demolition charges. The evidences of the Japanese occupation and the battle for Manila were everywhere, including unburied bodies.

The battle was still in progress when we arrived with the enemy just across the Pasig River. They took potshots at us from time to time. Individual enemy soldiers would infiltrate into the civilian life of the city, turning up in the mess lines of Philippine workers. They would be recognized and driven off. At one point, I found myself looking down the rifle barrel of a Japanese soldier hidden in the bushes around a cemetery.

I describe in awed detail to my mother the final days of the war. We lived through the days between the Hiroshima bomb and the final surrender in apprehension. We dropped the second bomb, and the Japanese still did not surrender. I knew well what would be involved in an invasion of Japan. I was in a position to know which units would be in on the initial landings. I believed my own outfit would go in shortly thereafter, the same as we had in Manila.

The night before the final surrender, my buddy and I were asleep in our tent near the Signal Center when we heard shouts and cheering. She and I pulled clothes on over our pajamas and made a dash for the center. We stood and watched as the announcement came in over the teletype that there would be a surrender. Others in Manila got the news almost as soon as we did, and we could hear the ships in the harbor blowing their whistles. The sky was filled with searchlights from the antiaircraft battalions.

When the great bells of San Sebastian Church began to toll, I started to tremble, realizing the end was near.

On November 8, 1945, I left by navy troopship for the United States and a tumultuous welcome home. I had acquired three battle stars twenty-two months after my visit to the recruiting office.

PART ONE

United States

St. Louis, Missouri and Galveston, Texas

I graduated from Webster Groves High School in January 1940, four months after Germany marched into Poland on September 1, 1939.

My first full-time job after gradua-tion was at the public library in Richmond Heights, Missouri, a small suburb near Webster Groves. My salary was paid by the federal government through the National Youth Administration, one of the big programs of that period, de-signed to scoop up the hordes of unemployed young people. Those were the days when every freight train that rolled past my house was covered with young unemployed men going someplace else to find work. My job at the library con-sisted of arranging magazines and shelving books, a totally mind-numbing way to earn a living. I was

Selene Harding Curd
Class of 1940 Webster Groves High School
1940 Yearbook Webster Groves High School

not allowed to learn anything that might make me a competitor for one of the librarian jobs. I quit after a few months. My mother was appalled that I would give up a job, any job, during the Depression.

At that point, my sister, Alice, came to the rescue, and paid my tuition to go to a secretarial school. She had graduated from the Washington University School of Nursing in 1938, at which time she started work as a private-duty nurse. She still lived at home, and her salary combined with my mother's for her work as a ticket agent for the Missouri Pacific Railroad was enough to support the three of us, however modestly.

In the fall of 1940 the first draftees were called up, and that took many of the young men from my high school class. At the same time the sleeping giant that was American industry began to stir and wake up. On my way to school each day on the streetcar I passed the Scullin Steel Mills that had been closed all the years of the Depression. One day someone was outside cutting down all the weeds that had grown. A few days later the big doors were open, and I could see the fires from the furnaces. I was thrilled. Jobs suddenly became more plentiful, and I was offered a job at Stix, Baer and Fuller, one of St. Louis's very nice department stores. I left school to take it. It was to work in the School Bureau, selling school uniforms to the children in the many Catholic schools in St. Louis. However, while I was still in secretarial school, I had taken a civil service exam, along with all the other students in the school, and promptly forgot about it.

In September 1941 I received an appointment as a clerk/typist at Camp Wallace, Texas. I resigned from Stix, Baer and Fuller and left by Greyhound bus for Galveston, Texas. I moved into the YWCA residence, along with many other young women who had received letters just like mine. It was a very nice place to live, and I enjoyed it immensely. Camp Wallace was still in the hands of the constructing quartermaster when we got there, and so my first job was to keep track of government property to be transferred over to the army, as the base was being completed. It was pretty primitive, but very exciting. I thoroughly enjoyed being a part of the huge undertaking that was getting us ready to go to war. One day I looked out the window of the building where I was working and saw my boss, a WWI captain, driving a huge piece of earth-moving equipment. I thought that looked like fun, and so I went outside and when the captain drove past, I shouted up to him, "Hey, that looks like fun." To which he replied, "Wanna try?" "Sure," I said, and climbed up. The captain showed me which levers to pull, and which pedals to push, and off I went. It was wonderful, and I thought, "Boy, now this is what I would really like to do for the war effort!" However, the best I was ever able to wangle was a two-and-a-half-ton truck at Fort Monmouth.

On December 7, 1941, my twentieth birthday, the Japanese bombed Pearl Harbor, and we went to war. Camp Wallace had originally been activated as a Coast Artillery training camp, but at some point, it changed over to antiaircraft training. When the base construction was finished, and handed over to the army, I moved from the constructing quartermaster to the army quartermaster and went on keeping track of property. When the transportation part of the Quartermaster Corps split off, and became the Transportation Corps, I moved again. I found I had learned a great deal from two parents who worked for the railroad.

My parents had divorced when I was quite young, probably about nine years old. I saw my father very rarely after that until I started to work at Stix, Baer and Fuller. When I started to work downtown, I took the commuter train from the little station where my mother worked, and my first day on the train, as I walked down the aisle looking for a seat, I heard a voice call out, "Hey, Selene." It was my father, grinning from ear to ear. From then on we rode the train together every day. We talked a lot about his work; I was interested, and I encouraged him. It paid off later. He worked in tariffs, and he explained what they were, and how to use them. A tariff is a schedule of charges for services rendered, and so they can apply to any number of things, but railroad tariffs were enormous books with the lists of charges for moving almost anything, and there were separate tariffs for people and things. When I was asked, many months later, if I knew anything about railroad tariffs, either passenger or freight, I could say, "Yes." I learned freight from my father and passenger from my mother.

All that led to an incident one dark night that I still remember with chills down my spine. I got a telephone call late one evening, asking if I could come to Camp Wallace. I had to find someone to drive me, but I went. They needed someone from the Transportation Corps to check in some freight coming in later that night. I stood beside the siding that came in to Camp Wallace from the mainline of the Santa Fe Railway and watched an immensely long freight train pull in, followed by a second equally long. Each car was a flat car with two humps covered with heavy canvas; each car had an armed guard standing at each end. When someone removed the canvas and showed me what was underneath, I was told, "These are our newest and most top-secret weapon. It was the forty-millimeter antiaircraft gun. My job was to go down the length of both trains, and inspect each gun and certify that it was there. I was awed by the responsibility, and thought, "I'm too young even to vote." I think back today about the responsibilities I held and the things I did, and I think, "Great Scott, the war was won by a bunch of kids!" I have two solid brass candlesticks on my sideboard made from shell casings from one of those guns.

I don't remember when I met Howard Treacy, but it was sometime during the winter of 1941–1942. He was simply one more young man in the mass of young people at Camp Wallace. He was a staff sergeant in one of the training battalions. I probably met him when I was checking in troops from a troop train, and signing them over to a battalion. We started dating, and he wanted to get married. In the late thirties and the early forties the peer pressure to get married was pretty horrendous. My friends really turned up the heat, and coupled with the pressure from Howard I agreed, and we got married in the base chapel in September 1942.

I knew within a few months that it was a mistake. I worked long hours, and often weekends, and was on call. I simply could not be the wife he expected. I could not do his laundry in the kitchen sink, shop with ration coupons, cook the meals, and keep the house and be a wife to him. I was resentful and so was he, and so, in the summer of 1943, I walked out and went to a hotel. In the meantime he got orders to go to Fort Ord in California, preparatory to going overseas. I believe we were together less than ten months. After he left for Fort Ord I moved back into our little apartment, and he left me his car, which simplified my life considerably, as he had gotten resentful of having to drive me back to the base every so often. We wrote to each other often and agreed to a separation. However, until a divorce, I would continue to receive an allotment as his wife.

During those months that we were together, I would stop by the recruiting office every so often to look at the recruiting posters, and talk to the sergeant on duty. I was definitely interested in becoming part of the army I had come to love, but there were two impediments that kept me out. The most important was the War Manpower Commission. As long as I was a civil servant in the army I could not join the Women's Auxiliary Army Corps. The other was auxiliary army corps. I was only mildly interested in being an auxiliary anything. In this case I could go overseas as a member of the WAAC, but if taken a prisoner by the enemy I would not be covered under the Geneva Convention. I would have no insurance and no veteran's benefits. In short I would not be a real soldier. However, in the summer that Howard went to Fort Ord, on the first of July, the WAAC was disbanded and the Women's Army Corps was formed. The WAC was part of the army, and the rights and responsibilities were the same as the men's. Now that was right down my alley! I knew that as soon as I could get free of the War Manpower Commission I would join up. That did not happen for quite some time.

Since I was all alone in Texas, and had not been home for more than two years, I got enough time off to go home for Christmas. I got myself one very precious berth on the Missouri Pacific train that ran between Galveston and St. Louis. I got home on Christmas Eve Day. It was a lovely Christmas with all the family present: my brother, Charlie, who was eight and one-half years older than me; his wife Evelyn and their baby daughter, Ann, who was just short of her third birthday; and my sister, Alice, six years my senior. My father had married again, and so I did not see him on that trip. We spent Christmas night at my Uncle Walter's. He was the second of my mother's four brothers. His two daughters were home, but my cousin Eunice's husband was in the army, I believe England at that time. He later went in on the D-Day landing and came home unscathed. My cousin, Jane, lived in Ohio with her husband and three children, and they had driven to her home for the holiday. My cousin, Stan Gore, and his sister, Mary Jane, were there with their parents. Stan was home from the army on an overseas furlough. He was also sent to Europe, and was wounded by friendly fire. Bob, my cousin Jane's husband, had a deferment from the draft because he was the father of three children. Later, in 1944 they had a fourth baby, but the government was so short of manpower, they drafted him anyway. He was thirty-six years old when he went in. Christmas presents that year were the kind everyone made. By that stage of the war everything was very hard to come by, and so homemade was the order of the day.

The day after Christmas Mother and I packed up her clothes and boarded the train for Texas. I had invited her to come and stay with me for awhile. She was delighted to accept, as she had fallen on some wet leaves in the late fall and cracked a bone in her hip, and she needed to walk. My apartment was built right on the Galveston Seawall, and that was a perfect place for her to regain the strength in that hip. On the way back to Texas, I broke two pieces of news to her. The first was that I had left Camp Wallace and gone to work for the Santa Fe Railway in downtown Galveston. Camp Wallace had begun shutting down preparatory to being turned over to the navy as a lighter-than-air-base. They had already started moving the army people, both civilian and military, to Temple, Texas. I explained to her that Temple, Texas was not where I wanted to go, and that I had taken the job at the Santa Fe with the understanding it would be temporary until I could get my release from the War Manpower Commission, and that when I did I was going to join up.

Mother was aghast at my going into the army. She used the expression, "*those women*" several times in the conversation. She said, "*Those women are not your kind,*" which was code for trash. I tried to reason with her, asking her what she knew about "*those women.*" Her reply was that everybody knew what "*they*" were. There was no convincing her, and so for the next month and a half she walked on the wall and down below the wall on the beach and made a gratifying recovery. When she left in February to go home she had lost all traces of a limp. My mother had been born in 1888, and so she was just fifty-five that winter, far too young to be so lame. I admired her diligence in walking hour after hour, day after day. It was good for me to see first hand what exercise could do. Mother lived until just short of her eighty-fifth birthday, and never limped again. I enjoyed her long visit, and because I had the car I could take her several other places in South Texas.

She became seemingly reconciled to my joining the army, and accepted it as inevitable. When I discovered that I would need a birth certificate to join the army, she very cheerfully went to the recruiting office with me and gave a sworn statement that I had been born at eleven o'clock the night of the seventh of December, 1921, in Adams County, Mississippi, and weighed in at four pounds. Because I had been born in rural Mississippi, I had no birth certificate, and did not get one until the state established records for all of us in 1952. Mother again swore to the date and place of my birth. I got my release from the War Manpower Commission sometime in early February, and showed up at the recruiting office in Galveston, in February 1944. At the recruiting station I was given a test of literacy and general knowledge. The recruiters wanted to know how much education I had had. I was able to tell them that I had six years of high school with a college preparatory diploma. In my day that meant four years of Latin, two years of French, four years of English, chemistry, biology, and physics, orchestra, choir, and two years of art. My work experience included two years of civil service with the army. After the test, I was asked to take a seat in the hall while it was being graded. I waited, and I waited, and I waited some more. Finally, everyone in the recruiting office came out and lined up in front of me, and someone said, "We will take you in the army. You did so well on the test, we thought a mistake had been made on the grading so we re-graded it to make sure. No one has ever scored as high as you did." Someone laughed a little sheepishly and said, "We just wanted to see what you looked like."

Between the eleventh of February and the first of March, I received orders to report to Houston for a physical. The exam revealed that I was underweight. The doctor said, "You're a healthy young woman, and because you don't weigh all that much doesn't mean you shouldn't serve." So he fudged a little on the weight. I may also have been pretty persuasive on the subject.

After I was sworn in, I turned in my resignation to the Santa Fe and went home to pack up everything. Mother helped me prepare our few possessions for shipment home, plus most of my civilian clothes. I took her to the station for her trip home on the train, with my big wooden crate of clothes and household goods in the baggage car. I must have moved back into the Y or gone to a hotel between the time mother left and the time I reported for duty in Houston. At some point I took the car in to have it prepared for storage. Then I left Galveston, and I have never been back.

Fort Oglethorpe, Georgia

A small group of recruits went by bus from Galveston to Houston where we caught a train to Fort Oglethorpe, Georgia, which was located just over the line from Chattanooga, Tennessee, on the old Civil War battlefield of Chickamauga. We spent the first few days in the reception center. The barracks were World War I, one-story buildings, with big coal stoves in the center. The latrine and

Pvt. Selene H. Treacy
WAC Training Center, Fort Oglethorpe, Georgia

wash house were outside. If I could have found the gate, I would have gone through it.

In one of the innumerable, alphabetical lines we formed to get our uniforms and everything else, I met Jean Ann. My last name was Treacy, T-R-E-A-C-Y, and hers was Thompson, so we were always next to each other. Jean Ann was from Morristown, New Jersey and would be my companion on every assignment except one for the rest of the war.

Pvt. Selene H. Treacy
Civil War Memorial, Chickamauga Battlefield, Fort Oglethorpe, Georgia

On this occasion, we were being issued wool OD (olive drab) uniforms, Hobby hats, and OD underwear. Believe me, that man's army knew zip about women's clothes. Nothing fit, and if you see the pictures of me in my winter uniform, including Hobby hat, you can see what I mean. They were grim and fit like bags; however, some were fun. The fatigues and the high-top shoes were great, comfortable and useful; the GI pajamas and robes, and the green-and-white seersucker utility dresses were great. But, those French foreign-legion hats looked like saucepans on most of us.

Pvt. Selene H. Treacy
Civil War Cannon, Chickamauga Battlefield, Fort Oglethorpe, Georgia

After the clothes were issued, injections given, more physical exams, and so forth, we were assigned to a basic training company on the south side of Fort Oglethorpe. The quarters were decidedly more comfortable than the reception center. No more alternately freezing and roasting from that coal stove.

Basic training was scheduled to last six weeks. Almost immediately I developed a bad case of shin splints from all the marching and drilling. I remember my commanding officer, Jeanne Holm, being very kind over those shin splints. We considered her a good officer and others must have agreed. She retired a major general. She called me an eager beaver—which I probably was.

On the sixteenth of March I wrote to my sister Alice at Oak Ridge, Tennessee. At that time I didn't know what Oak Ridge was but I have since learned it was one of the sites of the Manhattan Project. She was the first director of nurses at the Oak Ridge Hospital, which was an easy train trip to Chattanooga. I implored her to visit me.

In my letter I write how much girl scouting was helping me in basic training. Scouting in the days when I grew up was predicated on military forms, so that being expected to do things at a certain time, in a certain way, was something I had experienced. My summers at Girl Scout camp helped a lot, and I knew it at the time. I enjoyed basic training but the shin splints I got from marching pretty well put an end to the drilling and other strenuous stuff.

I wrote another letter to Alice on the 23rd of March 1944:

"Received your letter today. It was a swell morale boost. I know the last letter was a shortie, but you have no idea of the schedule here. There is practically no time for yourself. I like it, though, in spite of the fact that I'm probably the army's most unsoldierly soldier. The drill is fun, but rather tiring. We have classes in everything from sex to army discipline. It's funny how little I knew about this end of the army. Last Tuesday, we played another company in basketball and got beaten. Earlier in the day, we had walked twelve miles, been to classes, scrubbed floors and steps, all that during the day. After dinner, we had a class in rhythm to help us march. More hoof work. After that, the game, then home to polish shoes and buttons, wash hair, and iron a play dress. So, you see why writing is a little difficult. That is besides studying, the studying we're supposed to do. I'm no great shakes on inspections and stuff, but I do like it, and it is only five weeks. About your visit: the weekend of second or third would be swell, and I have made arrangements for that time. Let me know when you expect to arrive. I can't get off until about 1:00 Saturday afternoon, and will have to be at Camp 11:00 p.m. Sunday evening. If you come to the post, when you arrive, I could show you around a bit maybe. Well, honey, I'm counting the minutes, so let me know right away. Mother sent me the clippings about your engagement. That was swell. I really can't think of much to write about, because our schedule is identical every day. We work awfully hard, and I've lost ten pounds. So if you have any extra food lying around, send it to me. We only get three meals a day, and I've never eaten so much or been so constantly hungry in all my life. It's amazing how much food all the marching and calisthenics and scrubbing requires. Well Hon, let me hear from you real soon. Letters received are much appreciated, by the way. I look good in my uniform. Bye, now, Love, Selene. Is this letter a little better?"

Close to the end of basic training, in late March, I thought my military career was coming to an end. One Saturday, after our usual Saturday morning inspections, I was called to the psychiatrist's office. At the time I was not sure it was a psychiatrist appointment. It was Saturday early afternoon and there was no one else in the building.

I went into a room where a woman introduced herself as a Major. She was different from the women officers I had seen in that she was wearing an all-male uniform. This might be acceptable nowadays, but fifty years ago, women officers didn't dress like men. Immediately little red flags went up. To be quite honest, I was frightened of her. She was a sizable woman—I mean, not big, but certainly larger than I was. She had me sit down and asked, "Why did you join the army?" I told her I wanted to help win the war. It seemed such an obvious question. Then she started in on me. She accused me of having problems with my father. Well, this was ridiculous. I hadn't lived with my father since I was nine years old and had scarcely even seen him, so obviously I'd had no problems with my father. With my mother, yes, but that's not what she talked about.

She then asked me more about why I joined the army. I tried to justify myself for thinking that I could make a contribution, and that I thought it was important to win the war.

She told me that she was from Vienna and proceeded to really accost me. "What do you know about war, a little girl like you from a sheltered environment?" She didn't know a damn thing about my environment. I was starting to get very angry. She accosted me again about how her entire family had been lost to the Nazis. I expressed my sympathy, and yes, I knew what was going on in Europe. I thought, what did that have to do with me?

It occurred to me that she might be a lesbian, and maybe she was coming on to me. I was a pretty red-head, rather fragile-looking, which was misleading, as my subsequent army career proved. I was slim and had pale, red-haired skin. Probably it was an interview to screen me for going overseas, but at this point I had no idea I was being considered for that kind of duty.

I left the interview to go back to the barracks feeling frightened and threatened. I was sure I was going to be kicked out of the army. My buddy, Jean, was terribly upset about it in my behalf. I never knew if any of the other girls were questioned because Jean was the only one I told. I was horribly embarrassed about being called in by the psychiatrist, and I didn't want anyone to know.

Jean and I were very upset and so we decided we'd go to the country club. I should explain that Jean's parents were well-to-do. Her father was an officer of a large New York bank and had memberships in several clubs, including a country club, and so Jean had a complimentary membership at the club in Chattanooga. She and I enjoyed it much and often.

At the country club, for the first time in our lives, we got systematically and deliberately drunk. We had dinner, but were still drunk. While Jean was in the ladies' room, I slid quietly under the table. I don't remember how the country club personnel responded. It was all very vague to me, but probably they called a cab and sent us back to the post. Somewhere along the line I remember encountering MPs and later discovered I had lost a gold pen given to me by my family. I felt bad about that.

Back at the post Jean decided I needed a shower. She shoved me into the shower fully dressed in my coat, WAC hat and uniform, and emptied a box of Lux flakes on my head and turned on the water. I stood there and let her do it.

The next morning I awoke someplace other than my regular bunk. The charge of quarters came in to tell me to report to the officer in the orderly room. I couldn't move. I absolutely could not move. I was still that drunk. Pretty soon, the officer came in. She stood at the foot of the bed with her hands on her hips, looked at me and said, "Well, Treacy. I have to give you some company punishment for this. You were drunk and disorderly and out of uniform." I don't know what that was all about because I got back with all my uniform. Anyway, she said, "You're going to be confined to quarters for the rest of the day." Well, obviously that was not a problem.

1st Lt. Jeanne Holm (Front Row, Fifth from the Left),
WAC Commanding, Co. 14, 21st Reg., Third WAC Training Center,
Fort Oglethorpe, Ga., April 19, 1944

Fort Monmouth, New Jersey

One day, about two weeks before the scheduled end of basic training, I got called to the orderly room and told to pack. I was among five women at Fort Oglethorpe given orders to report to Fort Monmouth, New Jersey. Jean Ann Thompson, Willa Wasson, and I would be together for most of the rest of the war. The other two women did not survive the rigors of training at Fort Monmouth and washed out.

We left Fort Oglethorpe and went to Fort Monmouth by train. One night while we were sitting in the Pullman car one of the girls told a joke about the little bee that went from pansy to pansy, and when he got home, he couldn't make his honey. The girl who was sitting on the armrest was so shocked and surprised that she fell off into the aisle.

We arrived at Union Station in Newark, New Jersey, on a Saturday night and were met by Jean Ann's parents who had driven from Morristown. We visited with them, then took another train to the Jersey Shore where we were met and taken to Fort Monmouth and installed in barracks.

The buildings at Fort Monmouth were red brick, built in the thirties and surprisingly comfortable. The room where we slept was long with rows of double-decker bunks on each side. There were about forty women in our class, and so there was space for all of us in that one big room. We were twenty on each side, ten bunks with two women to a bunk, top and bottom.

Our first meeting at Fort Monmouth was the next day, on a rainy Sunday afternoon, in the WAC day room. We were told at that time we were a specially selected group of women who would be trained for top-secret work for an overseas assignment. We had been selected for our level of education, experience, and an Army General Classification Test (AGCT) of 135 minimum. We were told we had been cleared for top secret and what that meant. We were not to tell anyone what we were doing, nor were we even to discuss our work among ourselves outside of the classroom, no chat in the mess line, the latrine or laundry rooms.

I must say, we were all impressed. In the coffee hour that followed, I discovered that of the forty or forty-five women present, I appeared to be the youngest, and the least educated. We were told that another identical group of WACs was being trained at Camp Crowder, Missouri, and that eventually the two groups would be combined. The group that trained at Fort Monmouth included a like number of male officers, making a total of ninety students.

Those three months at Monmouth were wonderful. We were treated as professionals with no Kitchen Police (KP), or other duties, except keeping our own quarters up to army standard. Our training included theories of cryptography, techniques to increase speed and accuracy of our typing and pigeoneering.

One of the sessions I remember most vividly was the day we went to the pigeon lofts. I know now that pigeons were used extensively in the Second World War, and that there were pigeon companies in the Signal Corps. We were each handed a bird, and a little message on rolled up paper which was supposed to be inserted in a tiny tube on the bird's leg. I had never handled a bird in my life and was misled by the lovely silkiness of the pigeon's feathers. I didn't hold him firmly enough. That bird gave one almighty flap, and was gone. He arrived at his destination minus a message.

Those of us who already possessed a license to drive were given instructions in driving in convoy. None of us had ever driven a truck before and we had a marvelous day driving around the New Jersey countryside in a convoy of two-and-a-half-ton trucks. What a marvelous sense of power to drive by civilian traffic stopped at all the intersections to let us pass!

Another day was spent on a map-reading problem. Jean and I drove around the New Jersey countryside on a beautiful spring afternoon in an open Jeep. I remember the apple trees were in bloom.

One two-day period was spent on bivouac and was really awful. Jean and I shared a pup tent constructed of two tent, shelter halves. The whole area was a sea of mud, and it was cold. Our job was to man a field switchboard that was the shape and size of a big suitcase and came with a stand. When opened the actual switchboard was vertical, and the cords and plugs were in the half that was horizontal.

There we sat on metal folding chairs in about an inch of water. Every time a call came through we got shocked. We tried everything, cardboard, dry blankets, and dry clothes, but nothing worked. We simply had to endure the shocks. Little did we know that all the rain and mud were merely a foretaste of things to come.

Trainees Operate Portable Field Message Center Switchboard
Fort Monmouth, New Jersey

Signal Corps, *The Outcome*, p. 509

We learned to operate several types of cryptographic devices. There was one, a small device to be used in the field, called an M-209. It was a mechanical device of surprising complexity enclosed in a metal box. It came with a code book that included dates and times. For each appropriate date and time there was assigned a set of letters. Those were the settings for the machine. The receiver had the same code book so that the machines could be synchronized to enable each party to a communication to use the same settings and be able to read each other's messages.

We learned a lot of basic mathematics in which I did very well, surprising me because I'd never been interested in math. The most interesting part was the theories behind codes and ciphers. I never used it in the field, but, interestingly, many years later, in the '60s, I drew on this training to become a pretty fair, machine-language computer programmer.

Up to this time, the only thing I had ever known about codes and ciphers was from Edgar Allen Poe's story, *The Gold Bug.* That was the story in which he broke the code with a letter count.

During the time I was at Fort Monmouth, the Italian government capitulated to the Allies, making the Italian troops co-belligerents, thereby joining in the fight against the Axis in Italy. Suddenly, the Italian prisoners of war at Fort Monmouth became allies instead of enemies. To welcome the now ex-prisoners of war to the Allied side we threw a party in the Post Exchange (PX). The Italian prisoners of war showed up in nice, spanking, new uniforms.

The PX had a big central room where they served beer by the pitcher. I didn't drink beer but virtually everybody else did. Many of the American soldiers were Italians and had relatives in the group of ex-prisoners. There was dancing, there was singing, and a lot of beer drinking. It was a joy! My friends would order a pitcher of beer, and I would order vanilla ice cream with a cup of coffee that I poured over the ice cream. It must have been the caffeine, but I could get just as high on coffee and ice cream as my friends did on beer.

An added bonus to the fascinating spring at Monmouth was the New Jersey Shore and New York City. We had our weekends free, that would be the last time we did, and we made good use of them, with help from Jean Ann's parents. They took us on their sailboat a couple of times. We also made many trips into New York City where I had friends from Camp Wallace, Texas.

I wrote to my mother from basic training and from Fort Monmouth, but none of those letters survived. A letter I wrote to Alice about a trip to New York where I ran into Major Rust did survive.

Of Major Rust I wrote, "Whom I ran into on the corner of Broadway and 42nd the first night that I went to New York. I have covered the New York City nightspots pretty thoroughly. Maj. Rust was with the old 69th Coast Artillery that opened up Camp Wallace way back when, and he was still there when I went out there to work. He is now on his way over to someplace, but the night I met him, he was on his last leave before shipping out, so he wondered what he was going to do with himself for an evening in the big city, and would I care to go over to the Astor bar and wonder with him. I did, and we had a marvelous time: the 21 Club, the Stork, the Diamond Horseshoe, Jim Dempsey's, and Diamond Jim Brady's, and the top of Rockefeller Center at about midnight, and that was really beautiful. I like New York. Last Sunday, I covered practically the entire Central Park. It was a lovely spring day, and some of the arbors were covered with wisteria, all in bloom. There were so many people in uniform from all over the world, all enjoying a brief respite from the week's work in the sunshine. Well, dear, this period is almost over, so I'll close now."

This particular letter is interesting, because it was written on a typewriter that had only capital letters. We were trained to type very, very fast. This was accomplished by typing rhythmically, in all caps, and with no punctuation.

By the time we finished our Signal Corps training the last week of June 1944, we had developed a tremendous *esprit de corps*, which was to stand us in very good stead in the months to come. I had discovered my fellow WACs, with the exception of the five of us who came from a basic company, had been recruited from other bases and other specialties. I have surmised that there were simply not enough WAC Signal Corps types available to man even a small detachment in the Southwest Pacific. So they had pulled likely Signal Corps candidates from wherever they were available in the entire stateside Women's Army Corps to run through two otherwise all-male officer

Signal Corps training companies. Training highly qualified enlisted women with male officers had some interesting results. At the end of the course, the top three spots in the class ranking were taken by enlisted women.

About the 26th of June, after our three months of training, we were given furlough time. Taking the train at Little Silver to Newark we all scattered for home. From Newark, I took the Pennsylvania Railroad to Washington where I caught a train to Charlottesville, Virginia, to see my old friend from Camp Wallace, Walter Myden, before continuing to St. Louis.

Walter and I had been corresponding since he had left to go to military government school at the University of Virginia at Charlottesville. I arrived in Charlottesville late at night where I was greeted on the platform by a team of United Service Organizations (USO) ladies. Walter knew I was coming but I hadn't been able to give him the exact time I would arrive so there was no one to meet me. I needed a place to stay and a very nice lady named Lily Newell took me to her home. She had a son in the South Pacific and we talked a long time. She was very interested in what I was, though I could not tell her what I was doing. I did tell her I was having a final leave before going overseas and that I was in Charlottesville to see a friend. I stayed that night in her spare bedroom, or what I thought was her spare bedroom. It turned out to be her son's room. At some ungodly hour, probably 4:00 or 5:00 in the morning, I heard squeals and squeaks and carryings on. Her son, the poor guy, had flown home all the way from Australia to find a lady soldier in his bed. I had breakfast with them then moved to a hotel, which had been my original intention.

Walter and I finally connected and spent Sunday together and went to see Monticello. Walter had very little time off duty as his schedule was as busy as mine had been at Fort Monmouth. During the Second World War, you received a lot of training, pushed into a short period of time.

Monday afternoon I took the train from Charlottesville cross-country to St. Louis. Except for my sister Alice, who was home from Oak Ridge, I was not well received. Upon seeing me in uniform, my mother suggested, "Wouldn't it be better, dear, if you wore something else while you're home?" In war time, that was not possible. I was very disappointed and hurt, but in retrospect, I realize my family and friends thought I was just playing soldier and that my army service was not for real.

I was glad when my furlough was over. I carried orders to report back to Fort Oglethorpe for overseas training.

Pvt. Selene H. Treacy
Portrait taken at home on furlough, July 1944.

Fort Oglethorpe, Again

At Oglethorpe, I was happy to be back with my friends. We continued to develop an *esprit de corps* which proved to be uncomfortable for the officers, but served us well.

My first letter from Fort Oglethorpe after I got back is on the letterhead of the Monticello Hotel in Charlottesville. It was dated the 10th of July.

"Dearest Mom: Well, here I am back at Oglethorpe. Arrived yesterday morning to find Chattanooga restricted for WAC due to a fight the previous week. So, it's really a good thing that Sis didn't come. I wasn't even able to call her, the MPs brought several of us directly to the post. Jeepers, it was hot. I can't say as yet what cooks here. Jean and I are bunkmates again, and this is definitely it."

The "it" was overseas training, and so it meant that I would definitely be, or was already, on orders to go overseas.

"It is so good to be back with the gang again. The trip down was very uneventful and I slept very comfortably. That's about all there is, so I'll close now. Love, Selene."

I give the address as Headquarters and Headquarters Detachment, Battalion Pool, EFS, Fort Oglethorpe, Georgia. EFS stood for Extended Field Service.

There is a letter written on July 19, which was ten days later, and I say:

"Dearest Mother: I haven't a single thing in the way of news. We're stuck here in the pool waiting for the rest of the people that will make up our outfit. Result, the soonest we can possibly leave will be the 1st of September, so Jean and I, rather than just sit, have gotten ourselves a job as cadre over in a basic company. I don't know how we're going to like it, but it's something to do. I'm going to call Mrs. Newell, the lady in Charlottesville. I'm going to call her tomorrow. Alice is coming next weekend. Yippee. In re to the checks, I had to cash the small one instead of the others, because I couldn't get adequate identification. No telling when we'll get paid, and I have to buy three pair of shoes. Isn't that something?"

I had to buy my own dress shoes because I wore a size $5\frac{1}{2}$ AAA.

"I can't wait until those PJ's arrive, as it's hotter than h___ here. By the way, send my bathing suit PDQ. We have a swimming pool here. Also, any fruit. Not much else to tell about, haven't done a blessed thing, but sit and go to the PX. So, goodnight for now. Love, Selene."

I have another letter dated 21st of July.

"The PJ's are simply super. Really, they are just adorable. Just exactly what I had in mind. The kids are green with envy. They say they'll make good curtains when we get where we're going. Thanks for the bobby pins and the paper. Looks like we're going to be here awhile. We have to wait until the middle of August to start training, so Jean and I are going to do cadre work to pass the time. Must go."

The next letter was August 2nd:

"Surprise. Ha-ha, a letter. I have a few minutes to spare, so I thought I'd drop you a little line, and also please find the check enclosed. I didn't need it after all, so here it is. Not much doing today, except they took all the basics out of our barracks, and gave us a gang waiting for overseas assignment just like we are. Boy, a lot of them have ratings, and most of them are truck drivers and so forth. Oh, boy, they're a tough bunch. If Jean and I can do with this outfit, we can handle anything, I'm sure. It's interesting work, though, and we like it. We're all dressed up to go to the movies tonight now. Expect to see Bette Davis in *Mr. Skeffington*. Should be very good. Not much else to say, so we'll close now. Just ate the last of the oranges today. Love, Selene."

I wrote a letter the following day, August 3rd.

"Dear Mother: Pardon the pencil, but it's still quite early in the morning, and I'm in the office, and I don't have my pen with me. I know you won't mind. I just had a few minutes, and was wishing for this minute that I was at home and had never even met up with the army. I haven't felt as depressed as this in a long, long time. It seems as there has been some money missing upstairs. The long and the short of it is, one girl got out of the upper bunk to go to the latrine late the other night, and in climbing out braced herself on the opposite bunk. The girl asleep in the bunk screamed and grabbed the kid by the arm. The next morning, it was reported that the kid had been feeling under this girl's pillow where she kept her money. There were witnesses that would swear to the girl's innocence, but the result is that the poor kid has been through a terrible grilling with the MPs. No food or sleep. All of her belongings have been searched and her mail confiscated. It seems almost as bad as Germany, that suddenly an innocent girl would be grabbed by the long arm of the law and put under suspicion. It could happen to any one of us; however, there is one rosy side. All this girl's friends have signed a petition in her behalf. I'm very curious as to how that will be received in official circles. I'll let you know. It's funny that such a thing should knock me so hard. I scarcely know the girl, but its moral portent is something that can't be overlooked. It's at times like this when prayers really are a help. Jean and I went to see *Mr. Skeffington* last night, and I haven't cried so much in a long time at a movie. If you can get the chance, don't miss seeing it. Well, dears, I must close now. Thanks for the papers; they came yesterday. Love, Selene."

A letter to my sister, August 4th:

"Hi, Sweetie Pie: Just finished a letter to Mother. I'm so proud of myself; I've written her every day for a week. I guess she's surprised by the onslaught of mail, but I don't have much actually to do in this job—just be here. So, I have time to catch up on my letter writing. I'm afraid that our coming up to Oak Ridge is out of the question, as they have canceled all overnight passes, as we will be moving over to EFS to join a company any day now. I don't relish the prospect of the training, but it will be good not to have to sit around anymore, although Jean and I have managed to keep ourselves fairly occupied. I've been writing letters all week to people I've owed since the year one. Just finished one to Syd. Jean and I went to the country club for dinner last night and had a swell time. It was so lovely out there. We had dinner on the terrace and the moon over the Tennessee River was just beautiful. I guess we'll have that to look back on when things get pretty rugged overseas. When and if you see Eldon again, give him my best regards. Did I tell you that Howard has gone overseas from San Francisco? I wonder where from there. He went out as an infantryman. By the way, I'm feeling fine now, back to my old self again. Well Hon, let me hear, and be good. Let me know about the army."

That was when my sister Alice was talking about joining the army. I didn't know until many years later, that she had, in fact, tried. She didn't tell me that she was turned down. Just a few years ago, forty-some years after the war, I was told what had happened to both Alice and my brother Charlie, who had tried to join the Seabees. Charlie was turned down because of a heart murmur; it was his understanding that Alice was turned down for the same reason. There was resentment on the part of both of them and I can understand. The fact that I, the baby of the family, a most unlikely army candidate, would be the one who not only was accepted by the army, but went through all the training, and did extremely well. I was the youngest child, and I was a tiny baby born under most inauspicious circumstances on a plantation outside Natchez, Mississippi. It was unlikely that I would have survived at all, but I did.

Well, another letter on August 4, same day. This one is to Mother.

"Dear Mom: I guess this terrific onslaught of letters has got you somewhat floored, but I'm working up a reserve so when we start our training and I don't have much time, you can't accuse me of being neglectful. We're due to start August 15, so when the letters stop you know we've started training. Last night Jean and I went to the country club for dinner. We felt the need of a morale boost, so we took a cab and blew ourselves. We had a wonderful time, a lovely light supper on the terrace. The club is a beautiful sort of English-style building perched on a cliff overlooking the Tennessee River. Lookout Mountain is just opposite. It was a beautiful night, full moon, twinkling in and out between busy scuttling little clouds, sparkling lights from homes in the hills across the river, and a violin softly playing nostalgic things like 'The Merry Widow,' and 'Goodnight, Sweetheart.' It was a terrific morale boost from this dismal post. The final shot was when Jean put a quarter in the slot machine and won four dollars. Luck, eh, what? It really was a swell evening. As a result, we've been in a good humor today, in spite of the scorching weather. It's hot and muggy. Well, Sweetie Pie, 'bye for now. Haven't anything much more to say, so will close and go to dinner. Probably something horrible! Love and kisses, Selene."

Another letter to Alice. This was the 7th of August.

"Got your letter yesterday. This is going to be short. We moved today, and we will leave any day from now on. In re to the car: first, it's not really my car to sell."

The car was Howard's and I had been driving it in Galveston until I joined the army, at which time I put it into storage. The battery was taken out and all the other things which needed to be done to store a car. The plan was that later on Howard's father would come down from Michigan to drive it back so Howard would have it when he got home.

Alice didn't have a car, and at this time in the war, cars were as scarce as hen's teeth. I can understand why she wanted it, but it wasn't mine to give.

"In re to the car: First, it's not really my car to sell. For my part, it would be OK, but the title is in Howard's name, and as you know, he has left If you could get mother to send him the title and ask him for his signature, I won't be able to handle anything now, because I won't know whether I'd be here to receive your next letter or in Timbuktu. I'm so tired I'm just numb, so I'll close now."

Well, obviously, we had started the training. I don't know exactly what day it was. The next letter was August the 8th to Mother. I said:

"Well, I'm not quite as numb tonight as I was last night when I wrote to you, although running a close second. This is pretty rugged, and I don't mean perhaps. Right now, Jean and I are sitting under the trees in a little park in the battalion area. It's nice and cool and my clothes are dry for the first time today. The heat is terrific, although one compensation: We have awfully good mess. Tonight we had two vegetables and a salad, and it was all very good. On the whole, I don't think it will prove to be as rough here as we expected; pretty much on the order of basic training. Saturday afternoon, Jean and an older woman, Alice Conlon, and I went to the country club. It was a scorcher of a day, but it was nice and cool out there high on the bluffs over the river. Alice is 42, and a schoolteacher. Well-traveled and witty and an entertaining companion. In fact, Jean and I have become quite attached to her. She's a very genuine person. We had dinner on the terrace again, and in the course of the evening, I met a very attractive lieutenant and had a date with him for Sunday. He was awfully nice and very handsome, a big, blond Danish chap. He had a little sister in the WAC. We went bowling and had an awfully good time. He's an osteopath in civilian life, in the Medical Corps in the Army, Elbert Ashbaugh, by name. In re to the cans: Do you have any old cold-cream cans? I have to take a year's supply of powder and so forth in all-metal containers. If you have any, rush them right away. I can't remember any more questions you asked, and I don't have your letter with me. We have so little time to write now, that all of my letters will have to be brief. By the way, Jean and I have taken to reading her Bible. We read the book of Ruth the other day. Well, dear, must close now. Love, Selene."

Another letter dated 9th of August 1944:

"Dearest Mother: Hi, Hon. You'll have to admit that I've been doing very well with the letters. I'll admit that there isn't much in them, but there isn't much to put in them. We're just drilling and going to classes, just like basic, only more so. We go to bed about eight o'clock every night. Between all of that, we go over our clothes and so forth. All mine are still so new, I won't have to turn in very much. Pretty soon I'll be sending my suitcases home, but don't expect them until I've given you definite word. It's hotter here than the shades of Hades. It's terrific night and day. Thank heavens, though, the mess is super, best I've seen in the army. I heard a cute dirty joke the other day about the little girl who asked her mother where babies came from. The mother said that babies came from little seeds like little flowers. A few days later, the little girl went to the seed store and wanted to buy some little baby seeds. The clerk said, 'You go home and tell your mother that babies don't come from seeds anymore; they come from slips. After that, I'll close for the day."

Postcard from Lookout Mountain, 10th of August:

"Dear Mommie, just to let you know, I still see hills in Georgia. Hotter than h___, but believe it or not, having fun. No more time or space. Love, Selene."

August 19th, a letter to Alice. There was quite a period of time between this letter and the last one.

"I received your letter yesterday. Our mail was all held up; that's why I didn't get it any sooner. In re to the car: I couldn't let you drive the car without insurance, and it doesn't cover you. It wouldn't matter what happened to the car, but what if some child were to run across the street in front of you and be seriously injured or killed? In the first place, you could be sued for everything you have or will ever get, and so would Howard and I, as joint owners. In view of the fact that I can't change insurance or anything without his say-so, as joint owner, I couldn't have it changed to cover you. The keys are with the car, and I have the receipt. I'm sorry about the car, but I wouldn't be willing to have you driving the car around with no insurance, and stick Howard's and my neck out while we were overseas. I'm sure you can see my point on the matter. I wish I'd been able to see you again before you left these here parts. We'll be leaving any time now. The training here is not so hard, but very intensive. We do a great deal of group singing. We had a songfest the other night. We did a beautiful song, the children's prayer, 'Now, I lay me.' It was lovely. I must close now. Love, Selene."

August 19 was the last letter I wrote from Fort Oglethorpe. We were not permitted to write things home as to exactly what it was we were doing while at Fort Oglethorpe or Fort Monmouth. Therefore, my letters were full of trivia and personal things. But, the overseas training was pretty much like basic, except that we did some things there that we certainly did not do at basic training. One of them was the infiltration course during which we crawled along on our bellies dodging 50 mm bullets being shot over our heads. Boy, was I glad I was thin.

Another experience was the obstacle course. Most of the things I did, I did pretty well, with this exception. Someone would swing a rope; you were suppose to grab it; then swing across a water obstacle and drop on the other side. Well, my problem was that I was too small and too light for the rope to get as far as the other side. I always managed to drop into the mud or water.

There was also a wooden wall with a cargo net which is a rope net we were expected to climb. Later I was glad I had learned to use it because I would need the skill.

It was easy to go up—you only had to be careful that the person above didn't kick you, and that you didn't kick the person below you. The problem was coming down. We were wearing big, heavy boots and if someone didn't watch where they put their feet, it could be right on your fingers. That was a real pain.

I would like to quote from Mattie Treadwell's book, *The Women's Army Corps*, part of the World War II series, prepared by the army:

"Overseas training for WACs was patterned on that given men preparing for overseas shipment. WACs were toughened . . . by long hikes in the rain . . . they swarmed up and down cargo nets; they crept up on the enemy in the field, adjusting their gas masks as gas bombs exploded around them, and practiced dispersion and seeking cover. They studied first aid, map reading, defense against chemical attack and air attack, malaria control; they got practical experience in using a compass, messing in the field and extended kitchen police duty."

Ms. Treadwell didn't think much of this training for women. From personal experience she was wrong. I would have hated not having the training we did.

Our training did not always run smoothly. One incident involved the ubiquitous dogs found on any army base. On our morning marches through the Chickamauga battlegrounds we would be joined by a dog or two, which the officer in charge would diligently try to run off. One morning, each of us had pocketed our breakfast sausage and did we ever collect dogs that day. Dozens of them. From everywhere. By the time we marched back through the gate, our numbers had been doubled by dogs.

Early in our stay at Fort Oglethorpe, our outfit was separated from a German prisoner of war camp by a big field. The prisoners had been part of the Afrika Korps under General Rommel and had been taken prisoner at the fall of North Africa.

Before starting to work as cadre, Jean and I became very adept at hiding in order to avoid being hauled in to do KP duty. One of our favorite hiding places was in the tall, silky grass that grew under the mess hall. It was nice and cool under there. We would take a couple of good books and crawl back underneath the building which had been built on a hill.

One morning there was a work detail of German prisoners of war cutting grass around the mess hall. They discovered us but bless their hearts, they just giggled, laughed, winked and no one said one word about our being under there. They were enlisted men and knew exactly what we were up to.

One very hot, moonlit night when all the barrack windows were open we could hear the German prisoners singing. They were good and a group of us decided we would like to get a little closer. We had been doing a lot of group singing ourselves and were impressed with what we were hearing.

We climbed out of bed and still in our nightclothes, carefully, sticking to the shadows, approached the fence. We didn't get close enough to be seen, but we were close enough to hear better. When they stopped singing, we carefully, again sticking to the shadows, headed back to our barracks.

In the middle of this return operation, along came the Officer of the Day. There we were stuck right in the middle of the open area. We draped our arms over the nearby clotheslines and gently swayed in the breeze, hoping we would be mistaken for laundry. It worked because nothing ever came of it. We thought we were very smart and very funny. However, I suspect the officer who saw us simply chose not to report us.

Shortly before the end of training Alice came to Fort Oglethorpe for a weekend. We went to church, then to Lookout Mountain. While up there, I began to feel sick. My wonderful nurse sister called a cab and took me back to the post hospital where I was admitted with a high fever. Alice had to get back to work, but returned the following day. I remember almost nothing of being in the hospital except the fever. I had a strep infection and was given sulfa. I recovered quickly and finished training.

The morning before we were to board the train for the port of embarkation, someone dropped a powder puff on the floor causing all of us to fail inspection and to be restricted to quarters for twenty-four hours. This meant that we would not be able to go to town or to the PX for last-minute shopping and errands. It was a Saturday and word of our situation spread quickly among the other overseas units. WACs came from everywhere offering to do our shopping. As for us, we gathered in a group between our two barrack buildings and started to sing. We sang everything we could think of, and as time wore on, some of the WACs started making up rude verses to the songs. Finally, the officers gave in on part of the penalty and restricted us to the post rather than to quarters.

Interestingly, we had gotten a lot of practice singing, as we sang on our daily marches. One of our number, Sara Jane Cady, was a trained musician and by the time we left Fort Oglethorpe, we had become very good.

I was delighted to be able to attend a piano concert by Hephzibah Menuin (sister of Yehudi Menuin) that final evening on post. Hephzibah was married to Captain Rolf, a military police officer, and they lived on the post.

The next morning, we were hauled out of bed for breakfast about 4:00 in the morning, some of us were taken to the railhead by truck. Other members of our group marched to the train. If I or the other women who were sick had been anything other than cryptographers, we would have been taken off the orders, but all of us had been trained and all of us were expected in the South Pacific, and all of us got there.

We boarded a troop train that was pulled up on the siding at Fort Oglethorpe. To the best of my recollection, we were about four cars of WACs, with a kitchen car and a baggage car. We traveled in fatigues and were restricted to living out of musette bags, our duffel bags were in the baggage car. Somewhere along the way, we hitched up to a troop train loaded with men. We went by the L&N Railroad between Chattanooga and St. Louis. At St. Louis, we were picked up by the Missouri Pacific. This was familiar territory to me as I had lived all my life beside this railroad. I even saw my parents' house as we went by.

We got to Pueblo, Colorado, in early evening. The troop train pulled into the yards to change engines, and all the troops were decanted out to march up and down along the train for some much-needed PT, that's physical training. We were then told we would be staying overnight in Pueblo because our baggage car would have to be unloaded and reloaded into a Denver, Rio Grande and Western car, and there were no baggage handlers to do the job. With one voice the WACs shouted, "Let's go," and tumbled off the train. We formed into a bucket brigade between the two cars and the baggage moved in plenty of time to hook up to the D&RGW engine for the next leg west.

It was a wonderful trip and followed the route I had followed twice as a child. My father worked for the railroad, and so we had traveled on passes.

Because of my strep infection, I was not permitted to pull KP on board the train. In the days before penicillin, rheumatic fever following strep was a serious risk. The duty I pulled was guard, which necessitated standing on the platform between cars. It was glorious. I stood leaning on the lower half of a door, the upper half of which was open, with the wind blowing through my hair.

At one place in Western Colorado, the train pulled off on a siding to take on water. Alongside the tracks was a long line of packing sheds where cantaloupe and watermelon were being prepared for shipping. The packers came over to the train and started tossing melons through open windows to the troops. We ate as much as we could eat.

After six days, we arrived at Camp Stoneman, Pittsburg, California, very early one morning.

Camp Stoneman, California and at Sea

In the army, anytime troops either left or arrived someplace, they got fed. Any time after midnight, it would be breakfast. I remember very little about Camp Stoneman, California except its beautiful dun-colored hills, which changed to lavender and rose at dawn and sunset. We got our teeth fixed, new glasses, more winter uniforms and four Hobby hats.

At Camp Stoneman we acquired our escort officer. My memories of her are pretty grim. She was a tall, handsome, dark-haired woman. She talked to us about the trip and romanticized the beautiful steamship, which had been a luxury liner, that would take us to the South Pacific. She also glamorized going to war. That was a lot of rubbish and it didn't take us long to find it out. The real problem with this officer was she didn't give us the data we needed to be prepared for what was ahead of us.

On September 20, 1944, we were again hauled out of bed at 4:00 a.m. I rode to the dock on the Sacramento River in a truck while the rest of the WACs marched. From there we took a riverboat down the Sacramento River to San Francisco Bay. It was a beautiful trip. Each of us had been given a box lunch.

When we sailed out of the Sacramento River into San Francisco Bay it was dark and everything was blacked out; you did not see any lights except the red and green running lights on other ships. The riverboat we were on pulled alongside one of the piers at Oakland.

We were marched right through the pier from one side to the other, and boarded the *Monterey* which was docked opposite.

The *Monterey* had been built and launched in 1931. It may have been a wonderful ship, but all of the beautiful woodwork, paintings and other decorations were covered up with plywood. In addition, there were between five and six thousand troops aboard a ship that had been built for about seven hundred passengers.

Our cabin had been designed for four people and probably had had upper and lower bunks. However, all of the furniture had been taken out except a dresser and a basin with a mirror. There were four tiers with three bunks each. Shipboard bunks were rectangles of cast iron piping with a sheet of canvas lashed to the pipes.

Well, this wasn't what our escort officer had described. It didn't take us very long to figure out that officer had never seen where the enlisted women were going to sleep. She had talked about her experiences traveling as an officer, and it was probably nicer than what we were seeing, but I suspect it wasn't as grand even for her as she had described to us at Camp Stoneman.

We were absolutely floored. We had no porthole, or window. Air was blown through the cabin, but there was no air conditioning. We had been issued a mattress cover made of unbleached muslin, which was a coarse fabric and indestructible, but no sheets. We rolled up clothes, or our life preservers, to use as pillows and the mattress cover became a sheet.

We were given one or two canteens of fresh water daily but that is not very much in the tropics. With five or six thousand troops aboard, I'm sure we could not have carried much fresh water and that was before the days of desalinization. The short supply of water also meant we had no way to wash clothes except sea water. We had to bathe, wash, brush our teeth and wash our clothes in salt water. Because we could not wash off our own salty sweat, we suffered with terrible prickly heat.

I went aboard that ship with a strange feeling. It was the only time, and it didn't last very long, that I sensed the enormity of the decision I had made. I had never been out of the country but had traveled around the United States. However, going aboard that ship, seeing the conditions, and not knowing where we were going really struck me with a tremendous sense of awe.

Had we been told of the hardships in advance, and had we been told about things that could have made us more comfortable, like salt water soap, it would not have been such a shock.

Our two meals a day were served in a dining room below decks. We weren't exercising so we didn't need more than two meals but we sure would have enjoyed more.

The tables in the dining room were chest high and we stood. This eating arrangement was necessary because of our large numbers.

Many of the troops had trouble eating in the tremendous heat, with the smell of food, and the smell of unwashed bodies. The diet was, as army diets were overseas, very short on salads and fruits. We had canned fruits, but in those days fruit was canned with a lot of sugar. Others were seasick.

It was a very tough trip. And in fifty years' retrospect, it doesn't look any easier.

We spent our days on the promenade deck. A group of us had staked out a little spot where we would go after breakfast, or whatever meal was served us before noon, where we sat on the deck under the windows that opened into the ship's ballroom. There, bunks, like ours, had been set up for the men. Most of them spent their time sitting on their bunks simply because the windows were open and they were about as comfortable in there as they would have been on the deck.

The deck was a mob scene. Walking up and down involved stepping over people. There was astonishingly little friction. Everyone simply endured and was generally good natured about everything.

Our quarters were three decks down. The heat was unbearable, so we spent as little time there as possible.

With one exception, Lieutenant Lillian Steinberg, no officer ever came down to see our quarters. Our escort officer who had promised luxury and romance never came down. In fact, the only time we saw her, if we saw her, it was someplace else. It was her job to at least show she gave a damn about us. But she didn't.

At one point I was asked to sit with another WAC in the hospital section of the ship where she was locked in a cabin. I was told only that she was a nymphomaniac and had been in the ship's dental office to have some dental work done when she agreed to have sex with six men. I sat with her every day, and other people stayed with her at night. She seemed OK to me but we never talked about what had happened to her. However, I was uncomfortable about her situation. At one of the ports, where the ship docked, she was quietly taken ashore. I never heard of her again. Now I am inclined to question the explanation I was given. I believe she probably agreed to have sex with one and was raped by five.

We stopped for several days in dock at Hollandia, Netherlands New Guinea at Foxhole Dock Number Two while the ship was being partially unloaded. We did not go ashore. The mountains looked like they had been drawn by little children, just straight peaks. This was new geological territory and the mountains had been created by volcanoes. They came right down to the sea and roads had been scoured out on their flanks. The road from Foxhole Dock Number Two left the dock area and wound up the mountainside. Any ship in dock was clearly visible to traffic on the road as it wound back and forth around hairpin turns. The dock area was covered with piles and piles and piles of fifty-five-gallon drums and other materials for fighting the war. At that time the battle for Leyte was being supplied from Hollandia, the Leyte landing had taken place in early October. Ships by the hundreds were in the port and anchored offshore.

The deck above the promenade deck was called Officer Country. At the bottom of the steps was a chain with a sign "Officer Country" which meant no lowly enlisted person could enter. Jean and I found this very irritating. Well, one night we sneaked up the steps and then proceeded to climb one of the stacks.

No one on the ship could see us, but the guys unloading cargo on shore could. They were using floodlights and had a good view of the stack. They started to laugh, cheer and point. The MPs aboard began running all over trying to find us. To avoid capture, we separated and scooted down the steps where we got lost in the crowds on the deck.

Jean and I never analyzed why we decided to run up the stack of the *Monterey,* but I believe it was out of a combination of boredom and resentment. It was not the hardships *per se* that galled us, but we had begun to realize how badly we had been prepared for this assignment in comparison to the enlisted men. We not only had been totally unprepared for the conditions aboard ship, but we had been lied to. In addition, while we had been well supplied for Greenland, with all wool uniforms, including four Hobby hats, and four-buckle Arctic's, we had no clothes that were suitable for the tropics. The enlisted men had been issued six or eight suits of either khakis or fatigues, and a like number of cotton undershirts and shorts, whereas we furnished our own brassieres, and our army issue underpanties were rayon, which rotted in the heat. We looked on ourselves as badly treated slaves. It was a real comedown from the treatment we had received at Fort Monmouth.

We were at sea far longer than the trip would normally have taken because we were traveling without convoy making us vulnerable to enemy attack. We zigzagged all over the Pacific to avoid Japanese submarines.

Being most vulnerable to enemy submarine attack at sunrise and sunset, we stood on deck in lifeboat drill during these times. We would put on our life jackets and wait for the sun to either come up or set below the sea. In the tropics, you don't have dawn and you don't have dusk. The sun comes up and the sun goes down. When the sun goes down, it looks exactly like somebody dropped it over the side. Long, beautiful summer twilight's are phenomena peculiar to the extremities of the earth. You don't have them around the equator.

At night we were not allowed on deck because one lighted cigarette could be seen for miles at sea.

PART TWO

New Guinea

Oro Bay, Papua, New Guinea

Twenty-seven days after we boarded the ship in San Francisco, we were told to pack, we would be landing the next morning. Early the next day, the ship's engines stopped, and we heard the anchor chain drop. We were a long way from shore; all we could see was a line of blue raggedy mountain peaks, and the most heavenly deep blue sea in between. We were lined up on the deck in helmets with liners in place and packs on our backs; over the side we went. We couldn't believe it. We were actually going to make an infantry landing from a landing craft! Down the cargo net we went! We had no problems with going over the side of the ship and down the net, we had practiced that at Fort Oglethorpe, but no one had taught us how to hit a moving target. Some of us met the landing craft coming up, with jarring results; others, like me, dropped into thin air, with equally jarring results.

When we reached shore, the front of the landing craft went down, and we waded ashore. By this time, we were all laughing. It all seemed a little dramatic.

Fifty years after that memorable landing, I went on a cruise with my daughter-in-law's family, including my own nineteen-month-old grandson. We boarded the *Britannis* in Miami for a trip around the Caribbean and Mexico. The ship had an awfully familiar feel to it. I later found out it was the *Monterey*. In a chat with the captain, I learned that the landing at Oro Bay was occasioned by the ship's previous trip to Oro Bay in July 1944. One of New Guinea's many volcanoes had erupted, filling the air with fine powdery volcanic dust, leaving zero visibility. The ship went aground on the reef while trying to grope its way into the harbor. The captain, seeking to avoid a second encounter with that reef, sent us ashore in landing craft.

What a beautiful place Oro Bay was! It had heavenly blue crystal clear water and a glistening white sandy beach with coconut palms draped gracefully over the water.

I wrote an undated letter, my first from overseas. Because of the censorship regulations, we were not permitted to say where we were or when we had gotten there. I wrote:

"Dear Mommie: Your youngest progeny has, at least for the time being, ended her wanderings. We arrived today, and is it good to be here! The trip was terrible. The conditions and the treatment were the worst I've ever seen."

Of course, what did I have to compare it with? However, it was the worst treatment we had received in the army. It had been a shock.

"However, there were a few compensations. Jean and I are still together and we were able to talk to the fellows on the deck during the day. I ran into two fellows from St. Louis, lovely chaps, both of them. We had long, four and five-hour conversations on practically any and everything. I think that kept body and soul together. In another letter I will tell you more because I want folks back home to get a few things straight, but I'll do it tomorrow. This letter will be short, because although it is only 5:00 p.m., it's almost dark. I'm sitting out on the beach, which is our front yard. The country around here is quite lovely and isn't any hotter than Galveston, although when the monsoon season begins, no doubt it will be worse. Our barracks are just about fifty feet from the water. The coconut palms are all around the place and some of the fellows cracked some open for us this afternoon. Good, too. The trees are full of very gaily colored parakeets which make quite a racket. They are lovely to look at, though. Our barracks are long, one-story buildings, half screen and half plywood, and corrugated iron roof. Not beautiful, but nice and comfortable. Army canvas cots and—luxury of all luxuries—a sheet. The first we've had since Oglethorpe. We sleep on two blankets with one over us. I guess that sounds pretty crude. After conditions on board ship, it's pure heaven. We have nice showers and plenty of water;

another unheard of treat. The latrines are strictly country privies, but nice and clean. The WAC area is very new and raw, but I think after a time it will be very attractive, though I am afraid we will be picking sand out of everything here. There are lovely, rugged, raggedy looking mountains that loom up behind us. They are covered with fluffy looking mist what promises to be a good part of the time. That lovely mist is probably torrential rain. I don't know. The beach is lovely, and the water is warm close to shore, but wonderfully cool a little further out. We went swimming this afternoon. Thank heavens for my bathing suit. Some of the girls were so eager to get wet; they splashed in, clothes and all. I at least waited to change my clothes. I'm going to quit for tonight, and as long as I can't mail this yet, I expect to add more tomorrow. Perhaps we'll have mail from home by then. Here's hoping. It is absolutely all we have to look forward to. I know there will be something from you, dearest. You're so good about writing. It's been so long since any word from home and it's such a long way away. Night now.

"Good morning. It's a lovely day. The sky is bright blue and full of fluffy white clouds. Conditions here promise to be very nice, a little like Scout camp. Our mess hall is somewhat like the barracks, screens from about waist-high up, and cement floor. It's awfully pleasant, and so clean. It looks as though we won't be too rushed around here, as is the case in the States. The kids are allowed to smoke in the mess hall, and Jean and I loitered over coffee and her cigarette after breakfast this morning. It reminded us so much of our nice early morning coffee sessions at Monmouth. Although they've done a pretty good job on mosquito control here, we take atabrine, which in time will turn us to a terrible lemony hue, but it's not permanent and it's perfectly harmless. Very deglamorizing, though. In addition to . . ."

The censor blanked something out at this point. It's funny, they let me mention atabrine in one place and took it out the next.

"We sleep under netting. That's sort of fun, like a little playhouse. Last night after dark Jean and Sergeant Walker, our First Sergeant, and I, sat on the sand by the water and had a nice long talk. Sergeant Walker is a wonderful person. It was so pretty out there, bright stars and lapping water. Wondrously cool, too. We need a blanket at night, believe it or not. So far, we have not been assigned to duties and jobs yet, so our time is comparatively free, which is a blessing.

We have the most prodigious mountains of dirty clothes that need scrubbing. Our food is mostly dehydrated or canned, but it's very good. Hope we don't have any bacon, because no bacon—no bacon grease. And I've had so darn much grease in the army that I swear I was developing a curly tail and an oink in my speech. Coffee is wonderful, too. The well-dressed woman, white—that is, in New Guinea—is seen in green fatigue pants, khaki shirts, field boots, leggings, and fatigue hats. We look like Commando Katy, but they're very comfortable. As far as recreation, we don't know much yet. They have two dance pavilions right by the water. One we saw this morning is draped with gaily colored parachutes giving it quite a festive appearance. Judging from that, I presume dances are in order. Also, movies and a well-stocked PX. You remember, I told you the students at Monmouth were divided and some of them sent on before us? Well, they are here now, and maybe you think that wasn't a happy reunion. They have their work and really are looking wonderful. One girl in particular at Monmouth had a very pasty and pimply complexion. Also, she was very thin and nervous. Any little thing would set her off. I saw her last night and I didn't even recognize her. I have never seen such a complete change. She looked simply wonderful and her entire personality has changed. I wish her family could see her. It would certainly be gratifying."

Well, from the vantage point of fifty years, one wonders how much her family had to do with her original condition. She may have improved by virtue of being half a world away from her family. Anyway, going back to the letter.

"We had some natives working around the area. I hadn't studied them very closely because I didn't want to stare or seem unduly curious. But they get a hold of a bleach, and their hair is a violent yellow. Gee, it looks funny! They're fuzzy-wuzzies and no mistaking.

"Now here come the gimmies: a dozen pairs of white cotton socks, good ones. And would you make some white broadcloth panties? Good, durable ones. We have rayon panties and you know the voracious habits of ants. A pen, if you can find one, and my shower clogs. Those are things I need immediately. Things I'd like to have: any edible delicacies, canned or bottled; of course, Boston brown bread, particularly, anchovies, candy, particularly chocolate, if you can devise any way of packing it; and any other things you happen to think of. Toiletries of any sort. You know my favorite brands. Bath powder, particularly, and cologne or perfume, powder puffs, and any other little luxuries you happen to think of. However, bubble bath won't work in a shower. By the way, your idea of using boric acid powder as a deodorant is a wonderful one. I brought some with me, and it's been a godsend.

"I've thought of you constantly since leaving. I've wished so often that you could be here. It seems a shame that after all of the map and geography games we used to play after supper, that you and Charlie have to miss out on all of this. Here we were going to do our globe-trotting together. I certainly never thought it would be in this manner. It's a sad errand that brought me to this hither-to remote nook of the globe. We feel pretty subdued when we realize that every inch of this territory we occupy was fought for and hard-won, and that our fellow soldiers have bled and died for it. Speaking of fellows-in-arms, the boys here treat us like princesses. A lot of these boys have been here for a very long, long time, and they are as fine tempered steel. No monkey business. The girls here that have already gone to work say that the boys are so anxious to leave the office and get on up that they are most interested in getting the girls settled into their jobs. Well, dear, I guess this letter will get to you about the time of your birthday, so I want you to know I'll be thinking of you and the rest of the family celebrating. Eat a great big extra dish of ice cream for me. My mouth waters to think of it. Please, darling, have an especially nice party so you can write and tell me all about it. I'll think real hard and maybe I'll be there a little bit. I'll put a little birthday remembrance in the Christmas things. Well, darling, this letter has grown like topsy, and though I know you like long letters I'm afraid the censor won't. I'll write again real soon. Bye, now, Love, Selene.

"P.S. I also need a long clothesline, clothespins, and I'd like a new snapshot of Charlie."

About three nights after we arrived in Oro Bay, either Jean or I was assigned to the orderly room as charge of quarters. When one of us got an assignment the other went along to keep her company.

While we were sitting there, Jean Ann announced, "I'm hungry." This was a constant state of affairs throughout our army career. And so she went rooting around in the orderly room toolbox and came up with a screw driver and a hammer. Just as she walked out the back door, heading for the mess hall, the OD walked in the front. This night the OD was a WAC officer. Pretty soon, Jean was back with three plates, napkins, knives, a plate of biscuits and a tin of jelly. She offered the OD a plate, napkin, a knife, and some of the biscuits and jelly. She accepted. She never inquired about the source of the food, and when we were finished, she thanked us cordially and left. The truth of the matter was, Jean had gone to the mess hall and taken the padlocked door off the hinges. After getting what she wanted, she carefully returned the door to its rightful locked state.

The second letter I wrote to my mother was dated, 21st of October 1944, also from Oro Bay.

"Dearest Mother: I just received your third letter yesterday. It was manna from heaven. I laughed over Lassie's latest outrages."

Lassie was our very temperamental pup at home. She was half fox terrier and half some sort of spaniel, with pretty long hair and a sweet face, but she was the most neurotic creature God ever put on this earth.

"I'm really glad that Alice is not coming overseas. It's too bad for her to miss the experience, but it is a terribly hard existence and the civilians don't have the breaks that army personnel have. As yet, we have not been assigned to a job, so this is a wonderful vacation after the long voyage. We just loaf around and swim, eat, and sleep. The swimming is simply superb, and in spite of taking a quick dip and running back in, I'm rapidly acquiring an unwelcome tan, which everyone else, though, says is becoming. We have been restricted to the company area and the beach until today. We were allowed out, so Jean and I went to the PX and bought candy, overseas editions of popular magazines, and cute little cylindrical containers of tooth powder. Jean and I were simply in hysterics over trying to get ourselves straight on the Australian currency we are using. If the censor doesn't remove it, I'm enclosing a three-pence as a little birthday remembrance. I'm going to try and send a coconut later. Last night we decided to attend Jewish services. They came for us in a truck. We never did get to the services. It seems that someone misunderstood the time. But we had quite a trip through the jungle to the chapel. That was quite a jaunt—rough to say the least. But it was quite an experience, the trees meeting overhead and the silhouettes of palm trees against the sky. It was so black and impenetrable looking. The air was heady and warm with the smell of flowers. Let's hear real often. Letters are wonderful. What did you think of Lydia's marriage? I just finished a long letter to her. I think he must be the right one, although knowing Lydia it's hard to tell. In the same mail I received a lovely long letter from Walter. He will probably be down in this theatre sometime in the spring. You know, I've met a lot of men since I knew him, but I've never met anyone that could touch him. I also received a letter from Howard."

Private Treacy and Lydia Hobbs
Lydia was my closest friend. This photograph was taken when I was home on furlough after basic training.

Howard was my estranged husband; at that time we were legally separated.

"He's somewhere near here, but as yet I don't know where. I've left an opening for him to come and see me if he wants to. However, in view of the fact that his letters have become fewer and fewer, and more impersonal, I have my doubts as to whether he is interested in a reconciliation; I'm definitely not. And if he wants a divorce, I'd just as soon go ahead and finish this business off. I hate unfinished business. I have not met anyone I was very interested in, but I might sometime. Well, must close now. Will be waiting anxiously for word from you. Love, Selene."

I have another letter. Somewhere in New Guinea. 27 October 1944. This is written on a typewriter.

"Dearest Mother: This isn't going to be too long a letter as I'm working now and don't have too much time to myself. I don't have your last letter with me right now, but I'll probably start a short note in answer to your questions this evening and make this one just about me. First, I'm still in the same place and don't know how much longer we'll be here though. Some of our gang have been assigned to regular jobs, but Jean and I are still waiting for ours. It seems that we are destined to spend our army career in pools and staging areas. We are working in the company orderly room as clerks to help pass the time for us and to help out until a regular cadre is assigned. The work is pleasant and not too hard, but I'll be glad to get a regular job. Eight months in the army and still not working. This is really a swell setup, and Jean and I have been having fun. We've been swimming every day and it's wonderful. We are allowed to have dates from twelve noon to 4:00 in the afternoon, and from 6:00 to 10:00. We can't leave the area, but the men can come in. We've had several dances and last night some of the kids were having a beach party. We have a lovely recreation building right on the beach by the water. It is made of logs and roofed with palm fronds. It's really quite picturesque. Last night Jean and I had two of the loveliest dates—two of the nicest men I've met in a long time. We laid a blanket out on the sand on the beach and sat around and talked and sang. Then we laid on our backs and one of the fellows pointed out some of the constellations in the sky to us. It was so beautiful it didn't seem real, almost like something we had dreamed; the lovely white beach shining in the moonlight, palm trees and strips of white surf. The stars down here are so bright. It would seem almost as if we could pick them out of the night sky. It made me think of Galveston in many ways. I have found out where Howard is located but, of course, I can't tell you. It is quite some distance from here and the chances of our ever meeting are nil; I'm sorry in a way. I'd hoped we might be able to come to some definite understanding. I hate to have that problem hanging over my head, something unpleasant to reopen my civilian career. Your letter about Lydia and her marriage made me feel very much better about the whole thing. I know you don't make snap decisions. It seems funny to think of my little butterfly Lydia all settled down in married life. I only hope that she doesn't wait too long to have a baby. Under the circumstances Lydia would never want for a thing as far as her family is concerned should anything ever happen to Gordon.

"It seems too bad that he has to leave so soon. By the way, coming over on the boat I met Peggy Kaufman's husband, Sam Mosby. You remember he was in Sea Scouts, the ship *Sea Lion*. It was swell meeting someone from home and we had some nice long conversations. He looked awfully well and seemed to be with an exceptionally nice bunch of chaps. If you happen to think of it, I wish you would call her and tell her that I saw him, as she might be interested in knowing. Well, dear, there is not much to write about. The days slip by with languorous ease and we scarcely realize that they have come and gone. It is easy to see why the peoples in this part of the world are very backward. This climate is very conducive to mental torpor. It is more and more amazing to me every day how the men could have fought through all this heat. I don't see how they could have had the strength to. So far, the weather has been delightful, a nice breeze off the ocean all the time and cool at night. Practically no mosquitoes, of course. Mosquito control here is at an all-time high, oil spray and all that sort of thing. According to reports in the hospital this locality is now comparatively free of disease and germs usually associated with the jungles.

"Really, I'm getting very attached to our little WAC area here. We have a doll of a mess sergeant and the food is the best in New Guinea. It is amazing how a little ingenuity and imagination help out what otherwise would be dull, monotonous meals. After all, the supplies have to come from a long, long way off. Oh, yes. I wish you could have seen the natives building our chapel. The chapel is made of logs and when finished will be very attractive. But what amused Jean and me was the agility with which they climbed around on the log framework. Jean and I looked at each other with amazement when we realized how far away from home we are when we see some of the strange and unfamiliar sights.

"Well, dear, I must close now. I've run out of things to say so be a good girl and kiss all the family for me. Love, Selene.

"P.S. Please rush the white broadcloth panties. We are short on underwear and my rayon panties are falling apart already. I need the white socks, too. By the way, V-Ette bras, size 32, white. I need two."

In Oro Bay, as I said earlier, it turned dark about 5 p.m. The only place we had electricity was in the orderly room, latrines, and mess hall so there was no place to read and write letters. One night, another moonlit night, we noticed an LST had anchored just offshore. Jean and I were sitting on the beach and we could see it riding at anchor out there. I don't know who suggested we swim out, but we went into the barracks and quietly put on our bathing suits; nobody noticed us. It was so pitch-black dark that no one could see what we were doing. Then very quietly, we swam out to the LST and hailed the men on board.

They invited us to climb up the ladder that was hung over the side. That was a mighty surprised bunch of guys on that ship, but they were delighted. They fed us, we visited, had a great time, and then Jean and I climbed back down the ladder and swam back to shore. No one was ever the wiser.

I experienced one unpleasant incident at Oro Bay. When we first got there, we had enough space in the barracks so that you could walk between the beds pretty easily. We also had space for packing crates and boxes for our possessions.

One day another group of WACs was put into our building. It was going to be a temporary arrangement, but the period with both groups in the building was very crowded. We had to move our beds out from the wall and the packing crates had to go at the head of the beds because there wasn't any more than about six inches between any of the cots. In the new batch of WACs was a technical sergeant whom I did not know.

One afternoon as I was sleeping, she came to my bed and put her hand on my scissors that were laying on my crate. These scissors had been given to me by my mother when I got married. They weren't new scissors; she had used them during my childhood, and when she got another pair, she gave them to me. They came apart to be sharpened, so they were very nice scissors and something no one else had. When anyone needed scissors, they came and asked to use mine.

I said to her, "Sergeant, if you want to borrow my scissors, why don't you ask?"

"Oh, I didn't want to disturb you," she said, and left her hand on the scissors.

I said, "Sergeant, are you going to ask to borrow those scissors?"

She still didn't put them down. I don't know what else was said, but suddenly I had had enough. I was sure she was going to walk off with my scissors, and it was beginning to smell a little bit like she was pulling rank. I threw back my mosquito net, leaped out of bed, and hit the deck. Well, there wasn't room enough for two of us between the beds and I landed on top of her. She went sprawling across the next two beds flat on her back.

My friend Jean Ann saw what happened and went streaking through the back door headed for the orderly room. Because the back door was closer to the orderly room than the front door the sergeant used, Jean Ann reached the commanding officer before the sergeant. Jean Ann told the CO exactly what had happened so that by the time the sergeant got there, the CO was aware of the affair. I had been there longer and the CO knew what sort of person I was. When the sergeant came in and raised cain about how I knocked her down, the CO just smoothed everything over and said, "Look, it's better if you keep your hands off other people's possessions." Nothing further was ever said about it.

NEW BRITAIN

SOLOMON SEA

Kiriwino I

Goodenough I

Fergusson I

Normanby I

Milne Bay

Samarai I

CORAL SEA

NORTHEAST NEW GUINEA

Markham R

Loe

Salamaua

Sonananda

Buna

Gona

Dobodura

Ora Bay

Kokoda Trail

Pongani

Kinjake Borige Field

Embessa Field

Wanigela

Abel's Landing

Musa R

Kokoda

Ioribaiwa

Jaure

Kapa Kapa

Port Moresby

OWEN STANLEY RANGE

Kapa Kapa Trail

Abau Trail

Abau

PAPUA

PAPUA

MILES

50   0   100

The War Against Japan, p. 173

Hollandia, Netherlands New Guinea

The next letter I wrote to mother was written on the 7th of November and it's Netherlands East Indies.

"Darlingest Mother: As you can see, we've moved again. This time by plane, my first trip by air. It was quite exciting. In a way I hated to move, our former stop was so lovely with its white beach and heavenly tropical moon. We certainly do miss it. As for beauty here, there isn't any. The WAC area was cut right out of a jungle. It's on a hilltop of dark, red clay. As for trees, there's not one. Or even so much as a blade of grass. It's hot! We live in tents with the ground for the floor. As yet, we still haven't gone to work. Frankly, we're not too happy here. For one thing they don't need us. After all our training at Monmouth, I'll probably wind up in something else. Needless to say, after sitting for eight and a half months in the army, waiting for something to happen, I've come to the conclusion that it is a repetition of that little deal in Washington where they requisitioned ten WACs to replace five GIs. Result: so over staffed that no one has a damn thing to do. I think anybody joining the WAC is wasting their time. However, all in all, this is a nice vacation and we're gaining valuable experience. I'm glad I'm here. There is one job we can do, though. The fellows are so glad to see us. We've been treated royally. The fellows have given us everything from trousers to packing cases. We were very, very poorly equipped for this climate, so any extra clothes we can procure to supplement our issue is more than welcome. Well, darling, I'm sorry this is such a gripey letter but I'm so damn disgusted at the stupid inefficiency in the army. I'm sick of just sitting around. I was going to answer your questions, but in all the hustle of moving I've mislaid your letter. By the way, I've located Howard but he's too far away to ever see. Must close now and go to mess. I'll try to make my next letter better. Love, Selene."

I couldn't tell Mother about the trip up and our arrival in Hollandia. Twenty of us were loaded aboard a C-47, which we know now as a DC-3. We were all sitting along the sides in bucket seats and our duffel bags and other stuff were piled in the middle down the aisle. We were told before we left that we would fly over two combat areas and that we might take some enemy fire. We did. It was either over Aitape or Wewack, there was fighting at both places. We heard a loud bang, the plane shook mightily, and simply dropped. We did not go all the way down, however, and made it the rest of the way to Hollandia safely.

It was about eight hundred miles from Oro Bay to Hollandia. We landed on the biggest, longest airstrip I'd ever seen. It was huge! Just went on forever. We got off and the plane took off. There we stood. In the middle of the airstrip, all alone. As far as the eye could see there was nothing except across the field was a little operations shack but we couldn't see a soul. All of a sudden the door of the shack flew open and a bunch of guys came running towards us across the landing strip shouting, "We smelled you coming." In the process of jumping off the plane I had broken a little vial of Chanel No. 5 perfume and the air had wafted it right across the field.

They weren't expecting us and it seems no one else was either. Here we were, twenty WACs, and nobody knew anything about us. The men started calling around on the little field phones they used in those days. They called several of the regular WAC detachments but no one seemed to know anything about us until they called Base G, which was another outfit a little farther down the coast. It seems they were expecting some WACs so they sent a truck to pick us up.

We had made that trip with no NCO, and no officers or NCOs were there when we arrived. There were tents, but no floors. There was no mess hall and no orderly room. We were really shocked because this was the first time we had not been babied along and cosseted. We had never been left on our own, ever. The guys down the hill from

PACIFIC OCEAN

WHITE BEACHES

TAMI

Hollandia

Humboldt Bay

3

Pim

CYCLOPS MOUNTAINS

Sentoni

Lake

CYCLOPS

SENTANI

HOLLANDIA

HOLLANDIA

Tanahmerah Bay

RED BEACHES

2

Dépapré

5   0   5   10

MILES

The War Against Japan, p. 528

Hollandia, Netherlands New Guinea
Signal Corps Buildings

Signal Corps, *The Outcome*, p. 509

us were a black motor-pool company, and our first meal was shared with them. Little by little things improved. We were a group of cryptographers who went in advance of the rest of a headquarters. We moved in on the heels of the combat units; the fact that we had flown over fighting indicated that. I did not realize until I later read some World War II history how quickly we had come into Hollandia after it was supposedly secure.

I have a letter here 8 November '44.

"Dearest Mother: Summer has come to the tropics and they say this is only the beginning. The heat just shimmers like a living, breathing, thing and not a mere state of being. Jean and I went swimming yesterday. The beach is actually golden. I had always thought golden sand was the figment of someone's imagination, but it is so. The swimming is not very good. The bottom is so full of sharp coral, and it's very shallow between the shore and the reefs, with a vicious rip tide to boot. However, we had fun picking up interesting things off the bottom. The water is very clear and a beautiful shade of pale emerald. Some of the boys were diving along the bottom and bringing up huge chunks of coral with all sorts of funny little things clinging to it. One had a baby octopus on it. And another had the cutest little bitsy fish about three inches long with bright blue and orange marking on a gray background, tucked snugly into a little sort of a grotto. Last night we went on a beer party on the beach. We had a swell time in spite of the fact that I don't drink beer. There were about fourteen couples and they were all awfully nice kids. The fellows here are simply swell. I paired up with a first sergeant and he is going to take us riding in a Jeep this afternoon. This double-dating in a Jeep is sure fun, although an old-fashioned linen duster would certainly be in order. This red dust is terrible. My date this afternoon has a little opal ring from Australia he's going to give me, besides a big sheath knife and a locker for our clothes. He's so generous it's embarrassing. And all the fellows are the same way, just showering the girls with all sorts of life's little luxuries and native trinkets, to say nothing of prize Jap souvenirs. I already have two issues of Jap invasion money which I'll send home the next time I get a box ready to send home. By the way, I've sent a large box of woolen clothes home. Some are Jean's and some belong to two other girls. I'll send the addresses home in my next letter with a list of items to go where. Take the postage out of my money. I know this is a lot to ask, but we didn't know any other way. Of course, it will probably be months before it reaches there, so don't worry about it. Jean and I sent a little box of things to Jean's family and Ms. Thompson will send the things on home. I feel very bad that I couldn't send more, but there just simply wasn't anything more to send. So the bracelets are for you and Alice and the Aussie penny is for Charlie. I just couldn't get anything else for the rest of the family. But here in our new location I think we'll be able to buy more trinkets, to say nothing of some beautiful shells and coral. So when I've accumulated some more things, I'll send home a box for everyone. Well, chow time. Love, Selene."

Because of the censor, I never told my mother anything about my work. We were assigned to the Signal Center at USASOS, which stood for United States Army Services of Supply. I believe we were the first WACs assigned to that headquarters at Hollandia. The headquarters, where the Signal Center was located, was fifteen miles from where we were billeted at Base G. We were obliged to travel in an open two-and-a-half-ton truck over incredibly dangerous dusty roads each way, every day, seven days a week.

Holidays in Hollandia

The next letter is dated the 23rd of November. Netherlands East Indies. And I say,

"Dearest Mother: Well, today is Thanksgiving and boy is it hot. It seems funny for it to be so hot in November. We just had a swell dinner, turkey and all the fixings. I've got dressing coming out of my ears. Incidentally, what do you think of the letter paper? Needless to say, it's Jap notepaper and I presume their writing goes in the other direction.

"I received your letter of November 2nd yesterday, which means twenty days enroute. It did my heart good to know that at last you had heard from me and know that I'm fine. I have to laugh at the stuff the censor saw fit to cut out. I would have written more about the trip across, but it never would have gotten by the censor. However, I'm just as glad I didn't. For now it is just an awful and humiliating memory. And not really humiliating, because after all, I have you and Alice and Charlie and Lydia and Syd and Jean here, and all the rest don't matter. I'm glad that you don't come in for any of the ugly rumors about the WAC overseas because, after all, Jean and I are WACs, and the parents of the other girls have beloved and fine daughters in the army. Well, enough of that. I don't like it here but I'm glad I'm here nonetheless. Jean and I have at last been assigned to a job, believe it or not, in the work we are trained to do. And they were swell about putting us on the same shift. So T&T are still together and going strong. My, but we've been through a lot together! Our working conditions are very nice. I'm working with a swell chap from New York, or New Jersey, to be exact, by the name of Lieutenant Townsend. He reminds me of Walter and Van rolled into one, which, as you know, is a pretty good recommendation. He actually treats the enlisted WACs like ladies in the manner I feel they deserve. After all the treatment that a great many officers hand out, it's certainly not a reflection on us, but them. This letter is decidedly disjointed due to various and sundry interruptions. Coming back to Lieutenant Townsend, I'll have to confine my comments about him to impersonal observations in view of the fact that the censoring is done by same worthy gentleman. Suffice it to say I find working as his assistant enjoyable. The only thing about the job I don't like is the distance to be covered every day in an open truck over mountain roads. The dust is so thick you could cut it. The sun is hot. I believe in my last letter about living conditions—they're pretty rugged. But you know me, very adaptable. We have plenty of water and soap and as long as we have a twice-daily bath and clean clothes, the other things don't matter. I don't even mind the indigenous wildlife anymore. In fact, it's been a source of acute disappointment not to meet a forty-foot python walking around the jungle. We had detailed instructions on board the ship as to how to pick him up by the tail. Can you see yours truly swinging a forty-foot python by the tail? When this little WAC passes the time of day with Mr. Python, she's going to be running in the other direction. The jungle does look like I thought it ought: huge green ferns and big, tangled vines; tall, tall Banyan trees reaching for the sun, their funny roots rising up out of the still, black ooze. Banyan trees are peculiar looking things. Their roots are all mostly above the ground. I really do wish that I was back at APO 503. That was a lovely spot, the white beach and pale blue mountains rising out of the sea. Jean and I would swim out into the surf and just shout for the pure joy of being alive. One night there in the pale opalescence of evening, we gathered up lovely orange Hibiscus blossoms that had fallen to the ground and dropped them one by one into the surf and watched the white foam fold over them, carrying them out to sea. A wish accompanied each one. There was a flower for each member of our families. Speaking of wishes and such, in Burma there is a belief that butterflies are the souls of sleeping people. Consequently they never touch one. In the same connection they never wake a person suddenly, for fear the butterfly might have strayed too far away and not be able to get back in time. I like that, don't you? I like to think that some pretty little blue butterfly might be the soul of a little fat, cuddly baby, sleeping peacefully in his crib while his little soul flits gleefully in the sun. Lieutenant Townsend was telling me that one of his tent mates was expecting an addition to the family and every morning some silly bird took a seemingly perverse delight in heckling him by calling, 'Junior, Junior' at the top of his lungs. Incidentally, the baby was a boy. Lieutenant Townsend's comment to that phenomenon was 'Damn smart bird.' Speaking of birds, there is one fool fowl that can give the Bronx cheer in the best traditional GI manner, much to our amusement. One of the girls in our tent, Frankie, swears she heard a bird sing the first few bars of the prologue to Pagliacci, perfectly in tune, but sadly in the manner of a very worn-out tenor. I haven't heard that one yet, but I'll let you know if he should decide to increase his repertoire. I've been very fortunate in meeting a nice chap from Los Angeles by the name of Earl Thomson. He did all the sound recording for MGM. He's really swell, and we manage to have lots of fun on the beach and over in his office in the evenings. He's in the Overseas Motion Picture Service in connection with Special Service. Last night we saw a new movie right from the States on their little movie screen they use to preview pictures. It was such fun sitting around drinking warm, canned orange juice and the inevitable bread and peanut butter. Aside from his excellent company, he insists on keeping me supplied with practically any and every thing, from this letter paper to shell bracelets. It's wonderful. Well, angel, this letter has grown to astounding proportions. I haven't said everything, but I think I'll quit anyhow. Be good and give a big kiss to all. Love, Selene. Belated Thanksgiving. Regards."

I can say now what it was that I did. I didn't work as a cryptographer in Hollandia. I worked in the Signal Center, but as I said in my letter I worked as assistant to Lieutenant Townsend. His job was officer in charge, on whichever shift we were on, and my job was interesting. I logged in all the messages that came into the center to be encrypted and transmitted. Then I logged them as they went out on the wire with the time, which Headquarters they had come from, and where they were going.

The most interesting thing I did was in a sense a variation on the cryptography we had learned. Many of the incoming messages came in over radio and the reception oftentimes was not very good due to the tremendous humidity and high mountains that created interference causing them to be garbled. Often after a message had been decoded and typed for transmission, it still looked very much like it was in code. My job was to go through these garbled patches and try to figure out exactly what should have been said.

Virtually all of our messages had to do with incoming ships, or requisitions for materials. Because army communications were very stereotypical there were certain ways of saying things. Even though there would often be just a letter here and there that was correct, it was enough to be able to figure out the rest. My cryptographic training had prepared me well to do that, plus the fact I had a pretty good imagination. In addition, my first year at Camp Wallace, Texas I worked in the Quartermaster and had taken care of supply records so I was familiar with all the terminology. Most often I could send a message out to the recipient that made perfect sense.

That was the biggest part of my job working for Lieutenant Townsend. He was a joy to work for because he was a very considerate man. He enjoyed the WACs and he treated us all exactly as though we had been his sisters. As a matter of fact, I continued being friends with Lieutenant Townsend for many years after the war. Whenever I was in New York I'd give him a call and we'd have lunch.

This letter is a week later on the 30th of November 1944, and it too is written on rice paper.

"Darlingest Mother: Raining again. I thought awhile back we were going to lose the tent. It got to blowing. And these tents aren't anything more than a roof. We still have it but it really wouldn't make much difference. It's only a gesture in the right direction. The blamed thing leaks like a sieve. The mail just came in and all six of us got some. We had a fine old time reading choice tidbits aloud. Some of the families' reactions to letters from here are nothing short of phenomenal. Jean's mother wanted to know if our first stop here was a rest haven for rest and adjustment. That one brought howls. We did relax, but it was strictly on our own. You know, the fascinating art of goldbricking. It's an art to arrange to always be someplace else when they dream up a lot of stuff to spoil our fun. However, there is no goldbricking here: we work hard at our job and it's a relief. I just received letter number ten today from you, in which you told about Howard's father. Funny thing, I can't see any sense in Edna carrying on the way she does. I hope Howard doesn't know. I can't have one bit of sympathy. She and Howard are just alike. That sort of thing is weak minded, to say the least."

Edna was my husband's sister, and she was trying to get Howard out of the army. Howard's father, who had been widowed just six months earlier, was distraught over losing his wife and having his only son in a combat zone. Obviously, from my letter, I had little patience with that sort of thing. Howard stayed in the army until the war was over; either the army wouldn't release him, or more likely, he would not accept discharge while the war was going on.

"Well, I've got some news. I don't know how you are going to feel about it, but I think after due consideration you'll come to the conclusion, as I have done, that it's the only sensible course. I've written Howard for consent to get a divorce. If he consents, I'll send you a Power of Attorney giving you the right to get the divorce for me. You can turn the whole thing over to Mr. Noble."

Mr. Noble was a lawyer friend of ours.

"The only grounds needed is incompatibility. I hope you can see my point in this matter. This way it'll be all over a long time before either one of us returns home. It'll be long forgotten. Of course, I'll want my own name back. Household things should by rights belong to me, except perhaps the clock. However, if Howard wants any of the things, no doubt he will say so. I had a bitter disappointment yesterday to hear from Walter that he missed me at APO 503 by three days. I'm simply heartsick. Perhaps, though, we'll have better luck next time. I would give all the pay I haven't received to see him. He's a wonderful friend and I miss him. I miss him a great deal. He's all the qualities that I find important to me."

This letter was continued on December the 9th.

"I've been on night duty, and during that hellish time I've done nothing but try vainly to get some sleep. It was awful. The WAC officers seem to think that if you sleep in the daytime you're goldbricking. Consequently, we're hauled out at odd times during the day. Our officers in the company must have been ones that they didn't want back in the States. They are so awful and crummy. It's too bad, because I've known so many lovely officers, ladies through and through, long before Congress had anything to do with it. I know it's awful not to hear from me, and there is no excuse except I hate to write letters that reflect a bitter state of mind, because I know you would be disturbed, and needlessly. I find that if I fight it I can keep from becoming permanently warped. I never realized it, but before I joined the army I'd had a pretty sheltered existence. The people with whom I've come in contact have been pretty fine all in all. Over here, with conditions so basic and fundamental, people are either good or they're bad. It's been very disappointing to find some of my friends just haven't stood up at all. It's so easy to be rude and unkind and cross. I've been so annoyed at times. Some of the kids make no effort at all to be thoughtful or considerate of one another. Don't worry, though: not so Jean. She is such a fine person—genuine, kind, and so thoughtful always. She's the kind of a girl that brings out the best in others. Friendship is the only thing over here. I don't know what I would do without Jean. On my birthday I had KP, but it was only half a day and I didn't mind in the least since I could take the evening off. I read your darling birthday letter, and one from Alice, and one from Evelyn, that all had arrived the night before. I want to thank you all for the subscriptions. They will be very much appreciated. I don't agree with the current policies of *The Reader's Digest*, but I do enjoy their articles of general interest. *Time* is my favorite, of course. They're prejudiced, of course, but clearly so. I will read them both from cover to cover. During the afternoon, I read in the tent and wrote the family's Christmas letter in the evening. Earl took me to the Special Services Office where they showed the picture, *Mrs. Parkington.* It was splendid and I enjoyed it immensely. Earl celebrated my birthday by giving me a dozen oranges and six apples. That may sound funny, but it was the nicest thing he could have given one. Fresh fruit is so scarce. He went down on one of the boats in the harbor and bartered for them. All in all, it was a very nice birthday. Different, but very nice. Well, dear, poor Lieutenant Townsend must get so tired of such lengthy letters, so I'll give him a break and sign off. Love, Selene.

"P. S. I've enclosed some money printed by the Japs for the invasion of New Guinea."

This letter was written on the 7th of December. Netherlands East Indies. This is my family's Christmas letter.

"My Dearest Family: As the Christmas season draws near and my thoughts turn to home, I find myself taking stock of things from Christmases past. As I dust off memory by memory and lay them out neatly like Christmas tree ornaments, I evaluate each one. There in the middle, like the great big red ball that's been the favorite for so long, is the memory of the family, the four of us together . . ."

I'd like to comment on that. My father had left us when I was about nine, so he hadn't really been a part of my life for most of my growing up at home. The four of us that I talk about was my mother, my brother Charlie, who was almost ten years older than I, and my sister Alice, who was five and a half years older than I, and myself.

"The four of us during the Depression. Christmas presents then were homemade. Remember the blue velvet dress with the pale blue blouse hung on the bookcase for Alice? I feel all warm inside when I think how our able skipper [my mother] steered us through those rough times. Other families let Christmas slip by because of hard luck. They didn't know about the Christmas Spirit, did they, Mother? Isn't it too bad? No one ever told them that Spirit is for poor people. It's a big compensation. It makes up for lack of material things. Love costs nothing. There is the blue peacock that used to have a spun-glass tail. That's for Christmas nights at Uncle Walter's. How lovely were those drives through the park, the lights gleaming out in the darkness winking good cheer to all who would look at their gay colors. I can almost taste that Welsh rarebit poured in on an already overstuffed tummy. Uncle Walter is always such a genial host, almost like the English gentleman in the carol, 'God Rest Ye Merry Gentlemen.'' Or perhaps Washington Irving's version of 'An English Christmas.' Oh, yes, here's the cunning little China ski boy. Isn't that Charlie's? Or is it Alice's? Or was that ownership one of the weighty family problems never settled? Isn't that little thing for caroling with the Scouts, sneaking and slipping around surprising people. Remember twelve years ago, Mother, at the first rehearsal when Vernel told us about the mystery and suppressed excitement of caroling with them? I could scarcely believe my ears. It was so thrilling, quietly tiptoeing in back ways and removing wraps while Pepper surreptitiously tuned her fiddle. I laugh to remember the constant admonition about wax on the carpet. The dearest recollection of all is the one of Mrs. Lewis. She cried. It was Christmas and we were young, and then we wanted to cry because she was pleased. There are so many more, too numerous to put down here. But there they are, all laid out on the breakfast-room table ready to hang on the tree, shining with the patina of much loving handling and useful old age. Along with old ornaments and memories on the family tree, I have a few new ones I'd like to add. They're not new except to me. They indeed are ageless and of priceless value. See, here is a bluebird of spun glass, delicate and dainty, but of surprising durability. That's for love, the only thing that's worthwhile. There are many things love can do. My love for all of you has been a buffer between me and the bleakness of my surroundings here, the bitterness towards authority and the lack of consideration and gentleness among so many people here. My love for Jean is a nice, comfortable thing. She is so kind and understanding always, and she's here. She reminds me that there are people here who have not been touched with cynicism. Then here is Earl: he, too, is part of the bluebird, a nice gay part. It's the part that makes me feel protected and cared for. It keeps me wearing lipstick and perfume and desiring to be a lady. After all, any human relationship is only what it can make of the individuals involved. A kind and generous feeling constitutes a lovely friendship. Here is another ornament. It's all wrapped in white tissue paper. There. It's a gilt bird cage with a tiny, little, gold canary inside. This minute thing could have come from Baghdad, or perhaps it was the toy of the Kubla Khan in ancient Cathay. That's for beauty and all those who can see it. Always there is the sky, as moody and ever changing as a prima donna, sometimes flaming with sun and clouds, then it's gorgeous and exotic. Other times glittery and luminous with stars. There is beauty always for those who will look and listen. I can see not only what is here, but what I have seen before. And even the beauty and songs that dreams are made of. Now you have my . . .

"And kiss each and every one of you tenderly. Merry, Merry Christmas and good night. Selene"

The reference to caroling was one of my most joyous childhood memories. Between the time I was ten and become a Girl Scout and the time that I left St. Louis, each year I was part of a group of carolers. We were all Girl Scouts and were organized on a city-wide level. Girls who were deemed to be talented, who could sing, and I regret to say who were probably pretty, were asked to join the group. For the first couple of years I was one of the little carolers down in front.

We wore costumes and carried lighted candles. Our director and another member played the violin. We sang carols at the homes of people who were benefactors of the St. Louis Girl Scouts. The Ms. Lewis referred to in my letter was one of the people who had done a lot for Scouting. It was always a joyous occasion to sing, because people never knew we were coming. It would be arranged with someone in the family to let us in the back door. On the Sunday afternoon before Christmas we would sing at the St. Louis Art Museum in the beautiful Morlaix Court. We also sang at the St. Louis Athletic Club and any number of other public places on behalf of the Girl Scouts.

The next letter is 23rd December 1944, Netherlands, East Indies:

"Darlingest Mother. Long time no write. Also long time no hear—almost a month. Haven't heard from anyone except Bob McDonald down at APO 503. Remember I mentioned how darling he was to us down there? In case I didn't, he's the one we met one night when Jean and I were on duty in the Orderly Room. He was Officer of the Day. It rained and he stayed. It continued to rain, and he continued to stay. The result was next night he came in as a private and every night after that. Even crawling in through a hole in the fence. It was terribly risky, but fun. After all, you know the old adage about forbidden fruit. Well, he wrote me a darling letter. He was so swell to Jean and me. Gave us khaki pants and shirts from Officer's Store, to say nothing of candy and Scotch and Australian beer for Jean. Well, here it is almost Christmas. It's almost unbelievable. It's so dreadfully hot. It rains and steams most of the time. One nice thing, we've gotten floors in our tents and boardwalks around so that it's no longer necessary to wear huge knee-high galoshes to take a shower. However, food is still pretty horrible. It has been nearly impossible to write letters. I've been so horribly depressed by conditions as they exist here, both personal and otherwise, that the letters I've written to you and torn up would never have passed the censor. I wish it wasn't so, but it is. It has been necessary for Jean and me to reinstate ourselves in an entirely new outlook. It's been terribly difficult to fight off encroaching bitterness against existing conditions and treatment. It will be impossible for you to understand our viewpoint until you can hear it, if then.

"24 December: Good morning. Well, here it is Christmas Eve Day. When I came home last night Alice's package was there waiting for me. You simply cannot imagine my delight. It was really awfully funny. The girls were all sitting around quietly waiting for me to come home. They insisted that I open it right then. As the outside wrappings were wet and sticky, I did, thinking that something must have broken. But there was nothing damaged except the candy had melted from the terrible heat in the hold of the ship and had gotten a bit buggy. But everything else was OK, so with the exception of the hose, I went no further. The hose had gotten sticky, so I very carefully washed them out in my helmet. That sounds funny, doesn't it? For tomorrow we are going to be permitted to wear skirts, so I will wear my new stockings. However, don't let Alice worry. They will get plenty of wear when we move up into more civilized territory. Earl, and Jean's little boyfriend, six-foot-three tall, and one of the other girl's men friend, and I are planning on going to church tomorrow morning and then bringing them back to the mess hall for dinner. Jean has been going with a very lovely fellow. He is such a peach. The other girl, Sarah Jane Cady, has been keeping serious company with an Australian sergeant, Sir Ronald Humphries. If they get married she will be Lady Jane. Quite something, isn't it? Sally is a swell girl, golden eaglet and eleven years of scouting behind her, Episcopalian, too. So is Jean's friend and, of course, Sir Ronald, and Jean is by adoption. Isn't that odd? We were disappointed that there were no English services, so general Protestant will have to do. Incidentally, Jean and I have the day off through the generosity of Lieutenant Townsend. He really is a darling. I'm very fortunate to work for someone so nice. As you can see, I've enclosed the power of attorney and will send Howard's release along as soon as I get it. I would appreciate it very much if you would see Mr. Noble right away and let me know of developments. Also, I'm enclosing a money order for you to deposit to my account. I'm saving every cent I can get my hands on. Would you check up on all the money I have in the bank and in bonds? I'd like to have some idea as to where I stand. Are my bonds coming through all right? I should have eight, I believe, since I've been in the army. Jean and I are quite serious about this college business. We are taking a correspondence course on psychology and life. It will give us one credit. I haven't decided definitely on a school yet, but I think it will be Columbia. Northwestern is only good for football."

Gosh, such ignorance!

"I've been talking around, and Columbia is still 'the' school. Well, must close now, dear. Love, Selene. P.S. No money order. Sunday, so APO is closed. Will send it along in next letter."

I should make some comments about my marriage. I had met Howard, a very nice guy, when I worked at Camp Wallace. He was a staff sergeant then. We married the 25th of September 1942, in the base chapel. It was a lovely wedding. I had a white cotton dress my mother had sewn and I wore it over a hoop skirt with one of my great-grandmother's petticoats. I carried an orange blossom bouquet. Sydonia Stanislaw, who had been my roommate in Texas, was my maid of honor.

The marriage was under a lot of stress from the beginning because I was working very long hours at Camp Wallace. I couldn't be the wife Howard expected me to be, and I was resentful. There was just too much friction for the marriage to be in good shape from the very first. That never changed. In July 1943, when he went to Fort Ord, preparatory to going overseas as infantry in the American Division, we had been together only ten months.

This letter is also dated 24 December 1944, Netherlands, East Indies. This one is to my sister, Alice.

"My dearest Angel Pie Sis: Came home last night to find your Christmas box waiting for me. The outside was pretty banged up, but everything on the inside was fine except the candy had melted. But nothing was damaged in the least. Honey, everything is wrapped up so sweetly. So far, I can't thank you for anything except the cunning little ornament because I haven't peeked at a thing. Jean and I are the only ones to receive any packages so far, so it is with great anticipation that we look forward to Jean's and my package on Christmas morning. The mess hall and the rec hall are gay with Christmas decorations. Jean and I have tomorrow off. Isn't that swell? Thanks to our darling boss. He's not only an angel, he's cute, too. Of course, I can't say more because he's also the censor. Jean and I expect to attend church tomorrow morning with our friends and then invite our favorite men friends back to the mess hall for Christmas dinner. Wonder of wonders! We're going to be allowed to wear skirts on Christmas Day; it will surely seem nice. It's been three months with no skirts. You know, it's funny, in spite of the horrific heat, it really does seem like Christmas. You have never in your life seen such originality in trees, both in tree and decorations. One colored outfit has taken heavy leafy jungle vines and strung them up on a tent pole, then they decorated from there with bits of colored paper. Quite effective. It's quite exciting getting greetings from other headquarters this theatre on the teletype. One headquarters played "Jingle Bells" on the little bell, a bit out of tune, but unmistakable. Last night we picked up San Francisco on the radio in time to hear them play Christmas music. It seemed odd so far away, half way around the world. Well, Angel, will close now. Love, Selene."

This letter was written Netherlands East Indies, 26 December 1944. This is "Dear Garden Club." My mother was very active in the Garden Club most of the years that I can remember and they had sent me a box.

"Dear Garden Club: I want to thank you for the lovely Christmas box. It was so thoughtful. It came just before dinner Christmas Eve after the regular mail call. Opening it was such fun. All my five tent mates sat around eager with knives and scissors to open the wrappings. It is amazing how you all could know just the things most appreciated. I know Uncle Sam never intended mess kits to be used for popcorn poppers, but they did wonderfully last night, over a little electric plate. So far we haven't tasted the plum pudding, but that will come tonight. We have built a little fireplace in back of our tent and have spent many an enjoyable evening cooking up a brew of filched coffee in a big number-ten can. So the plum pudding will be a most welcome addition to our little tête-à-têtes. Of course, reading material here is terrifically scarce. Books and magazines are read until they fall to pieces. That reminds me of one of our first stops here before we got off the boat. We anchored out in the harbor a few days. Of course, we lined the rail to catch our first glimpse of foreign soil. By the same token, boys from shore installations came out in little boats to catch their first glimpse in over a year of white women, for many, the first American women in three years. We had magazines from the trip which we had read. Finding that their newest periodicals were six months old, we madly scurried around and made huge bundles of literature tied up with belts and neckties and anything we could find, and dropped them overboard to them. It gave one a sort of peculiar feeling to have something that they could use and we could give. Thank you again and accept my most sincere wishes for a happy and prosperous new year for all of you and your families. Sincerely, Selene H. Curd Treacy."

The next letter was also written on December the 26, 1944, Netherlands, East Indies.

"Dearest Mother. Well, another Christmas come and gone. It was a very nice day in spite of the terrific heat. We came home Sunday evening to find that some of our tent mates had procured some red and green crepe paper and decorated the tent. It looked quite festive. Even our two brooms were dressed up with an immense crepe paper bow on each. The six of us sat around batting the breeze. Someone started a Christmas carol and then another. We looked up to see two more girls standing outside to listen so we invited them in. Then three more from the tent next door come in to wish us well and they stayed. Before we knew it, all the beds were occupied, and the floor and the front porch, and the area outside in front. There were girls we didn't even know who heard the singing and came to see where it was coming from. Someone had the idea of serenading, so we went, as was, pajamas and housecoats, up to the officer's area. It was then about 2:00 a.m. We tiptoed very quietly until we were just outside our CO's tent, then burst into song. She was so surprised. When we finished she gave us a can of boned turkey and a half-pint of Four Roses. She said, 'It isn't much, but it's all I have.' You have no idea how scarce those things are over here, so it was a great sacrifice. Well, we went back to the tent. By this time we were about thirty strong. We sat and sang until 3:00 a.m. It was so lovely. Next morning we exchanged presents, which consisted mostly in a swap of personal belongings, then I dressed up in my new stockings, freshly ironed skirts—it was wonderful—and hied us off to church. This installation has no chapel, nor a Protestant chaplain, so it was held in the officer's club with a borrowed chaplain. As always, general Protestant services are an acute disappointment. They are so lukewarm. The music was nice, though.

"After that I brought Earl over to our mess for dinner. The dinner was lovely; turkey and all the trimmings. The mess hall was decorated so nicely and all the girls and fellows looked so clean and shiny. After dinner Earl and I played several games of checkers in the rec hall and then I returned for a much-needed nap. In the evening we popped corn over a little hot plate of Earl's in my mess kit. We had a nice evening talking and eating popcorn and drinking coffee. Needless to say, the popcorn was from the garden club. That box was the most delightful surprise. It arrived late Christmas Eve. So far we haven't eaten the plum pudding, we've had so many other things. But don't worry, we will. As soon as I finish this letter to you I am going to send a thank-you note. It was so thoughtful of them and most appreciated. I was so fortunate to receive two packages. Jean only got one and the other girls none at all. All in all it was a very nice Christmas, different, to say the least. Well, honey, I hope you had a lovely day, too. As I write this I realize that according to the differences in time you all should be at Uncle Walter's about now. Let me hear soon. I've only had one letter from home in over a month. Of course, there are circumstances which caused that. Bye now. Love, Selene. P.S. I've enclosed the money order for $80."

There is more I'd like to say about this Christmas Eve. With fifty years' hindsight, that recollection of Christmas Eve with the other WACs has stayed in my mind as one of two absolute highlights of my entire service career, all twenty-two months of it.

I worked the evening shift on Christmas Eve and came home after midnight and took a shower. When I came back the girls were waiting for me. One of our number, Marianna Pipkin a girl from Greensboro, North Carolina read from the Bible, from Luke. She knew it so well that I'm not sure she read it, I think she recited it. It was beautiful. We had no electricity in our tents so we had put a candle in a beer bottle for light. To look up and see other girls standing outside the tent in the candlelight was lovely.

We had three officers, one of whom was Captain Frances Hardisty, our commanding officer, a really sterling lady. Another was Lieutenant Eleanor Conners who was a Signal Corps WAC, so she was not one of our company officers, but she lived with Captain Hardisty. We enlisted women were concerned about our officers. We knew that the WAC Officer Corps in the South Pacific was terribly understaffed and that they had very little support or help from any of the higher headquarters. We thought they must have been very lonely. As a matter of fact, we all were glad we were enlisted women because we had each other. These were officers we really liked. We wished them well and we wanted to show our appreciation so the thirty or so of us made our way, very quietly, down the company street to the officers' tent.

On the left side was north, and we could see the Big Dipper and the North Star way down near the northern horizon. To look the other way we could see the Southern Cross.

The officers' tent was on a little hillside so that when we got there we were below them. We sang and when they came out on their little porch, we were looking up at them. To show her appreciation, Captain Hardisty opened a can of turkey and put it into a mess kit, breaking it into fragments with a fork. She then poured the Four Roses, a half-pint, into a canteen cup and passed it around. We each took a morsel of turkey and a sip of Four Roses. It had all of the emotional content of the Holy Communion, and everybody felt it.

As we walked quietly back one of the girls said to me, "I have seen the Lord." We all felt the same way. The Holy Spirit was there with us. Fifty years later, I have never ever forgotten it. Many years after the war I saw Jean Ann again. When we greeted each other, the first thing she said was, "I know what you're going to ask me: Christmas '44." And I said, "Yes, Jean, you're right." She said, "It's the same for me." And it still is.

Some other things I didn't put in my letter to Mother happened Christmas night. As I said before, Lieutenant Townsend gave Jean and me the day off on Christmas. However, because of a change of shifts, we went back to work at midnight on Christmas night. Jean Ann, Walter Bowman, my friend, Earl, and I had one of those funny old personnel carriers with a high center of gravity that had come out of the First World War. We had a few of those in the South Pacific. In New Guinea there were constant cycles of rain and sun, which meant you were up to your knees in mud, but with dust in your face, but the mud was predominant in the roads. The mud had an extremely fine, almost silky texture which made it very slippery. Under that layer of very liquid mud was rock. At one point on one of those horrendous mountain roads, with the mountains straight up on one side and straight down on the other and no guardrails, our vehicle started to slip and it kept on sliding. No way was it going to stop. We jumped out as the vehicle kept on going over the side. There we were, the four of us, standing in the middle of the road laughing like loons. What else are you going to do when your vehicle goes seven hundred feet down to the sea? Fortunately there was enough traffic on the road, even at that hour, that someone picked us up. I had done something to myself when I jumped out but I couldn't tell what it was. All of a sudden I had a terrible stabbing pain in the lower right abdomen. Someone took me to the dispensary but the doctor on duty was too drunk to do anything about me. I was upset and disgusted because he was drunk on duty so we all went back to work and I went on sick call sometime later.

Out of the Signal Corps

This letter is, Netherlands East Indies. January 3, 1944.

"Dearest Mother: I have your two last letters here. Mail here is so irregular. Sometimes three weeks go by without mail. I've been in the hospital since the day after Christmas. Nothing serious, just a recurrence of the trouble I had before I was married. Don't worry, though, I'm all right now, although still in the hospital. The doctor says it's caused by physical strain of some sort. Your letter of the 13th was an especially nice one. It makes it interesting for you to comment on the things I say. I try to think of the pleasant things. After all, I know you know living conditions and the treatment of enlisted women is pretty rugged, so there's no point in elaborating. In answer to your question about the last move I made; thank heavens, no boat trips were involved. I've had enough ocean travel to last me a lifetime. In answer to your questions about the trip over: I know you are familiar with the type of second-class accommodations aboard a big liner. Well, they moved the two bunks out and installed regular troop sleepers, three-tiered, four rows. It got pretty hot towards the Equator with the porthole closed, but it was bearable except for the smell of unwashed bodies. No one thought to tell us to bring salt-water soap. Try dissolving a piece of soap in a glass of salt water. It forms a sticky slime. Our eating was done on the next deck down so we didn't have far to go. We ate with the men at long refectory tables, standing up for our two meals a day. In answer to your other question, I spent part of the time on board in the hospital as a special attendant to a patient suffering from nymphomania. I felt very sorry for her. That is how come I was eating three meals a day toward the end of the voyage. I heard from Herman today."

Herman Agostini was a Puerto Rican family friend of ours.

"The first letter in quite some time. He is in Italy. You can imagine my acute disappointment—he had thought he might come this way. It does my heart good, though, to know he has at last gotten a good deal and the overseas service he desired so much. He had his foreign duty at Camp Hulin. He works hard and likes it. He is enjoying to the fullest extent the beauties of Italy. I'll give you his address so you can write. Please do. I heard from Van,"—that's another family friend—"who was at that time giving New York a thorough going-over after a pleasant but short sojourn in France. He is still plying the Atlantic as a transport officer. I have never received an answer from Howard about the divorce. I believe he must have moved. Today I received a birthday card from his family and a bulletin from the high school. I was so distressed to learn the death of Ms. Winifred Tonner. School won't seem the same. By the way, would you give them my new address and take the one at home off the list? I receive two copies at the same time. Also, tell them I'm no longer at Fort Oglethorpe. It looks like Ruth Danielson and I are just about the only Webster girls overseas." Webster Groves is where I lived. "Nice to know she made Captain. I believe I told you about missing Walter by two days. He's in the Philippines, lucky cuss. I'm afraid this letter sounds a bit sour, don't laugh, but it's raining again and I'm anxious to get back to work. I loathe hospitals, as you well know. One of the nicest things I have here is Lieutenant Lillian Steinberg, a lovely, charming young Jewish woman. She was our CO coming over on the boat and I got to know her very well. My best description of her, other than looks, is a feminine version of Walter. We go to talk to her when Jean and I feel the need of some intellectual conversation. She was so swell on the boat; the only WAC Officer who would come down to our quarters to see us. It reminded her of the thirteenth century. She reminds me of Rebecca in *Ivanhoe,* except she's a blond. Well, nothing much new. Nothing happens in the hospital here, so I'll close. Love, Selene. P.S. I know you worry about my long silence, but there are times when letters just can't be written. If you will go back and reread any letters from way back in Galveston, I never mentioned anything unpleasant. I guess maybe I've been wrong, but it has always seemed so futile writing letters complaining of things you couldn't do a thing about. But perhaps I've been wrong. I've torn up many more letters than I've ever sent. I hate to think of you worrying. After all, I'm not suffering unduly. I have Jean, thank God, and Lieutenant Townsend is a delightful person who's lent me several books since I've been here. Earl is also still here so I'm very well off as far as companionship. So far I've not received any boxes other than the one from Alice and the Garden Club. The cute little things in Alice's box delighted me to no end. Well, here come the requests. If Aunt Jane will send soap, I'd appreciate it. I would prefer Yardley's. Also, how about some bath powder, Dr. Lyon's tooth powder, and some Scripto ink? You pack bottles in hunks of bread. It works fine, or packed with toilet paper in a can or tin. Powder better be the same way. Also some Yardley's cologne. Please, also some V-Ette bras, cotton, size 32, large cup, about six. Also my cotton slips. I guess that's all this time. Love, Selene. Over."

Oh, and I write the address to Herman Agostini.

Hollandia, Netherlands New Guinea
Wooden-floored tents, occupied by the women

Special Studies: WAC, p. 428

On that one I didn't tell the doctor that I'd had to jump out of a vehicle. I know now that it was probably an ovarian cyst which burst when I hit the road.

Netherlands, East Indies, January 5, 1945. Two days later.

"Dearest Mother: Well, I'm still in the hospital but I expect to get out tomorrow, thank heavens. I just finished buying something for you from a native and as soon as I accumulate some other things I'll send it home. I'm anxious to know how you liked the bracelets. Was there an Aussie penny in the box? I sent one but I'm afraid the censor took it out. And how about the six-pence? The box we used was one Jean had brought with her into the army for bobby-pins. She emptied them into a cheese ration tin and we used the box. By the way, I could use some bobby-pins. Don't have but about six. By the way, has Sis ever looked up Syd? She's out at Brooks Hall."

That was Columbia University.

"How about having some snapshots made of the house, Charlie's house, and the whole family? Do you ever hear anything from Dad? Does he know I'm overseas? I suppose I should write to him but it would only be from a sense of duty and I guess the sense just isn't strong enough. Well, dear, it's hot today and I'm not very literarily inclined, so will close with lots of love. Selene. I know all these bits of information are very disjointed, but you asked me to write things as I think of them. Read this letter in conjunction with my last and it will make more sense."

This is 31 January 1945. Netherlands, New Guinea.

"Dearest Mother and Alice: First of all, I had all your recent letters in my pocket in my raincoat to take them to work to answer, and lo and behold, someone stole my raincoat, letters and all, so I'll have to do the best I can without them. I'll probably get the raincoat back. People seem to think that it rains harder on them than someone who had the forethought to carry protection. Business first. I'm enclosing the two lists of things belonging to the other two girls. As for Jean's and my things, they should all be easy enough. Hers are marked T-1919 and mine T-0828. The girdles are hers. When I mailed that package we were leaving at 2:00 p.m. on the plane for here and it was then one o'clock. I had just gotten the box at noon so the oversight, I hope, was pardonable. As for the nails, they were Australian and Bob McDonald made the box for me. Nice, don't you think? Now, good news. I have today received five packages: the first from Alice, in that everything was fine except the loose candy had melted, and the bulbs had rotted and bugs had taken a nibble from one hose. However, it was at the top and easily mended. The cute little Santa and the candle and bits of Evergreen were in fine shape. And best of all was the book, *The Prophet*. I love that book and Jean and I have read and reread it. Everything in the Garden Club box was perfect and the two boxes from you, Mother, were perfect. I got both of them on the same day. I was so thrilled. They arrived about a week ago. Honey, you and Alice just did yourselves proud on your taste and packing. I can imagine the time it must take to fit all those tiny little things so they won't rattle around. The little bracelet is just what I wanted. It's so dainty and the engraving is lovely. I love the bracelet, but I'm ashamed to admit it, but I got a bigger kick out of the little Christmas tree and all the little fixings. It was so like you, darling, all the little stars and plastic ornaments, even to the candles. I have very carefully packed all my little Christmas things away in a tin can for next year. I wonder where it will be? China, maybe. The kids didn't like the whole-wheat wafers, and I'm glad, because now I can eat them all myself. Horrid, aren't I? The little sock with all the stars, even to the tarlatan bag of nuts. Honey, you do know me pretty well, don't you? The fifth box was from Edna. It was lovely and showed so much thought and effort. Well, honey, even though a little late, the Christmas Spirit was certainly there. When your letter about Christmas at home arrived it came simultaneously with one from Jean's mother. We read them out loud and laughed and wept. I had wondered if my Christmas letter would hit just the way I wrote it, and it did. Honey, everything at home was just the way I wanted it to be. Mother, when your letters have kept coming right on, even though mine have been sporadic I realize that with no basis for comparison it's nearly impossible to understand conditions and why people's minds work the way they do. I'm looking forward to the day when you and Alice and Charlie and I can be together again, then I can tell you things that I couldn't put on paper, things that make letter-writing at times impossible. You know, honey, I've been so afraid that when I come back I'll be so changed that I won't seem to belong anymore. I think now my worries are not justified. If there were more mothers like you, the kids over here would have a darn sight easier time. When some of these people write letters they should perhaps try and visualize circumstances surrounding arrival of that letter. First, a long wait in the mail line, maybe the rain coming down in buckets and you're up to your calves in mud. Well, a cross or whiny letter from home just isn't worth all the drenching. That's putting it mildly. There are times when the army is so stupid and unjust you feel so helpless. After all, we're just privates, the world's lowest animal, and supposed to be the most imbecile. A great many things depend on swallowing distaste and carefully choosing buddies. Earl left for the Philippines not so long ago. That acquaintanceship had a very sad anticlimactic ending, but that will come another time. I have made another fine friend—don't laugh—the Jewish chaplain for the base.

"One evening one of the girls came over to bat the breeze awhile, and she got to talking about this remarkable man, so we decided to go calling. We went over to his office and there sat this very small man with pale gold hair and bright blue eyes, about 28 or 29. There was something in that face and those clear eyes I liked and trusted immediately. Something made me say, 'What do they call you? Pat? Short for Padre?' 'Yes. They call you Ginsberg, I take it,' was the quick comeback. We hit it off immediately. After that evening I went over every evening and we read and talked. He is a remarkable man. He was born in Brooklyn of Polish Jewish parents of very humble origin. He has the most terrific combination of earthy wisdom and wit and sophistication. He has the perfect approach to life, here as well as elsewhere. He has a very puckish expression coupled with a quick and ever-ready wit. I don't know when I've met anyone that I admired as much. I went to two Jewish services. Didn't get much out of them, but I did enjoy the music. What impressed me most, though, was the ease and cordiality with which they made me feel genuinely at home. That group of young people gathered quite frequently at the chaplain's office and I enjoyed their conversation. It made me feel very proud that they felt they could discuss their point of view on world affairs and the Jewish problem with me. It gave me a new outlook and certainly a keener sympathy and understanding. I really feel that I've come a long way. Jean came with me once but she didn't enjoy it. She has that general feeling, not exactly prejudice, but she "had an uncomfortable reserve. She's a snob, but I guess she can't help it. Certainly doesn't change my feelings about her in the least.

But we don't enjoy the same people, nor hold the same viewpoints. She cannot accept people or situations according to anything but her own standards. For real understanding those have to change with each incident. Well, dear, it is getting late, so must close now. By the way, all that about the chaplain is in the past tense because he's gone north. By the way, Allen Beck works in my office. Isn't that something? Love, Selene."

Allen Beck was the brother of a life-long friend of mine and when he walked in the office one night I almost fell out of my chair.

Netherlands, New Guinea. 7 February '45.

"Dearest Alice: Received your nice letter two days ago and I'm just now getting around to answering it. It's not that I'm too busy, but it's so hot that except for the few hours a day we spend working life seems to be just one long siesta. I suppose being always sleepy is nature's way of preventing our overexertion in this climate. Don't think our mouths didn't water and drool over the description of snow in Central Park. It sounded heavenly. I'm glad you're going home, but what I wish is that you'd be more explicit about your plans. Now that you've finished your training what do you intend to do with it? As long as I've got a part investment in that education I would like to maintain some interest. Could you take some small pictures of the house and the neighborhood? I get awfully homesick sometimes, and as I've told mother, I've nearly worn out the pitiful little snapshots I have. Have I mentioned before that Jean is planning to be married? She has met a fine man, Walter Bowman. He is a peach if I ever saw one. Of course, getting married over here is so complicated it will probably takes months for the papers to go through. First, after all the investigations, legal, financial and otherwise, they have to have a Dutch civil ceremony first with a Dutch colonial marriage certificate and license. Then the religious and American ceremony, all very interesting but a lot of trouble. Tell mother that it slipped my mind to thank her for the darling Valentines she sent Jean and me. Jean's young man made her a footlocker, staid olive-drab color on the outside, but a heavenly baby blue inside. So we posted the Valentines on the inside of the lid. They add a very gay touch. Also tell mother that the whole-wheat crackers were wonderful and I hope she'll send some more. Well, Angel Pie, let's hear soon. Love, Selene."

I have one comment about that letter. Alice had given up her job as director of nurses at Oak Ridge. I never did hear exactly what happened, but she quit. I was very disapproving of it. She had decided to give up nursing and go into photography. She lined up a school in New York and mother took the money for her tuition out of my account. I was not very happy about it because I thought, and I think probably realistically, that if she wanted to do that she really should have hung on to her own money and paid for it.

This was the beginning of a lot of very serious problems between my mother and me over money. Just recently I've talked to other former service people and it seems that this was something some parents did. They assumed the money coming home from their children was theirs. I find that I'm not the only one who came home in poverty.

This is 8th of February 1945.

"Netherlands, New Guinea. Dearest Mother: In answer to number 31"—that would have been my mother's 31st letter—"where do you think we get such things as Cokes and liquor? I've had about two drinks of both in six months. We don't see any Cokes and the officers have been known to pay as high as $40 a fifth for whiskey. You know, Ann's birthday completely slipped my mind."

Ann was my niece who had been born in 1941, and so she would have been three.

"I wish I had something to send her but I don't. If she needs any little thing why don't you give Evelyn a couple of dollars or get her something yourself. If she likes books, a nice illustrated *Bible* or *Book of Arabian Nights*, if you don't think she's too young. By the way, do you remember the book about the brownie we had from the Kanakas? Have you ever read that aloud to Ann? I would imagine that she'd enjoy it. On the subject, I wish you'd get something nice for the new baby for me."

My sister-in-law, Evelyn, was expecting a second baby.

"I only wish I could pick something out myself. Be sure it's something useful, something around $5. Hope it's a boy." Since they already had a girl. "About the natives here. They aren't Fuzzie-Wuzzies, but they resemble them in build and features, except the hair is short. Where did you get your preconceived notions about NEI?" That's Netherlands, East Indies. "This place, like British New Guinea, is as wild as a March hare. Plantations were widely scattered. Of course, as you say, it's rather difficult to imagine what it was like before the Japs and we took over. However, I believe that most of the towns listed in geography books were probably just missions and an occasional harbor for a rare tramp steamer. Don't know much, however. By the way, when that baby arrives be sure that Charlie takes pictures, and often, for me. Honestly, honey, I've practically gazed the image off the little snapshots I have. Well, dear, I haven't much new except it's hot and dusty and muggy all at the same time. It's too hot to move. When we hit the tent, off come our clothes down to undies. It's gotten to be a joke. I've just finished *Sapho* and *Manon Lescau*— pretty torrid stuff. My, but aren't men fools? I've been trying my darndest to cut down a pair of men's GI trousers to fit me. What a job! I never realized gentlemen's apparel was so complicated. Well, dear, I'll close now. Love, Selene."

8 March 1945.

"Dearest Mother and Alice. I'm enclosing a peace offering of two pictures of yours truly that Lieutenant Townsend took last fall out in front of the office. I had forgotten all about them until he came in today and handed them to me. I have no very good excuse for not writing except that I have been in the hospital again. It doesn't look as though the army and the tropics are agreeing with me. The doctor says that I have developed a very severe allergy to dust from the terrible trip every day to work in the open truck. My eyes were almost swollen shut and I was a very unhappy WAC. However, I have since been transferred to the quartermaster office, which is just across from our area and I can walk to work. I don't like the work at all. In fact, it is so menial and boring that were I civilian I wouldn't have stayed half a day. All I do all day is just type from straight copy. And after my nice, interesting job at the Signal Center I'm about to go mad. I don't think I ever held a job that I disliked so intensely. Well, my darling fellow 'T' has deserted me for a very desirable 'B'. Yes, Jean Ann was married a week ago last Sunday to Staff Sergeant Walter A. Bowman. I'm so happy for her I could simply pop. I guess it is a matter of sort of projecting my own unhappy state into all her lovely dreams and plans. It almost makes me believe in fairies again. It is nothing short of magic, how beautiful love can make a girl look. When she and Walter are together it is as though they had set up their own little personal sun. I guess it sounds sort of funny, but some of the other kids were worried about me because they were afraid that I would be jealous or left out or something. But thank the Lord, at least I've been blessed, I believe, with a generous nature. Anyway, it has the same effect on me as though I had. Now, for another piece of phenomenal news. I was up in the hospital entertaining a group of wounded men around the bed from the next ward when I saw another GI join the group. It was Howard. Needless to say, I almost fell out of the bed. I couldn't have been more astounded had it been you. He looked awfully well. Tropics agrees with him. He has the most perverse habit of making the very best of any situation. It was nice to see him and we had a nice chat, although his stay was only a few hours long. We decided definitely on the divorce and as soon as he reaches his new station he's going to send me the necessary affidavit. I hope that you will see fit to go ahead with the favor I asked of you. You see, as long as I'm overseas the divorce should cost me nothing. And with the schooling I'm looking forward to in the offing, money is quite an important consideration. And Howard is quite agreeable to it. He had finally realized that there is no longer anything whatsoever there. It seems amazing that I should have so little feeling about a man whom I married for the rest of my life. I've just about reconciled myself to being a career woman, and not from choice, but from necessity. After all, I should have married a man like Jean's Walter. But a man of his type won't touch a divorcee with a ten-foot pole, and most any other man who will comes under the heading of wild oats. Either that or they're much too sophisticated to make good husbands. Another thing, of all the swell men I've met in the army, not one of them would I ever care to see in civilian life except perhaps Lieutenant Townsend and Bob McDonald, and that is just a swell friendship because they are very much interested in their wives. In fact, so much so that it makes them quite capable of having a platonic friendship. So you tell Evelyn that it looks as though she will have to make the Curd family second generation all by herself. Speaking of second generation, I am anxiously awaiting word of the new baby. I know you want to hear more about the wedding but I'm writing it all up in story form for Jean's family and I will send you a copy of that when I've finished it."

Unfortunately I never did, so I'll have to put it in here.

"There's another bright spot on my horizon. I met an interesting girl in the hospital, Charmian Montross. Her mother and father are both well-known writers and so is Montie. She and I just clicked it off. I know that she is a person that I will keep track of. Somehow the stimulus of another creative brain has set me off and I've written two short stories and have started two more. She has sent them off to her agent and I know they won't be accepted, but she seemed to think that one of them in particular had such a degree of originality that it would. It was a little tale about a lonesome and amiable dragon, a lady, and a very stuffy knight. The lady goes off with the dragon instead of the knight. The other story is a serious, bitter sort of tale with a peculiar twist at the end about the prostitutes I used to see in Galveston. The story I'm working on now is a tale about an old chap who runs an engraving shop. I'm enjoying myself and it makes this dismal hole a little more bearable. I guess it would come under the heading of an escape mechanism, but those things are justifiable under such circumstances. I've been seeing a very cute navy flyer lately. He's a very handsome and jaunty sort of devil, not very deep or anything. But devil may care, good for the morale. I've been asked to speak on a panel discussion over the Jungle Network Special Services Radio Service. As yet I don't know what the subject is, but I was very flattered that someone in the army actually thought I had sense enough to wear rubbers in the rain. I always have the feeling that I'm being presumptuous if I show that little spark of intelligence that sometimes lurks around the dark corners of my brain. After all, I'm only a private. The other night at the hospital Montie and I were sitting out in front just listening to the jungle night, when we saw the MP at the gate, just a few yards away from where we were sitting in the moonlight, stiffen with a scarcely perceptible sound. He flashed on his light just in time to see an alarmed mouse dash across the beam with a cat closing in on its tail. The expression on the face of the MP was so comical that we broke the silence of the evening with loud and long guffaws. The other day I went into the orderly room. It was around noon. It was empty. Just as I was leaving I heard a very sociable voice say, 'Want a drink of rum?' I jumped, turned to see the curious little face of a very sociable green parrot perched on a typewriter. Remember, this is the jungle we live in. Well, last but not least, I want to thank you, Sis, for the pictures. They are all so good. When your letter came it was so heavy I knew right away it had photographs in it. You never know, darling, how much those pictures mean. I find that family mean more when they're not around than I ever thought they could. The picture of Charlie up in the tree, the one facing the cameras, darling, he looks a lot like Jean's Walter. He, too, is a tall, lanky chap, heavier than Charlie but with the same sweet, boyish expression. Also, the ears. Any more prints will be so desirable as to even be better than food, and you know what that means. I had a quarter of an apple today. I mean a real one, the first since my birthday. We also had fresh cabbage today, almost as much of a rarity as apples. Well, darlings, I'll try and be good and write more often now. My eyes and sinuses are in much better condition and I've been able to read and write more, although my eyes were weakened considerably. But they're getting better, so the damage was neither serious nor permanent. I hope you like the pictures. Be sure and don't lose them as they're the only ones I can get. Must close now. Love, Selene. P.S. I have received both sets of pictures."

Some comments about all of this. Howard and I were never able to get divorced until after the war, because my mother would not cooperate. She was bound and determined that I was going to stay married and so would not help me at all. When I did get the divorce I had to pay for it. I had very little money to pay for it with when I got back.

The next letter is dated 9 March 1945 to my sister and I opened it with this: "Ode to a happy marriage. A little home upon a knoll and you and me and birth control."

That was a little verse written by my friend, Charmian Montross. This was to Alice and I said,

"Don't read this out loud, Darlingest Sis. First, just to make sure you know how thrilled I am with the pictures, I'm going to thank you all over again as well as in the letter to you and Mother together. The ones of Charlie in the tree are so cute. It's a good likeness of Mother, too, although the one you took last year in the living room is the best that I have. Secret: I'm enclosing a money order and I want you to buy Mother a white orchid for Easter to wear to church. If you can't get one, use your own judgment. I don't believe she's ever had an orchid and it's high time. I have all I can use here. The other day in the jungle we saw two gorgeous ones. I'm enclosing some poems of my friend, Charmian Montross, and I wish that after you read them you'd get Mother to lock them up in my metal strong-box. They're part of a book of war poems that is to be published shortly. I thought you would like to read them over. I want to make sure that nothing happens to them. In connection with poetry, sometime if you get the time would you send me a copy of some of your best poems? Well, darling, this is just a little note so I will wind it up for now."

I didn't see my friend, Charmian Montross after New Guinea and I don't know what ever happened to her. She was not a Signal Corps WAC. I met her in the hospital, and she came from one of the other headquarters. I think she may have come from USASOS, which was fifteen or twenty miles, and was where we worked. I don't know whether any of her writings were published but if they were I never heard.

This would be a good time to talk about Jean Ann's wedding. Jean Ann had intended that I be her matron of honor, but unfortunately I had been in the hospital and had just gotten out the day before the wedding. She chose one of our other Signal Corps friends to be her matron of honor. As I said in one of my letters, the Dutch required a civil ceremony before a church wedding in Dutch territory. Jean Ann and Walter had to drive about 80 miles over jungle roads, and probably through enemy territory, to the nearest station where Dutch civil authorities were located. She told us about standing at the ceremony in their khaki uniforms. She had on a skirt but no stockings, just bare legs and shoes. The perspiration was running in rivers down the backs of her legs and all the time the Dutch official was marrying them, in Dutch, a big collie dog was licking the perspiration off the backs of her legs. She made it sound terribly funny. The only thing she understood was when he spoke her name, and it was pronounced, Yahn Ahn. "Yahn Ahn, do you take Walter", et cetera, et cetera. She didn't look upon that as the real wedding.

The American wedding was in the chapel at Walter Bowman's outfit, and it was lovely. The chapel was perched on a promontory overlooking the sea and so the sides were all open to the ocean. The roof was Nepa Palm and log, which was pretty common construction. There was a wheezy little field organ that played the wedding march. Jean was in her tropical worsted uniform with the most gorgeous bouquet of orchids. The guys in Walter's outfit had climbed up into the canopy of the rain forest—the canopy is where all the action is and where you get all the sun—to pick those gorgeous orchids. She had several beautiful scarlet ones and some little green ones. It was the most beautiful wedding bouquet I've ever seen. When I think of the risks those guys took climbing up into that canopy! It made my hair stand on end, and still does. All of us were dressed in freshly ironed uniforms. We had a wonderful party at the recreation hall in Walter's outfit which had been decorated and the mess sergeant produced a real wedding feast.

The guys built a honeymoon cottage for them of plywood and screen similar to what we had down in Oro Bay, but on a smaller scale. Four of the guys stood guard over the cottage because the Japanese were still very, very close. They assumed, and I think correctly, that the Japanese, who knew everything everyone was doing, also knew about the wedding.

Walter had made their wedding rings out of highly polished Monel steel. The last time I saw Jean, in 1975, they were still wearing them, and I assume that wherever they are now, they probably still are.

I don't think I had ever said where Jean Ann and Walter met. She had been hitching a ride somewhere around Base G, and Walter drove up in a big two-and-a-half-ton truck, stopped and gave her a lift. That was the beginning of a life-long marriage.

We were very restricted in Oro Bay, as my letters reflect. However, the letters from Hollandia and my memories indicate that the early months in Hollandia were as free from restrictions as we would have been in the States. If we needed or wanted to go someplace, we signed out and went. We walked where we had to or hitched rides when we could, which was most of the time. Our outfit was essentially unguarded, and people could and did come and go with freedom. No one seemed concerned about that state of affairs, least of all ourselves. Until one day Base G got a new commanding general who regarded us WACs as his children, or worse, his grandchildren. This gave rise to a lot of the bitterness I felt. No one was particularly concerned about our morals or safety when we first arrived at Hollandia, they had more urgent concerns. We did our jobs and went about our business. Then suddenly, we get a stateside-type general who showed up and started treating us as his children. The WACs nearly mutinied.

Essentially, he restricted us to quarters, except when we went to work. If we were allowed out at all, it had to be with armed guards, and at least two men. It put an end to hitching rides all around

Hollandia. It ended wandering down to the beach for a swim, going over to the dispensary when we needed to, private dates, or the meetings with the Jewish chaplain which we all enjoyed so much. Everything had to be planned and approved in advance.

Our response to all the restrictions was that instead of being upset, we regarded them as challenges. One particular night, I had a date with the attractive navy lieutenant I mentioned in one of my letters. He and I had his Jeep and joined some other friends in a whaleboat and went out to a ship anchored in the harbor. It was absolutely forbidden for WACs to go out on ships, but we did it anyway, and were always treated royally.

This particular night there were eight or nine of us in the whaleboat. Somebody had a friend on this particular ship and so we went to look for him. Everyone except me and the coxswain, who was running the boat, was an officer. We had a great time. We visited with everyone on board, then went over the side of the ship to return to shore.

On the way back I was sitting just behind the coxswain and next to me was an officer of some sort, he didn't have on any insignia because his shoulder was in a cast. He was very nice and we had chatted a lot during the evening.

En route I noticed we were heading towards a line of white surf where I had been swimming since my arrival in New Guinea. I knew the reef was located there and became concerned because the tide was out. Tapping the coxswain on the shoulder I said, "Look, coxswain, we're heading towards the reef." He gave me a withering look and ignored me.

Within a few moments he too realized how close we were to the reef. Realizing we were in trouble, he tried to come about which caused us to smack the reef broadside throwing us all into the water over the reef. The rip tide had created a deep hole on the land side of the reef where the man with the shoulder cast ended up. His cast took on salt water like a sponge, pulling him straight to the bottom. I reached across him in a cross-chest carry and pulled him into shallow water and we walked ashore.

My friends and I climbed into the Jeep and headed back to my outfit. I thought, oh, boy old, girl, you're in trouble, you're soaking wet. How are you going to explain this. But someone was watching over me. At the bottom of the hill on which the WAC area was located, a cloud came over and the rain poured down in buckets. I walked into the gate dripping water, threw the Officer of the Day a snappy salute and she responded, "Treacy, you got caught in the rain." I said, "Yes, ma'am," and went on to my tent.

There was a second chapter to the incident involving our trip out to the ship. Many months later when I was in Manila, I was walking down the street and suddenly caught sight of the man who had been in the shoulder cast. We recognized each other immediately. He waved and came across the street to where I was walking. I looked at his collar points and saw that he had two stars. "What's this?" I asked pointing to the stars. He laughed embarrassedly about being an admiral. He took my arm, saying, "Come on, let me buy you a cup of coffee and we'll talk about it."

"Sure," I responded.

We went to the Red Cross coffee shop in downtown Manila where you could always get good coffee. He explained to me that he was an admiral in the Inspector Admiral's Department in Washington and that he had been sent to New Guinea to investigate the sale of repatriations in the Seventh Fleet Navy Hospital. I wouldn't have known anything about that.

He had been on the *Nashville* when they took enemy fire on New Year's Eve and in the melee fell down an open hatch cover breaking his shoulder. He wound up in the Seventh Fleet Hospital as a very legitimate patient which gave him the opportunity he needed to investigate the hospital without people realizing what he was doing.

One night, we held a meeting in the mess hall, and our overbearing general came to explain his policy regarding WACs to us. It was a disaster, he was condescending in the extreme. He actually said, "I have daughters, and I look upon you with the same care and affection." He was greeted with absolute silence. Obviously, his daughters were not soldiers in New Guinea. Finally, one of the grandmothers in the group couldn't stand it anymore. She got up and said, "General, I have grandchildren," and sat down to uproarious laughter and applause from every WAC in the building.

At that same meeting, we asked for some other things, which we received to make our lives more bearable. The mess hall was to be opened twenty-four hours a day, with a permanent supply of hot coffee, this gave us a quiet place to read and write. Our tents never did have electricity and were not suitable for anything other than sleep as we were all on different shifts and someone was always trying to sleep. We had the recreation hall, but that was used for games and dates, so was never quiet enough to read and write.

I don't remember if he eased up on the regulations after this meeting or if our officers simply failed to enforce them, but we pretty much returned to doing what we had been doing before. One thing that always worked in favor of the Signal Corps WACs was our shift work. It was hard for anyone to keep track of where any given WAC was at any particular time.

My navy lieutenant friend came to a tragic end and I still feel sad about it. He had the most beautiful honey-colored hair which he wore in a crew cut. He wasn't as frivolous, or as light-minded as I had said in my earlier letter. He later told me that he had been part of the original bombing of Tokyo and that he was the only one of his outfit left. He had tremendous feelings of guilt about being alive when no one else was. One day I heard a plane fly over where I worked in the Signal Center. I rushed out as he buzzed the building where he knew I would be working, waggled his wings, went out to sea and crashed. I do not believe he crashed deliberately, he was not suicidal, but took a negligent risk. He was flying so low that I believe he got caught in the down draft over the mountains and was unable to pull out.

About this same time there was a very striking young woman in our outfit. She was tall, slim, and elegant with long, dark hair. On one or two occasions, I saw her in the bathhouse with her hair down, and it came to well below her waist. It was lovely, chestnut hair, with a wave in it, of which she was very proud. I would never have paid any particular attention to her except that she was always in immaculately clean, starched, khaki uniforms. Nobody had starched uniforms, even the officers. The word was out that she was having an affair with a high-ranking officer. I assumed that it was a general. At the time, I probably knew who it was rumored to be.

The rumor had it that the general had an enlisted man who took care of his clothes, and he took care of hers, too. None of us really cared about that. If she wanted to go to bed with a general, OK. But things got difficult when she pulled her lover's rank on us.

She wanted a promotion from Captain Hardisty, our CO, which Captain Hardisty was neither willing nor able to give her. A rating was something no one else was getting, and so there was no reason why she should. She threatened Captain Hardisty.

Some of the WACs thought they'd have to take care of this lady. Things began to happen to her. I was in the mess hall one day, when somebody tripped and dumped a whole mess kit of beets in her lap. Everybody swore it was an accident.

According to some of the other WACs, she didn't get the message, and so someone left the top off the grease pit behind the mess hall, and one night she fell in it.

She kept on threatening Captain Hardisty, and everybody was getting upset, because Captain Hardisty was a good officer. We had had our fill of bad officers earlier, and we wanted to keep the good one we had. The WACs were not going to sit by and let this girl, through her lover, get our good CO transferred back to the states, or Australia, or anywhere else.

And so one night, when she came into the latrine, the lights went out, and when the lights came back on again, she had a butch haircut. That must have gotten through to higher authorities; the general disappeared, and so did she.

I've always had mixed feeling about that incident. Though I was not involved until the last night, I knew what was going on. It seemed to me that in the army, in the South Pacific, we WACs, including the officers, were totally powerless, and so we could not think of any other way of dealing with that particular problem.

Another incident I did not tell mother happened when I was sent farther down the shore to the General Hospital, which was the Johns Hopkins hospital unit. Like most places in New Guinea, tents were pitched on the tops of the mountains, because that's where you got whatever breeze there might be. Of course, like everything else, there was no air conditioning in any hospital, even a general hospital.

Once they got you in the hospital, you had all hell to get loose. However, at the General Hospital it took me awhile to get over the allergies and get my eyes so I could see again. While there I was fully dressed most of the time and simply sat on the bed. The hospital consisted of big tents that held an entire ward. They had old-fashioned metal hospital beds with a stick that held the head of the mattress up to make it possible for you to sit up in bed. There were dirt floors. It was primitive, but surprisingly nice and the medical care was superb.

The last couple of days before I was due to get out, we began to hear the sounds of trucks coming up the mountain road in second gear. We went to see what we were hearing. At the base of the hill there was an LST anchored. Coming up the road were bumper to bumper ambulances bringing wounded from the landing at Lingayen on Luzon. These were the seriously wounded patients, and we heard them coming all night, all the next day, all the next night, and the next morning.

Those of us who were not sick enough to be in bed decided we'd heard enough, so we walked onto the ward next door to us, where they were being brought, and told the nurse on duty, "We're here to help." She couldn't think of what we could do.

So we said, "Never mind, we'll find something." We went to the cupboard, got wash basins, washcloths, towels and soap and started washing. The poor patients stunk to high heaven. They had been on that LST for a good two weeks. One poor girl had a weak stomach and after trying to wash around a cast she had to go out and throw up. But she came back, and went on working. We held the basins while the nurses changed dressings. We helped out all that day and the next until everybody got washed and settled in.

I don't remember how long we'd been at Hollandia when a beautiful big, male, Irish Setter showed up in the WAC outfit. He came from out of the jungle and went straight to the orderly room. He was in surprisingly good condition, except his coat was matted and pretty ragged. The girls gave him water and food, which he ate and drank gratefully, then disappeared. A day or so later, he showed up again and they fed and watered him. On his third trip into the WAC outfit he brought another Irish Setter, a little, pale-gold female. The girls were delighted. They dubbed them McGillicutty and Murphy. Murphy was a little female. In a few days Murphy gave birth to a litter of beautiful little Irish Setter pups. Because they matched my red hair, the girls named the runt Treacy.

We all thought the dogs probably had been abandoned by the Dutch when they had been interned by the Japanese. But the dogs had obviously made it handsomely for a considerable time on their own in the jungle. After the birth, they stuck around.

When the Signal Corps WACs went to Manila, there was still a large contingent of WACs in Hollandia, and I think they were at Base G

56th General Hospital, Hollandia
Selene and friends

until all the WACs were repatriated back to America. I know there was a contingent of WACs that went back to the States directly from Hollandia. And so I have to assume that the dogs went back to the States with somebody because a lot of dogs did.

One of the interesting things I remember about Hollandia, was that things had a way of appearing, like the dogs. We had a washing machine that was fascinating. It was like a big wooden churn, and like a churn, the sides were slanted in at the top. It was tub shaped, however unlike a tub, the opening at the top was smaller than the bottom, and, like a tub, it was shallow. It had a hinged, wooden lid that could be clamped down by a heavy iron bar. Inside the lid was what looked like a four-legged milking stool set in heavy iron gears. When you put the top down and fastened the bar, there was a handle that worked back and forth. The gears turned the milking stool round and round. That was the most effective washing machine I have ever seen, including the new fancy modern ones. It really got clothes clean. We cut up GI soap with a knife and even in cold water, it got the mud out. It was wonderful.

I assume that it, like the dogs, had belonged to the Dutch, and like so many things the Dutch had left behind in their homes, got picked up somehow and made its way to the WAC outfit.

At Base G we seemed to get all the transients. I think there were several reasons. In the first place, we had space; we had empty tents. From reading the section on South Pacific WACs in Mattie Treadwell's book, I believe we had one of the most appealing locations. For all the problems we had, we did have a view, we were on a hilltop, so that whatever breezes there might be, we got and after we'd been in the area awhile, things did get a lot better, and they got better fast. The army moved quickly to make our life more bearable, including floors in the tents and elevated walkways. By Christmas, we had white gravel between the tents and down the company streets. We also had plenty of water most of the time with comfortable showers and washing facilities.

So it's easy to see why when the USO company for *Oklahoma* came to Hollandia the women from the cast stayed with us. Many of the WACs sailed in to wash, starch and iron all those ruffled petticoats and long full skirts. *Oklahoma* had opened on Broadway just a year earlier.

The night *Oklahoma* opened in Hollandia in a very nice outdoor theatre, built by the Seabees, it poured. Fortunately, the stage, backstage and orchestra pit were all covered. But the audience was not. We had logs built into the hillside for seats. There we sat watching *Oklahoma* open with full orchestra, full cast and all the beautiful starched and ironed petticoats and costumes, in the pouring rain. It was terrific! Many of us had never seen a Broadway show. I grew up in St. Louis so had seen light operas at the Municipal Opera in the park in St. Louis, but it wasn't the same. *Oklahoma*, with its marvelous choreography by Agnes DeMille, was the first of the modern musicals. Though it rained on opening night in New Guinea, we were snug and dry in helmet liners and ponchos.

Oklahoma is one of my fondest wartime memories. I've seen it several times since then. As a matter of fact, it was still running on Broadway when I came home from the war and when I went to New York in 1946, I saw it again.

When the Allies rescued the internees and prisoners of war from Borneo the first we knew about it was when we heard children's voices. We were astonished. We hadn't seen children since we left the United States. They were a small group of women and children that the Allies had liberated. In that group was the author of a wonderful book on Borneo, *Land Below the Wind,* which I had read. She was very shy and I did not get to meet her but I did talk to other people in the group who said the Japanese had tortured her terribly. They knocked out all of her teeth and I don't know what else.

It was heaven to see those children from Borneo. They became the most beloved and spoiled kids you can imagine. We tried to do for those children what the guys had done for us. Anything we could find they could wear or could play with, they got. They had left the camps with only whatever clothes were on their back and those were in tatters.

March 12, 1945, and it's Hollandia.

"Darlingest Mother and Alice: Have two of your swell letters here beside me to answer. Honey, if you've never done a single solitary thing for me all my life, and if you never did anything more, your darling, homey, sweet letters would be ample. When I find letters from you in the box, my day is just made. Well, I see from your letter that we're not the only one having rain. Although the entire base is today a sea of gummy, red mud, and the roads are like glass. Glad I don't have to ride to work anymore, although I'm so lonesome for my nice job in the Signal Center, I still hate this damn Quartermaster, with a purple passion. About the unmarked hose, yes they belong to Jean Ann and the shields to me. By the way, should I ask you to send me the tropical uniform sometime, be sure to include the shields. Someday we may possibly need those uniforms, but right now the possibility seems very remote. Honey, I wish it was possible for Mrs. Thomspon to see Jean now. Last night, as per usual, the power went out and we had no lights and we were sitting around the tent batting the breeze by candlelight. Incidentally, the red Christmas candle. And I just studied Jean's face as she sat there talking. I don't think I have ever seen a face so lovely. She has those lovely scholarly features with almost a patina of serenity and love in that soft candlelight. I couldn't help but think that is what love and marriage should be. The conversation would have made you and Mrs. Thompson howl I'm sure. Jean and Walter are planning on having a baby right away. They're working on the supposition that Walter may go to the front, which is unlikely, as his outfit does a different type of work. But anyhow, he doesn't want to leave here, and leave Jean all by herself. So as Jean says, 'If I'm going to have those five children, I expect that I had better be getting started.' You see, when a WAC is in a family way she is sent home and discharged as soon as transportation is available. Walter is from Pittsburgh, Pennsylvania, and he's a teacher of industrial arts in civilian life. He's quite an expert welder and all sorts of things like that. He has a hobby like Charlie's, of woodwork. After the war he's planning to take advantage of the GI Bill of Rights and get some more education before going back to teaching. I understand his family is pretty well fixed, and so is Jean's, so things should run pretty smoothly. In the army, Walter is in an ordnance company and he makes repairs on gun parts, I believe. It is very delicate work on instruments, as I understand it. He's very clever and he made the two wedding rings out of Monel steel, and they're perfectly beautiful. He had the tools and the equipment to get a high polish on them.

  "About the sand at APO 503. There was practically no coral at all, only the occasional little stray piece washed ashore. So the sand there was all white, while here it is nothing but coral. Consequently, the sand is all yellow. Besides, APO 503 is about 800 miles away. We work eight hours a day. No, I haven't seen a cassowary. At least if I have I didn't know it. Darling, would you please send me Lydia's address right away? I've written her several times at her home address, but have never received an answer. Of course, I know she is busy being newlywed. Letters just don't get written. How well I know. I got a nice letter from Herman yesterday, only 16 days all the way from Italy. Some time I'd say, he is working very hard and has a WAC stenographer. Some people have all the luck. He loves it in Italy and has been able to see a great many of the beauties and historical sites around Rome, Pisa, and Florence. Evidently he has quite a bit of transportation at his disposal. He has been to the opera in Naples several times. It seems funny that we should be half a world apart and yet only separated by 16 days. I also received a lovely long letter from Art Richmond, who was here in New Guinea but at another base. He, you remember, was the boy I got to know quite well on the ship from St. Louis. He knew Eunice out at Washington. He writes lovely letters and I look forward to hearing from him. The mail also included the second issued I've received of *Time* and *The New Readers' Digest*. Well, darlings, I will close now and I think I've covered all the news, except that I went down in the mud on my derriere a little while ago. Most undignified. Love and great big kisses to all. Selene."

Comment. Eunice was my first cousin. And Washington was Washington University in St. Louis.

15 March 1945. This was still Hollandia.

"Dearest Mother: It seems as though you have two letters to my one, no matter how often I write, but that suits me just fine. Your letters are always so lively and homey. Thank you very much for the clippings. I enjoyed them very much. About the washing facilities, there is a row of tubs set up with plumbing. They are 50-gallon oil drums cut in half long ways and put in wooden frames with wide planks extending forward between each tub to set things on. Showers are in another room. Sample day here is very difficult because all anybody does is work from 8:00 to 5:00 and come home and eat supper and hope that the light stays on long enough to get in a little reading. But mostly lately they haven't. Other evenings we go to the show and wash our clothes when the water happens to be on, be it either 6:00 in the morning or 12:00 at night. The water goes off periodically. And lately it has done nothing but rain so nothing dries anyhow. Of course, most of us send our clothes, except undies and socks, to the Quartermaster Laundry. That is one of the most popular luxuries around here. When we have no lights we light candles and bat the breeze. By the way, Minerva's name is not Adams, but Donald. She's a very thin girl, more so than I ever thought of being, and very blond. Exceedingly plain, but a lovely personality and well educated. We all like her so much. She has spent quite a few years around Europe. She's a PFC. All the girls with lots of brains are mostly privates and corporals and things. And that is no lie. Most of the girls who are Phi

Beta Kappa are privates. I've already told you that I received both magazines, enjoy them very much, particularly *Time*. It's the only news we get. Speaking of news, could you find me a clipping about the contents of the new Missouri constitution? I don't believe I have ever known just what the changes involve. It has rained every day for 37 days now. Three more days and we will win an ark. Three more days of rain, we'll need one. The mud is the consistency of malted milk, and brick red. It is simply bottomless. I have never seen anything like it in my life. Jean and I have been debating the advisability of inventing some sort of adapted snowshoes, with leather thongs, wide strips of inner tube, so it would give and could be washed when the mud got caked on so heavy you couldn't get your feet off the ground. The most interesting thing that happened recently is last night's discussion group. I believe I mentioned it in an earlier letter. We drove out through the blinding rain to the radio station, set up in tents. The discussion was broadcast over the Jungle Network. It was about veteran's organizations, pros and cons of the existing ones, and new ones just coming into being with the veterans of this war. The other three members of the group were lively, well-informed young people and the discussion was quite a success, getting quite heated in spots, thanks to yours truly. But that was the idea, of course. The funny part of it is the guy on the other end of the heated part actually agreed with me, but took the other side for the sake of an argument.

"So it was fun all the way around. Afterwards we had sandwiches and the others had beer with the studio personnel, and a continuation of the argument that got over the air. I enjoyed that more than anything I've done for a while. It is the first time that I have had the opportunity of meeting people that I found really mentally stimulating. Reminded me of my association with Walter and Otto earlier. Speaking of Walter, I had a lovely long letter from him yesterday. It seems funny, I haven't seen him, but the few days in Virginia, for over a year and yet he evidently finds my end of the correspondence interesting enough to hold up his end quite regularly. I think I have more all-round respect and liking for that man than anyone I've ever met. This is the conceit for you, but I feel that he is the only one that is definitely my superior in every way. That is, of course, of my own particular friends, barring, of course, Syd. Good grief! Here come the rain again with a vengeance. Guess my clothes won't get dry again today. Been hanging out for four days now. Give Miss Pickel my very best. When I think of really progressive teachers I think of her, one of the very few. Well, honey, you and Alice take good care of yourselves and I'll try to do the same. Love, Selene."

Ms. Pickel was my English teacher in high school and someone with whom I went on having a friendship for many years after the war.

March 17, 1945. Hollandia.

"Dearest Mother and Alice: This is going to be a little shortie because I don't have anything much to write about except that it rained so hard last night I thought our tent was going to come down around our ears. I just finished a letter to Mr. Nelson. Ye gods! This damn job at the Quartermaster is terrible. There's nothing to do. I sit and write letters until I'm blue in the face. I've written to every single person I can think of. I'm still trying to get back in the Signal Corps. I don't know whether I will or not. I expect to know sometime today.

If I don't, the kids will probably move on up and I'll be left in this dismal place. I never hated a job in my life as much as I do this one. There's absolutely nothing to do most of the time, and when there is, it is just copying stuff on the typewriter. I think I'll have a nervous breakdown if I don't get out of here. Well, darlings, as I said, this is going to be short because I have no news except as I said before, more and better rain. So I guess I'll wind up for today. Love, Selene."

27 March 1945. Ten days later.

"Dearest Sis: Where did you get the pink paper? Right sporty, don't you think? I'm terribly upset about that business of the V-Mail. V-Mail to us takes about six weeks to reach us while Air Mail reaches us in about eight to ten days. Another thing, I've never received all the V-Mail written to me from the States. Michael Aliotta has written me five letters and I've received one. It is very discouraging. Mail is about the only thing we have, and then to fix it all up like that. Tell mother not to write so small on those V-Mail forms. One of her letters on V-Mail was absolutely unreadable. There isn't much of anything new to report except that it has finally decided to quit raining all the time. It just rains a little every night now, which is an ideal arrangement. I don't know why they didn't think of that sooner. Coming back to the mail. I received your letter dated 11 March day before yesterday, and I haven't received the V-Mail at all yet. Your letter with the clippings arrived the same day. It was sweet of you to send them. We have the originals of the pictures tacked up on our bulletin board. The paper was all wrong about the whereabouts of the bride. She is now somewhere between here and the States at present. She and Carl are going to be proud parents in about seven months. How is that for cooperation? Carl and Hylo are both swell kids and it's nice that it worked out that way, as Carl is expecting to go home on rotation in the very near future. I didn't attend the wedding because I had to work, and then, too, I don't know Hylo that well. I haven't had a letter from mother now for about ten days, I think, but having heard from you is almost as nice. I am anxiously waiting news about the new babies. Have the kittens come? Well, dear, I have nothing new, so we'll make this a little shortie. Love to you both."

Hylo and Carl were another couple that married in New Guinea and either she or her husband was from St. Louis, so the papers were full of pictures and articles about the wedding.

That was the last letter I wrote from New Guinea. All the Signal Corps WACs were put on orders for Manila and I was not on them. I was heartsick. I was upset and terribly depressed.

They left on a Sunday, I don't know which one. The day that they were to leave, we all had breakfast together in the mess hall and everybody sat around talking. Across the table from me was a Signal Corps WAC named Rosalyn. She was sitting at the table with her face resting in her hand. When she took her hand down there was a black and blue hand print on her face. I looked at her in absolute disbelief, and said, "Rosie!"

"What?"

"You've got a hand print on your face; it's black and blue." Captain Hardisty was nearby and heard the girls getting excited. She came over to see what the excitement was about. She took one look and took Rosie to the hospital since we didn't have sick call on Sunday.

I helped my friends get ready and went down to the ship to see them off. I was crushed. I didn't know when I'd get to leave and I thought, my word, here am I stuck all by myself. I didn't want to stay in my empty tent so I went to the mess hall. It was the middle of the afternoon and I was sitting by myself with a cup of coffee when Captain Hardisty walked in. She had the most devastated look on her face. She came over to me and said, "Oh, Treacy, I have terrible news. Rosie has leukemia."

Rosie died four days later without ever being able to go back to the States.

PART THREE

Philippines

Manila, Philippines—
Return to the Signal Corps

A couple of days later I was on orders to Manila as a casual. I went down to the ship carrying my own orders with my musette bag, very glad to leave except that I was being transferred not as a Signal Corps WAC, but as a quartermaster typist. I was depressed as I got on the ship—it was the *Maui*, another Matson Line ship—and went down in the hold to where we were supposed to sleep. I did not know one single soul on that ship. There were other WACs but I didn't know where they came from. I don't know that they even loaded on at Hollandia, but they were not anyone I knew. They were being moved as one unit so I was simply odd man out.

There were racks of hammocks. I tried one. It was fine, except that the minute I fell asleep, I fell out. I couldn't get the hang of it. Every time I dozed off I got dumped. I thought, this is for the birds, and went up to the deck where I discovered the ship had been deck loaded.

On the forward top deck there was a big hatch cover, covered with canvas and all lashed down. On top of that was a piece of road-building equipment. There was space for me to crawl underneath, and it was high enough so that, while I couldn't stand up, I could sit up very comfortably. So I moved in.

I had a large tin of chocolate chip cookies from my mother so I stayed under that piece of equipment day and night reading Tolstoy's *War and Peace* and eating cookies. When necessary I would go down to use the bathroom, get meals, change clothes, wash and that sort of thing. Everyone seemed to understand that that was my turf. Nobody touched my possessions, nobody challenged me for this choice spot. It worked fine for me.

By the time I got to Manila I was feeling much better. The trip was a long one and I know that two weeks would have been ample time to make the trip, but I think it was longer because we were traveling in convoy, and when you travel in convoy you don't go any faster than the slowest ship. I don't know when we arrived in Manila. I know that I was aboard ship on the 12th of April, when President Roosevelt died.

One night as I was rolled up in my blankets under the truck it rained so hard that my blankets acted like a down spout and I suddenly found that I was soaking wet. I had kept my books on the wheel of the vehicle so they were away from the rain. The next day I took the blankets out and hung them to dry on the hood of the engine.

We dropped anchor offshore in Manila. The white walls looked so beautiful as the sun came up behind the city.

At the end of my walk down the gangplank were three Signal Corps WACs, Jean Ann and two others. They grabbed my bag, grabbed me by the arm and said, "Come on," and literally dragged me across the dock to a Jeep—God only knows where they had highjacked that. I said, "Hey, wait a minute, I've got to check in." They said, "No you don't; no you don't. Come on, come on, come on." They absolutely hustled me. Talk about highjacking! I was stuffed into the Jeep and told, "You're going to the Signal Corps." I said, "Wait a minute, I'm on orders for the Quartermaster." "Oh, no, that doesn't count; you're going back to the Signal Corps." I was driven to the Message Center at the University of the Far East and there were all my old friends except Lieutenant Townsend who had gone someplace else. "Welcome back!"

Although I was on orders for the quartermaster, my MOS (Military Occupation Specialty) for 805 and 808, which were for cryptographer and cryptanalyst, took priority over any other specialty. I had been transferred to quartermaster in Hollandia because working in the Message Center required a long drive in the dust every day and my health wouldn't allow it. My colleagues realized that condition didn't exist in Manila because the Signal Corp WACs were working and living on the same grounds.

So that's how I got back in the Signal Corps. There were some inquiries, but everyone would answer, "Private Treacy? Who's that?"

Life in Manila

25 April 1945. Philippine Islands.

"Dearest Mother and Alice: Well, I have so much to tell you I hardly know where to begin. Of course, you noted the change of address. That is why you haven't heard from me for some time. Yes, I am living in the same room with Jean Ann, although we didn't come on the same boat. The trip up wasn't too bad. Much, much better than the one over here. When I got here I think about every V-Mail you ever wrote is here. So I have another niece! Well, I'm tickled. I hope Alice will take a picture of her. I got two packages two days before I left Base G. Also, Louis's letter. The packages contained food, petticoats, soap and Yardley's. They were in perfect condition, and oh so much appreciated. This is going to be a short letter because I am so tired from the trip I can scarcely keep my eyes open. It is wonderful to see children again and civilization, especially busses and streetcar tracks and sidewalks, and hear all the noises of a city. I will tell you more later when I know what I can say. Love, Selene."

It says turn over.

"Please send tropical worsted uniform and brown pumps PDQ. We wear dresses off-duty. Don't forget the hat."

I cannot remember the exact state of the war when I arrived in Manila but I can give details of things I saw. There were definite signs in the various rooms of the Far Eastern University of their use as torture chambers, such as blood on the walls. Most of it had been

109

washed off before we got there but you could still see the stains on the walls and on the cement floors.

We had running water in the latrines of our quarters and thought it was great. Showers, basins and toilets! What we didn't realize was that the Filipinos, in cleaning up Manila, had thrown the bodies of dead enemy soldiers into the sewers. So when we got a combination of torrential tropical rains and a high tide the sewers backed up. I don't have to tell you what happened. The floor drains and the toilets backed up with bits of human flesh and bodies. There was absolutely no mistaking what it was.

The army took a very dim view of this and the next morning came to close those bathrooms off completely. They poured concrete down the floor drains and toilets so it could not happen again. The bathrooms were locked and sealed. They quickly built latrines and a wash house on campus which was separate from the sewer system of Manila.

27 April 1945. Philippine Islands.

"Dearest Mother: Well, I guess this is as good a time as any to sit down and write you a longer letter than the last one. The trip up here was not so bad, nothing to equal the one coming over from the States. We had three meals a day and they left us pretty much to ourselves, thus I had time to read and write some. I was pretty lonesome as all the Signal Corps kids had come on an earlier boat and I didn't know a soul on board. And since I've been in the army I find it rather hard to meet people. In large groups I find my own thoughts more inter-esting. Our living conditions here are very nice. We live in what was the dormitory of one of the big universities here. It is of very modern construction, all fireproof cement, four stories high. There are twelve girls in our room and it has two tremendous windows looking down onto the campus, or rather what would have been a campus it if didn't have tents pitched on it. The windows opened, practically make a nonexistent wall and the ceilings are pretty high, so is as cool as any place in town could be. And that isn't saying much. It never cools off even at night. The mosquitoes are terrible, but I don't believe they are the malaria-carrying variety. Outside one of our windows we have a cute little balcony where we hang our clothes to dry, or rather will until they decide we can't do it anymore. Under the window there is the loveliest little tree. The foliage is so fluffy and dainty. It looks almost like a maidenhair fern. It throws such lovely, soft, lacy shadows on the pavement below. There are the most tremendous trees around the office building that look like magnolias, but I never knew that they grew to be so huge. they are lovely and with the white buildings and blue sky make a pretty color combination. The building where I work is just a few steps away from our quarters and we reach it by a covered passageway. Not bad if it should ever rain. We don't have any work to do. No KP, or cleaning details. There are Filipinos hired by the government to do that. It makes it nice, but I never can get used to having servants around. I was brought up to do things for myself, and while I like all the leisure it leaves us, it is hard to get used to it. All of our laundry is done by the Filipinos very reasonably and they do a wonderful job on it. The food promises to be good. Our mess hall has been a former Jap torture chamber and with some unmistakable signs of such around. I can't help but think of that every time I go to a meal. Our building had been a former Jap Headquarters building and the top floor was another torture chamber. It seems so funny to see Japanese written in chalk on the walls, et cetera. Right beside my bed I think there must have been a desk with a telephone on it because all of the wall has Jap doodlings in pencil. As for the city, there just isn't anything left standing to speak of. All of the lovely public buildings and the medical center near us, that you can see had been beautiful modern buildings, have been systematically destroyed. There was nothing left standing. The Japs had trained demolition crews in here, and they started at one end of the city and went block by block to the other. You can have no conception what it is like. Not just a few blocks, but a whole city leveled. I find that the terrible poverty and ragged naked children very depressing and it takes the edge off my delight in being here. The first afternoon we arrived, Frankie Cors and I went out walking around and talked to a few soldiers, but that was all. The next day, which was yesterday, two of my other roommates, both Signal Corps kids that ran around with us at Base G, Clyta Davis and Jimmie Hammel and I, went walking in the morning and made the acquaintance of a little cafe where we were able to purchase fair coffee for ten cents a cup or twenty centavos, Philippine money. We also bought bananas, but everything is so prohibitively expensive that I limit my eating to the GI chow. I'm only making private's pay. This afternoon the three of us hired a little pony cart, a funny sort of little wicker affair with a very diminutive horse. A two-wheeled specimen. At the reins was a dirty little Filipino driver that made queer kissing noises to get the pony to do what he wanted. That was fun, although a bit rough over the holes in the street. And heavens knows when the cart had last had new tires. So we jiggled along eating bananas and enjoying the ride, although, as I have said before, all there is to see here is this and that building and site—what that building and site used to be. It was very disconcerting. The first time we went out we oriented ourselves with distinctive piles of rubble, only to find that when we went out the next day they had all been cleared away, so we had to start all over again. We went into a lovely church that, for some unknown reason, had been left intact, although in very bad repair with holes in the roof and so forth. It was simply gorgeous. The altar was solid silver with gold candles and statuary. I had heard of such churches, but it was the first time that I had ever seen one. Then we went into a little shop and bought ice cream, one nickel scoop for fifty cents, or one peso. That little dish of ice cream is going to have to last for the duration of my stay in the Philippines at that price. What I can't figure out is what the Filipinos themselves are doing. Surely they don't have that kind of money. After that, we hailed an MP and rode home in a Jeep. By that time our feet were so sore and tired from tramping on the hot pavements, after the dirt in New Guinea, that we could scarcely navigate. Well, I am back working in the Signal Corps and it looks like Jean and I will be together for the duration of our stay in the army, as we have been formed into a Signal Company. Of course you know how delighted I am with the way things have turned out and it makes everything look pretty rosy, especially with this last bit of news that I have been saving for last. One of the fellows looked up Walter's outfit to find that it is only six blocks from here, so I am going calling the first thing in the morning. I am so excited I can scarcely wait. After all it has been ten months since I've seen him, and you know how much I've always enjoyed his company and his letters. In short, I find myself being terribly fond of him even though it has been such a long time. I will tell you all about the visit in my next letter.

"I only hope that he hasn't been transferred or something equally horrible. It is such a piece of luck that it just can't happen to me. And I keep thinking that there must be some mistake and that I will find he isn't there or something.

"Well, darling, I think I have covered every phase of the news, except, of course, the tragic death of our President. We heard about that on the boat and I can scarcely believe it was true. It seems so tragic that he should have had to die before he could retire to his home and have a much needed vacation and time to do all the things he no doubt would have loved to do and just never had the time. But he died a great man and one of the world's ablest leaders. I didn't always agree with everything he did, but he did so much more than any other one man could have possibly done. I can't help but wonder just what kind of man President Truman is going to be. He is working under very adverse conditions succeeding such a man, but he has been responsible for some very good legislation in the Senate and that is very indicative of the way the wind blows. I will close now, darlings, and be good. Love, Selene."

About this time we got a new officer who decided the Signal Corps WACs, and whoever else was around, should get up at eight o'clock every morning and do physical training. She had just arrived from the States and didn't understand what doing physical training in Manila's heat was going to be like.

She also didn't understand that at eight o'clock in the morning all the Signal Corps WACs were either doing something else, like being on duty, or sleeping after having come off duty at 7:00 a.m. If you had been on the evening shift, you would have come home at 11:30 p.m. or midnight and you were also going to be sleeping. Eight o'clock in the morning it was about as cool in Manila as it was ever going to get making it the only good time to sleep. If you couldn't sleep then, you sure as heck weren't going to sleep later.

I assume the First Sergeant and some of the non-COMS had probably told her this, but it didn't make any difference. Orders were issued for us to report for physical training at eight o'clock the next morning.

I don't remember us all getting together to discuss what to do but the next morning at eight o'clock everyone stayed in bed with

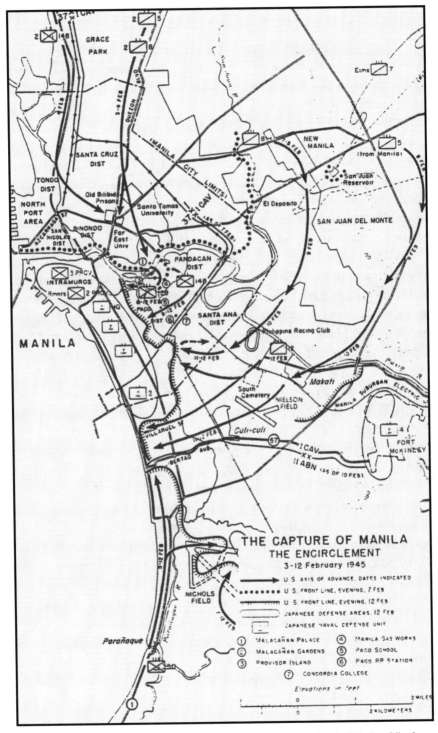

THE CAPTURE OF MANILA
THE ENCIRCLEMENT
3-12 February 1945

→ U.S. AXIS OF ADVANCE, DATES INDICATED
•••••• U.S. FRONT LINE, EVENING, 7 FEB
⎓⎓ U.S. FRONT LINE, EVENING, 12 FEB
⎓⎓ JAPANESE DEFENSE AREAS, 12 FEB
⌐⌐ JAPANESE NAVAL DEFENSE UNIT

① MALACAÑAN PALACE   ④ MANILA GAS WORKS
② MALACAÑAN GARDENS   ⑤ PACO SCHOOL
③ PROVISOR ISLAND   ⑥ PACO RR STATION
⑦ CONCORDIA COLLEGE

Elevations in feet

0   2 MILES
0   1   2 KILOMETERS

Triumph in the Philippines, folio of maps

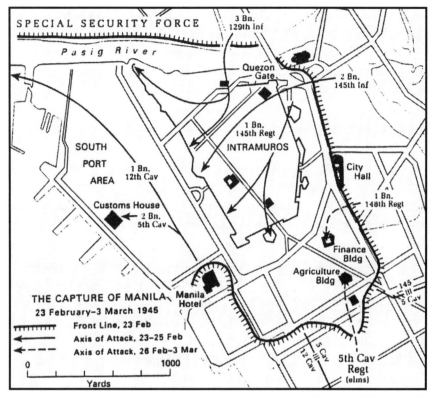

SPECIAL SECURITY FORCE

Pasig River

3 Bn.
129th Inf

Quezon
Gate

2 Bn.
145th Inf

1 Bn.
145th Regt

INTRAMUROS

SOUTH
PORT
AREA

1 Bn.
12th Cav

City
Hall

1 Bn.
148th Regt

Customs House

2 Bn.
5th Cav

Finance
Bldg

Agriculture
Bldg

THE CAPTURE OF MANILA
23 February–3 March 1945

Manila
Hotel

Front Line, 23 Feb
Axis of Attack, 23–25 Feb
Axis of Attack, 26 Feb–3 Mar

0   1000

Yards

5th Cav
Regt
(elms)

Triumph in the Philippines, p. 298

mosquito netting carefully tucked in. In our building we had one girl at the window to spy. Later she told us the officer walked up and down on the pavement below blowing a whistle to summon us. No one went. There she was pacing up and down by herself.

Finally a non-COM was sent upstairs. Our spy made a bee-line for her bed and tucked herself in. When the non-COM came in, everybody—every WAC in the place was fast asleep. We hadn't heard the whistle. We hadn't heard a thing.

There were consequences that could have happened to us, but they didn't. It was dropped and we never heard a word about physical training again.

I suppose for someone who has not lived through that kind of thing, it seems we were a rebellious bunch. But you know, it was the only thing we could do. Or it was the only thing we could think of to do to make our lives work. We had had a terrible time at Base G in the early days when we had officers who simply couldn't stand to see someone sleeping in the daytime. But when you work all night you can't function the next night at work unless you have slept. Our work was a very important part of the war effort. And those silly officers would come in with no idea of what we did or how we did it. The Signal Center was open twenty-four hours a day, seven days a week. So we nipped this one in the bud.

29 of April 1945.

"Dearest Mother: Well, the business of seeing Walter was indeed a false alarm. Needless to say, I am bitterly disappointed, but then what can you expect of wartime? Yesterday morning, armed with the directions to the place his outfit was supposed to be, Jean Ann and I started out walking. But finding the distance much too far for walking hailed a passing Jeep, but they could only take us halfway. So then we got out and hailed another. We drove around and around asking everybody where this place was. And, oh, yes, they all knew, but when it came to arriving we just didn't. So finally we went to one of the Headquarters Buildings in that neighborhood and called the Headquarters of PCAU, only to find that he is on some very minute island somewhere south of here. So there went my hopes crashing again. In the meantime Jean Ann had had to go home, so there I was halfway across town from our quarters and hot and dusty and mad, mostly at my own stupidity at not checking up first and saving my time and my feet.

"Well, another day and I will finish the letter I began last night. Well, as I said, Jean Ann had had to go home so I came out of the Headquarters Building with my chin dragging the ground and feeling quite dashed, when some cute little private walked up and asked me the way back to the business district, or what would ordinarily be the business district. And then he suggested that we go to the Red Cross and have coffee. So we did and then I felt better. And I also found out that he was from St. Louis and knew Art Richmond and Dick Fry and quite a few other people from Washington University that I knew. So all in all it wasn't quite all wasted time. Oh, yes, we played a game of Ping-Pong and I beat him quite off the map, as I had been playing for seven months down in New Guinea. Well, by that time, my little 19-year-old private, Chuck Nassau by name, had to go before an OCS

Board and wanted to go home. And also I didn't relish missing noon chow. So I hired a little pony cart and took myself across town to our quarters. The little cart I had this time was much cuter than the one I had before. It was shiny black with bright yellow wheels. And the pony was just as shiny as could be with a beautiful harness all studded with brass nails, and gay little pieces of brass that jingled merrily as we trotted smartly through town. Oh, yes, the little Filipino that was driving was cleaned up within an inch of his life with a bright yellow silk shirt and a long whip studded with brass to match the harness. We also had a bell that the driver used without discretion, so all the other little carts had to give way before such grandeur. And there was I in solitary splendor. Jean thinks I'm positively nuts to get such a kick out of those silly little carts, but somewhere back in my mind there must be some association with trotters and two-wheel equipages. That night Jean Ann and I had a date with Bill Fornwald who was a friend of Bob McDonald's, and was also very nice to us down at APO 503. He is here now and took the two of us out and we had a perfect evening. We went to a little night club just around the corner from our quarters, which makes transportation unnecessary. It is called the 'Princess.' It evidently had been an old home of some proportions, because we went into the first floor, which was all open to the street, and paid our cover charge. And then with a little Chinese waiter carrying a little kerosene lamp went up the most imposing staircase I've ever seen. On each landing there was a lamp on the floor to guide your footsteps up the stairs safely. On the second floor there were three rooms, the middle one of which had an orchestra and a place to dance. The walls were all folded back to let in air and dappled moonlight, and the heady smell of tropical flowers, plus the smell of flowers that all the WACs in the place were wearing. Some of the girls had the loveliest leis made of some small, dainty, sweet-smelling white flower. The ceilings were very high with heavy mahogany beams that gleamed in the soft lamplight. The walls were sort of screens of slatted bamboo that could be folded back, I imagine; they were painted pale green with pastel flowers and things on each one. All the little tables had white cloths and little lamps. I neglected to mention that as yet there is no electricity in the city except what the army has. Thus the lamps. I liked it better that way. There is nothing like lamplight and a dash—to add a dash of romance. All the girls looked so pretty and clean with their flowers and clean, starched shirts open at the neck. Of course I may be prejudiced, but for just downright good looks I think American women have it all over any other nationality. They always look so clean and dainty. Our waiter was a smiling, obsequious little man that bowed to us, which somehow annoyed me because it is a relic of the Japanese occupation. But there was a little Chinese girl hostess in a white silk dress, a perfect specimen of Oriental beauty. She was really lovely. Well, the three of us had a few drinks and danced and talked and had a perfectly marvelous time. I have another date with Bill tomorrow night, and so my stay here promises to be unusually pleasant because Bill is a swell guy with a lot of personality and no romantic ideas. Well, not yet anyhow. Tonight I have a blind date with a Naval Lieutenant, who is a friend of Jean's, and I expect to have a pleasant evening. So I see where my time will be well taken care of, especially with the fact that Pat, my little Jewish chaplain friend, will fly up from his little island south of here to see me. It is only an hour by air from here. Well, angels, that about takes care of the news abroad so I will wind up for this morning and call it a day. I hope you don't mind the letter written on the teletype, but it is so much quicker that way, although I expect a little harder to read. But then you can pretend it is a news bulletin."

1 May 1945.

"Dearest Mother: Well, I just finished a letter to Charlie and Evelyn about the Chinese cemetery, so rather than repeat, you can call them and hear all about it and I will tell you about last night. Today is May Day and it must be quite a celebration, because I woke up this morning to the sound of church bells. They sounded so nice and civilized. Just lying there in bed it was hard to realize that it wasn't just any prosperous city going about its daily business, and that the bells came from nice, well-kept churches. So many of them go right on having services and parish affairs without a roof. It rained last night and I went out on the balcony and had a look around, and everything looked so fresh and clean. And the buildings across the way just gleamed white in the sun. It was pretty cool then, too. Last night Jean Ann had made arrangements for me to go out with some navy lieutenant friend of hers, but somehow we missed each other at the gate. They came and we were there, but we messed up anyhow. So we were wandering around just about deciding to go over to the mess hall and have coffee, when a nice-looking chap walked up and asked us if we cared to go out. He was a civilian employee of the army and was doing criminal investigation. Most of these chaps are lawyers and professional fellows, so it wasn't too much of a risk and we were all dressed up and no place to go, so we said yes, we would. He had a friend and a Jeep so we went to a place called the Club Manila. It was very expensive, not nearly as nice as the little Princess Inn that I told you about in my last letter. Last night they were getting fifty cents a shot for about two tablespoons of diluted whiskey. Not very good. So I, for one, was perfectly satisfied to play with a glass of water. We are fed pretty well at the mess and have snacks at 9:30 in the evening, and also at 11:30, so we don't have to buy things to eat out in town when we get hungry. Nice, don't you think? We had fun dancing and the boys bought us lovely leis of flowers. The same, I believe, that I told you about in my last letter—small white ones with a heavenly fragrance. Well, last night I found out that they are the Philippine national flower, and they are called Sambaguita. The 'G' is pronounced hard with the accent on that syllable. The legend is that two Filipino lovers were denied the permission to marry by their families, and they made a death pact, which they carried out. Their families, stricken with remorse, buried them together and from their grave sprang these lovely little sweet-smelling flowers. If a Filipino girl gives a man a lei of these it means that she loves him and will be eternally true to him no matter what. I told Jean Ann that she should send Walter a lei. Well, except for the fact that my laundry was just stolen I guess that was all the news. Someone just helped themselves to my clean clothes waiting to be delivered to me, and now I don't have a single stitch to my name. Not one thing. I'm so mad! I had my nice white navy towels and sheets, navy shirts that fit, and about seven pairs of pants that I had simply taken apart and remade to fit me. So help me if I find who took those things, they're going to be picking themselves up in pieces. Well, I must close now. Love, Selene."

My letters mentioned the Chinese cemetery several times and one of those trips had some very interesting details that I couldn't put in a letter. First place I wouldn't—it wouldn't have gotten through the censor—and second place I'm not sure the censor, who usually was my commanding officer, would have been very pleased about it.

When we arrived in Manila the American troops only had control of parts of the city and there were many areas we were not allowed to go. But those in command didn't stop us and, I guess, we just didn't seem to think there was much danger.

Anyhow, one day a group of us took a picnic to the cemetery. When we took picnics, we went to the mess hall for cans of tuna, cheese and a loaf of bread. I still had the big sheath knife Earl had given me in Hollandia. I don't know how I would have managed the war without that knife. This day I used it to open cans and slice bread.

I remember sitting on the grass under a tree eating when all of a sudden Clyta Davis reached over and quickly took my red head and simply pushed me down. She said, "Get down, Treacy." And I did. But with a bit of a struggle. She said, "Don't look now but there's a Jap over in the bushes." Well, I sort of looked up from under my eyebrows and I was staring down the barrel of a Japanese rifle. I could see the face of the soldier just as clear as could be and I could see his cap with a little red pompom on it. Our eyes met. We were close enough that I could see the features of his face, and he could sure as hell see my red head. Suddenly, he got up and disappeared into the bush and that was it. We departed in a hurry and that was our last trip to the Chinese cemetery.

In later years I've wondered why he did what he did. I've wondered if he saw that we were unarmed women and just simply didn't see any point in taking a pot shot at us. But at that point in the war the Japanese were still putting up a good fight. Believe me, they were. Maybe that soldier just didn't see any gain in shooting unarmed women. But for whatever reason, I guess it was the Lord's will I come through intact, because this soldier was certainly taking a bead on my head.

May 3, 1945.

"Dearest Mother: This is in the nature of a business letter. Seven months ago Howard agreed to a divorce and I sent you the necessary power of attorney to get it for me. Well, Howard has simply not done a thing about getting the affidavit. He hasn't even had the courtesy to answer the letters I've sent him. I had one letter from him since I saw him at Base G. So what I want you to do for me is get from Mr. Noble the necessary information that the court would require from the defendant and get it to me as soon as possible. I'm tired to death of fooling around and I want to get it over with. That situation has been hanging fire now for better than two years. If you get me the necessary information for the affidavit then I can have it drawn up here in the Judge Advocate Section and send it to Howard for his signature. Only this time it will go to his Commanding Officer and then he will have to either sign or drop the whole thing. And if he does I'm going to demand more of his pay for my support. I know that you hate doing all of this, but it won't cost me anything this way, or very little anyway. While, if I waited until I got back to the States I would have to bear the full cost of lawyer's fee plus court costs, and as you probably know that isn't cheap. Besides, I expect to be over here for another 18 months at least, and it is quite possible that I might meet someone else I would like to marry. After all, it has been two years or thereabouts since Howard and I separated. In another two years I most likely will meet someone. After all, men, nice ones, aren't that scarce. Well, honey, I would appreciate it very much if you would do that right away and get it to me here. Love, Selene."

Another letter. May 3, 1945.

"Darling Mother: Well, my laundry was returned to me, so my disposition is up accordingly. Evidently somebody picked it up by mistake. Either that or they found my clothes were much too small around the waist for them. Well, yesterday was my day off and that is why I didn't write a letter. Night before last Bill and Jean and I went out walking. We have all three decided that drinking around here is much too expensive, so we're sticking to coffee. We started out sitting in a little hole-in-the-wall with a candle in the middle of the table and talked and drank our coffee. And then we went out to the former mansion of one of the high officials that is open for public inspection. Of course the building was closed but we walked around the grounds and the smell of Black Locust in bloom was simply heavenly. It was such fun walking around that lovely garden, with its clipped lawns and tremendous trees, in the cool of the evening. Finally we picked out the front steps of the house and sat there and just talked about home and plans for after the war. It was nice and peaceful and quiet.

Such a difference from the army. We took Jean Ann home about ten as she had to go to work at midnight, and Bill and I went and had some more coffee and discussed religion. And he recited poetry, which, by the way reminds me that I have a poem I wrote just for you on the ship coming up, and if I ever have it when I happen to be writing you a letter I'll get it in somehow. Yesterday, as I said before, was my day off. So Bill and I went out to that mansion where we had been the night before to see it in the daylight. Although I enjoyed the garden more than I did the palace. We sat on a sort of terrace—built right on the river. It was cool there and so that is where we stopped to rest. After that we went into town to see what we could find for our families in the way of distinctive souvenirs. It's very difficult because the things they have are mostly American. But Bill bought me six lovely little shells and one large one. We are going to use four of the small ones for buttons and the other two he's going to have fixed into earrings and then the big one will be put on a silver chain for a pendant. They will really be lovely. So far that is the only thing I have seen that I wanted at all, other than some wooden shoes. But they want much too much for them. Last night I had a date with one of the chaps here in the office who knew how much I love music. So we went to a little place called Felix's Tavern, where Felix's son played both the violin and the piano. And it certainly was way over and beyond my fondest expectations. He was marvelous. We had real honest-to-goodness limeades and I have never in my life tasted anything so good. they really hit the spot with a bang. In short we had a very pleasant evening. Well, let me think. What else is new? Oh, yes. Bill is going to make me a little cabinet and bookcase combined. Isn't that sweet of him? He gave me a book yesterday that promises to be very interesting, *Christ of the American Road*. Bill is a combination of Methodist and Christian Scientist, with the Scientist predominating. You know, Christian Science certainly must have a great deal to offer in the way of spiritual sustenance, because both Jean Ann and Bill seem to have so much spirituality and gentleness. You would like Bill. He's a very cute chap with bright blue eyes, unusually wide-set, and a nice wide grin. Unfortunately, though, he's quite bald. He's only 30 but somehow you never even think of that. I've been enjoying his company more than anyone I've met for a while. I only hope they don't start clamping down on officers and enlisted personnel dating like they did at APO 565. Then we would have to sneak around and that isn't much fun. By the way, if you should happen to be downtown and see some cute, gay, printed material could you send me a couple of pieces about two and a half or three yards each, with matching thread? I have so much spare time on my hands I could really use some little playsuits to wear around the area, and before too long we will have pools for swimming. There are a great many around town, but so far they haven't been able to spare that much water to keep them filled and clean. I've got a bathing suit in the process of being made. I made my double-bed sheet into a single-bed sheet and I'm going to use a white towel for the lining. I am trying to find some gay binding to trim it with and I think I know where I can find some narrow blue bias binding. Well, honey lamb, I guess I'll wind up for today and get to work. I have been a good girl. You know as much about what this place is like and what I've been doing as I do myself. Love, Selene."

Another letter dated May 3, 1945. Manila. This one is to Alice.

"Darlingest Alice: I want to wish you a very, very happy birthday and may you have many more of them. I only wish I could be there to help you celebrate. I have a little remembrance that I will send to you, but it will take longer to get there than this letter. It seems funny for me to be so far away from all of you knowing that it is just spring at home, that the mock orange is in bloom and the early June roses. I can remember going out on your birthday and cutting a bouquet of both and a bouquet of the light lavender iris that you always liked so much. The iris went in a crystal-cut glass vase and the roses in the little fish bowl. I remember the cake mother made for you one year with a basket on the top and all different colors of icing. I take it for granted that you will have ice cream and birthday cake and mother will make up some games for the family to play. Gee, you have no idea how much I miss my family. I don't remember whether I mentioned in a letter or not, I don't think I did, but just the day before I left Base G for the Philippines, I got the picture of mother that had been on the way since November. I had forgotten that you had sent it, so it arrived as a complete and elegant surprise. It occupies the place of honor now on the top of a little rations crate that I use for a dressing table, along with a cute little bowl made of a polished coconut shell with a little lid that is cut out like a star and has a little cork for a handle. Something like a sugar bowl. One of the Filipino crew members on the boat coming up made it for me. Wasn't that nice? I believe I mentioned in my letter to mother that Bill Fornwald is making me a bookcase and a cabinet combined for my books and junk, trinkets and cosmetics that I have accumulated along the way. One of these days I will have a wooden box made and send all that stuff home. I'm getting quite a collection of Jap-invasion currency that will come home, too. I have two brass candlesticks that I wouldn't take anything for, made from 50 caliber machine-gun shells with a 40-millimeter shell cap for the base. They are solid brass and weigh several pounds. I have a native comb from New Guinea and a lovely little Jap compass. All the figures are in Jap characters. Coming up on the boat I had fun figuring out the course for myself. I had that tall square tin that mother had sent with cookies and that made the shadow, and then a crack in the floor, or rather deck, made the other angle. We were so close to the equator that the other angle of the sun was negligible and I ignored it. I knew I had something I wanted to tell you. When we were out in the harbor at Base G, just before we left we could see the lovely harbor ringed with mountains. The nearest shore was a sheer limestone cliff, lovely, aged, and gray. The water was a deep blue. Then across our line of vision sailed the most beautiful two-masted schooner in full sail, with an auxiliary sail set. It was painted a beautiful light green and the sails were a darker shade of emerald green. It was so lovely as to be breathtaking. And then with saucy disregard for the dignity of this picture, a little catboat with a red sail, gaff rig, came panting up at a good clip behind the schooner, relieving the somber colors with the red sail. I only wish that you could have seen it. Only in the South Sea Islands do you find such scenery and such skies. When we arrived in the harbor here it was too dark to see very much, but we could see some dark little things moving around the water. And when it got light we saw that all those myriad's of tiny things were tiny little sailboats with outriggers. The sails were mostly white with a few other colors thrown in for good measure. It resembled a puddle where a lot of butterflies have settled. They were all over the place, actually hundreds of them. Well, dear, I will close now and go to lunch, and, again, have a lovely time on your birthday."

There were two Paul's in my correspondence. One was Paul Kneffley and the other was Paul Greenlund. Paul Kneffley was one of the men in my outfit, a really delightful guy. He had trained for the priesthood and then resigned and married his childhood sweetheart. She had married someone else in the interim, had a child, and had been widowed. So Paul came back from the priesthood, married her and they had a child. I think there was a difference of about thirteen years in their ages.

I remember this because his wife was probably the best letter writer known to man. Every time Paul got a letter from home he read it to everyone in the Signal Center. Those letters still stick in my mind. She knew how to write a letter to a service man. If she were putting up new curtains or something, swatches of material came in the letters. And she wrote all the funny, hilarious things that happened with the children. Paul's child was about eighteen months. I think it was a little girl. His stepson was about fourteen.

Paul had gotten to know any number of people and several of the places we went to visit were friends of his. The Gil Estate was one of them. The Gil's were a well-to-do Spanish family. They were Spanish, not mastisos, or part Filipino. At the time we were in the Philippines there were still families left over from the Spanish empire that had never intermarried.

We hitched a ride to what must have been a magnificent estate. The house was in the Spanish style built around a beautiful patio. The inside of the house faced the patio and had balconies up and downstairs. All the rooms opened out into the patio. There was a fountain in the middle and it had been planted in gardens.

The thing I recall about this visit, was that here was this big Spanish family with all kinds of young people both male and female sitting around. The patio was an absolute wreck. I saw one of the young men peel an orange and toss the peeling into the fountain. I was speechless. There was rubbish everywhere. Nobody did anything. They didn't even pick up after themselves. An American's view of this was absolute shock and disbelief.

There was only one servant in the household and she was a tiny Negrito woman whom I saw standing on a box at the sink washing a mountain of dirty dishes. It was obvious that she was expected to do it all. I couldn't believe all those young, able-bodied people doing nothing.

Negrito is a pigmy race from the central islands of the Philippines. They are small with kinky black hair and black skin. A full-grown woman might be no taller than four feet. This woman was awfully small to have to do all the work in this Spanish house that was designed for full-scale people.

4th of May 1945.

"Dearest Mother: I got your letter yesterday about Mr. Beck. Of course you realize now that I'm no longer in New Guinea and won't be able to see Allen at all. It is so sad. Mr. Beck couldn't have been very old, was he? Poor Mrs. Beck, she must be just lost. They always were such a companionable family and now with Mr. beck gone and Allen over here she must just about be crushed. Do you suppose that Lynn will stay home now or what? I started a letter to the family last night and will get it in the mail today. Well, Darling, this is going to be a short letter because I spent a very uneventful day at the office yesterday and stayed home and went to bed last night. High time, I guess. I knew I had something funny to tell you. You remember in my letter to Charlie and Evelyn I told about the party we were going to next Tuesday. Well, the last time that Jean and I went out with Bill she thought it would be nice to ask him to go along, as the host had said bring your dates. So we thought we could share a date in Bill. I also said that the party would be held in the Chinese cemetery. So out of a clear sky Jean asked Bill, 'How would you like to go to a party in a cemetery?' Needless to say, poor Bill was flabbergasted. He thought she was kidding, having the occidental view towards cemeteries. Oh, yes, another thing. We had a set of swinging doors. What I meant was swinging doors installed between the lobby of our building and the hall. On one door is the sign, 'Out, watch your nose,' and on the other, 'In, watch your nose.' I thought that was pretty cute, don't you? Yesterday afternoon here in the office we weren't very busy, so I wrote the silliest story about a little nymph that lived in the fountain at the president's place in Manila, all about what she did when the Japs came and about her bit toward winning the war. I wrote mostly for the entertainment of myself and the kids that live with me. Love, Selene."

Pasig River
Manila, Philippines

I should say here what I didn't say in the letters. The building I described was the Malacañan Palace, which is the presidential palace of the Philippines. At this point the president of the Philippines was still in Australia. He had been evacuated along with MacArthur and his staff. So the palace was unoccupied at that time.

6 May 1945.

"Dearest Mother: Well, I had the day off yesterday, so didn't write to you. But we had a most interesting day. Night before last Jean Ann and I went to the movies and saw an awfully cute picture, *Frisco Sal*. It was the first movie I had seen in some time and I enjoyed it immensely. It was a cute musical with more and better dialog and story than most. Yesterday morning I got up bright and early and got all dressed up. And, Bill, and a friend of his called Pete, came by in a Jeep and we went way out to the suburbs of the city where Bill had some friends. They lived in what had been a magnificent place with two houses and a tennis court and swimming pool. As I say, what had been lovely grounds. It had so many lovely trees that hadn't been damaged. During the occupation it had been occupied by two Japanese generals and in the true Jap tradition they let the place go to wrack and ruin. They never did repair or take care of anything. I don't know what they expected to do if they would have continued living here if they didn't keep their own quarters in repair. Well, anyhow, the Japs had turned the garage into a small apartment, which was a good idea. It has all cement floors and a concrete construction and good sheet-iron roof, which is very cool in the tropics. Has one big bedroom and three small ones and a bath. At present it is occupied by an English friend of Bill's who has been returned to his home after three years internment, but he is planning to move into one of the big houses with an American and his wife. So they are turning over the garage to Bill and Pete and one other friend with a sort of gentlemen's agreement, which should turn out to be a pretty nice setup. After having visited Mr. Skoe, who is the Englishman, we went out to what had been one of the largest plants in the Far East. Of

Escolta Business District
Manila, Philippines

Street Scene
Manila, Philippines

course, the damage is tremendous, but they are starting up production again with what they have. Out there we met several more people
who had lived in the Philippines for years. There were two Americans, three Englishmen, two Swiss and a Spanish. All of them were
men, of course, as it was during business hours. They too, of course,
had all been interned and it was wonderful to see how these men,
fellows about your age, had made a comeback both physically and
mentally. Of course, work is always a good cure-all and they were full
of plans as to the eventual enlargement and improvement of the plant
over the post-war situation, or rather pre-war. A little Filipino house
boy brought us real honest-to-goodness drinks, rum Collins, real old
rum that had been buried in the yard from the Japs and real ice in lime
and crystal cut-glass highball glasses with one-pre-war cocktail stirrer, commonly known as a swizzle stick. They didn't tell me where
they had hidden the glass and the swizzle stick but the stirrer they
spoke of tenderly as Mrs. Murphy, and laughed hilariously over some

private joke. All in all it was a very festive occasion and a real taste of what pre-war life here must have been. Gee, I only wish that you could have heard them talk. It reminded me of the *savior faire* of the French nobility during the Revolution. They didn't dwell on the horrors, but in the fun they had heckling their Jap jailers. Got a big kick out of regaling us with death-defying stunts they pulled off to get in food as if it was another type of cops and robbers. However, little things that would slip out made it very easy to understand how men of intelligence and ability suffered under the treatment. They managed to keep themselves busy by working around the place. During the entire three years, there were three radios in the encampment, but even until the last the other prisoners didn't know where they were. However, from reading between the lines I think that they had had one of them. Well, anyhow, they would listen to the broadcast over the short wave from the United States. There would be what they called the Daily TP. Obviously you can guess what the news was

Botanical Gardens
Manila, Philippines

City Hall
Manila, Philippines

written on. And they passed it around in the latrines and when—then if they had gotten caught it would have been very easy to dispose of it. But that is the way they were able to keep up with the news. The one thing they won't talk about, though, is their feeling when the American paratroopers came into the prison after three years and rescued them with the Jap-fired prison burning over their heads. One man told me that he and his wife had kept a tin can hidden from the Japs all during the internment, with $20,000 worth of her jewels, and then at the last when the prison was burning they had to leave everything and they didn't even care. What was also most interesting to me were the two Swiss. They were, of course, not interned, being neutrals, but they were watched like hawks all the time. In spite of the vigilance they were able to direct the tremendous sabotage ring that went on here all the time, just a constant heckling. I presume this was in conjunction with the guerrillas. They also helped to get supplies to the people who had taken to the hills and were fighting there. He laughed and said that even three weeks after the Americans came in when he was on the streets at night he would duck into a dark doorway at the sight of the headlights on a car. Then he would feel so silly. I wish I could remember all the things they had to say, but it will come back to me from time to time. Well, back again. After having several drinks we had dinner served on a sort of used-to-be terrace. Anyway, there was a lovely breeze, and it was nice and shady. We had a real damask tablecloth and pretty dainty civilian dishes and silver-and-cut-glass tumblers. They have to use the best all the time because it is impossible to get anything else, and those are the things they had hidden from the Japs. Food, of course, was GI, except for the onion soup. The onions may have been GI, but the soup sure wasn't. It was a wonderful clear dark brown, with real butter in it and plenty of onions floating around. Then we had the traditional GI sausages and stuff, and then a big platter of fresh, ripe cantaloupe. Boy, don't you think Bill and I didn't make sheep's eyes after all that time with nothing fresh at all?

Finance Building
Manila, Philippines

St. John's Episcopal Church
Manila, Philippines

After dinner we had to get back as Bill had to go on duty at 4:00 and thought he needed a siesta after drinking rum Collins in the middle of the day. He wasn't tight, but just sleepy, and so was I. Boy, if they keep that up it's no wonder they need a siesta. Durn good idea, though. I wish the army thought so, too. Oh, yes, I forgot to tell you about the bathtub the Japs had built at the plant. It was about eight feet square and about four-feet deep. On the outside there were little steps leading up to the side, and then around the inside there was a seat. All of this was white tile. It seems the Japanese officials of the company used to all get in the bathtub on a hot afternoon to discuss business. Rather too clubby for me, but I can see where it might have its advantages. I had to laugh. Bill and I went in to look at it and one of the chaps nailed the door shut so we'd have to climb out of the window. They hadn't had any freedom in so long they got a terrific bang out of the prank. Of course, the door was only beaver board and wood strips, so don't think it was vandalism. Last night I went up on the roof and just sat thinking a long time. What is it that makes people keep on fighting even after they've lost everything; money and possessions and family? What inborn trait is it that makes men like that so strong when they've always had everything so easy with more than enough money for every whim and desire. Is that what you would call '*noblesse oblige*'? I try and think how I would have acted under such circumstances. I like to think I would have done as they did, but my mind simply can't encompass such terrors, even when I am here and its manifestations are always and constantly around us. Well, darling, the censor isn't going to appreciate the length of this letter, but I guess that's tough. We have all sorts of nice invitations to dinner and cocktails and tennis when they get the courts finished, and swimming when they—when the Japs get out of the dam and can get enough water for such luxuries as lawn sprinklers and swimming pools. Those people said some mighty nice things about the WACs. I'm the only one they've met socially and I certainly was made to feel welcome and at home."

Legislative Building
Manila, Philippines

American and European YMCA
Manila, Philippines

I am amazed that the censor let that one slip through because one of the things we were never allowed to talk about was the progress of the campaign in Luzon. When we got to Manila the Americans had only secured part of the city. Much of the city was still in Japanese hands and every so often they took a shot at us. They held the Ipo Dam, which was the source of water for the city of Manila. Up to the time that I wrote this in May we were still very short of water. We had enough to bathe and to drink but there wasn't enough for swimming pools.

"Now, for a few requests. If I didn't already ask you for some dirndl skirts and thin blouses and my white sandals, I'm asking you now because the kids wear civilian clothes around the areas on our off-duty hours. They are cooler, to say nothing of saving our precious laundered uniforms. Could you put in each one of your letters a package of flower seeds? One in each letter would be quite a few. These people have no seeds to replant their gardens and I think that would be such

Ipo Dam
Triumph in the Philippines, p. 412

a small thing to repay their generous hospitality, particularly their small and precious stocks of liquor and scarce fresh food. These are the ones I would like: Zinnias, Marigold, Cosmos, Sweet William or Phlox, whichever it is, and any other nice bright flowers. After all, shrubs and stuff will have to wait until the war is over, but lots of gay flowers would help to cover up the bullet holes and lack of paint. Also, you might stick in a few watermelon and cantaloupe seeds and other vegetables and tomatoes. If you could just put in a handful of vegetable seeds, particularly melon seeds, in a letter. Just a couple would go a long way. Well, darling, if you would do this for me I can't tell you how much I would appreciate it, and my friends, too. After all, seeds are such small things for the tremendous return. I will call it a day and wind up this letter. Love, Selene."

May 7, 1945.

"Dearest Mother: Yesterday I dated my letter the 7th. It should have been the 6th, but I guess it doesn't matter. I haven't very much to write about today. I was so tired last night that I resisted all endeavors to get me out on a party. Was all ready to crawl in at 7:00 and call it a day when a message came that Pat Winokur was at the gate to see me. I was so surprised because, while he had come north a few weeks ago on business, I didn't expect him back so soon. So I dragged my weary self out of bed and bathed and dressed and went down. We went around to the Princess Inn and drank lemonade. As I said before, no more of that green whiskey for me. Wow! That stuff was cooked up yesterday and not much before. The evening with Pat was not wholly successful. I was tired and he was so disgusted with the deal they've handed him that he doesn't know what to do. He has been south of here in a small sub base where there was already another Jewish chaplain, who he outranked by quite some time. Of course, obviously that was stupid, particularly when some of the line

Approaches to Ipo Dam

Triumph in the Philippines, p. 406

outfits are desperately in need of a chaplain of any description. Now he is being transferred to another base about 150 miles north of here, but also he thinks there is another chaplain there already. However, it is supposed to be pretty country up there, but not much else. In spite of those facts, I was awfully glad to see him. But I'm also very glad that he isn't going to be stationed here as he originally thought, as things are getting very serious from his side. And aside from the fact that he is just a nice friend, I can't see myself getting serious about a rabbi, not that I could be married to any kind of a minister. I guess I'm too much of a heathen for that. Well, Angel Pie, needless to say, I'm feeling a bit rough this morning and have a date this evening with Bill. And tomorrow I'm going to the Philippine party I told you about. And the next night, to a real honest-to-goodness symphony concert, provided, of course, they still have tickets. It is to be given in the ruins of a church and the program is to consist of Beethoven's *Eroica,* Dvorjak's *New World* and should be very good. Those two complement each other very beautifully. Well, honey, I will close now as that is the latest news up to now. So until tomorrow, same station, same time, this is your announcer, Selene Treacy. Love, Selene."

8 May 1945.

"Darlingest Mother: Well, thank God the war in Europe is over. It seems so funny that after three-and-a-half years of fighting in Europe there was no celebration here. I guess we are all too numb to grasp the full import. The only thing we think of now is what—in that connection is now all those men and material can come over here and help us fight our war over here. The feeling is pretty grim because we weren't in the States so long ago. And we know that people sort of forget that we're over here and that some of the men have been for better than 40 months and have seen six and seven campaigns. I just hope that everyone doesn't figure, well, it will all be over soon, and start quitting their war jobs and going to civilian industry. After all, it will be a damn long time before any of us will put away our uniforms and go back to work. I expect to be in until the last dog dies. I will probably see a hash mark on my sleeve before this is over. Well, enough of the war. I got my duffel bag the other day, finally. The darn thing must have sat in a puddle for three weeks. Everything was simply soaked through. All my books are ruined and, needless to say, so are a good many of my clothes, which doesn't worry me too much because in my mind I know that I've always done the best I could to keep my clothes in the best possible condition, even to mending my socks and little holes in my underwear, rather than turn it in for salvage, simply because I was brought up that way. So I refuse to lose sleep over something over which I could exercise no control. The smell of all those mildewed clothes was enough to knock you down, but I sent everything to the laundry. Then if I can wear any of the stuff when it has been washed, I will, and turn the rest in or use it for rags. Last night Bill and I walked all over the city and finally wound up in our little coffee shop where we spent the evening drinking a cup of coffee, and about a dozen of water. After all that walking and perspiring I was completely and thoroughly dehydrated. I told Bill the proprietor would make more money if he gave us the coffee and charged for the water. We had a nice time. It is such fun sitting in that little place with its half-wrecked walls painted with whitewash right over the bare masonry, and the whole thing open to the street. I never thought I would see the day when an exotic Oriental city would become familiar to me. The streets are still completely dark and it isn't scary a bit, because you can hear the nice, soft, scuff-swish, scuff-swish of barefooted people padding along in the velvety darkness and smell all sorts of smells peculiar to this place. The Sambaguita flowers always seem to dominate the lesser smells, like coffee and liquor, and just people living close together, and burned-out fire. And occasionally, in some small dark corner under a heap of rubble, the smell of death. I never believed a city could possibly be so dark. I'm glad that I have never been afraid of darkness and strange people and dirt, because I certainly would have missed a lot. I find that I'm just as relaxed walking hand-in-hand with Bill through the darkness, and over holes in the sidewalk, and people sleeping on the street and in the gutters, as if I were walking down Clark Avenue. Needless to say, we are not allowed out after dark without escorts. Well, tonight is the night for the Filipino party I told you about. I only hope everything goes as planned. If it does I will have a lot to tell you about in my letter tomorrow, so I will wind up today with just lots and lots of love. Selene."

May 9, 1945.

"Dearest Mother: This is going to be a very short letter as I haven't much of interest to say, and besides that I'm pretty busy. Well, something happened to the party last night, we messed up somewhere, or perhaps the guy was stringing us or something, but anyhow we went out to the Chinese cemetery any how, and I got to see a lot of the places. Some of them are gruesome combinations of the oriental and the occidental. They were terrible but the structures where they had stuck to the Chinese art exclusively were lovely. It is hard to describe any of those things, except the beautiful workmanship, and the materials used were perfectly gorgeous. However, the entire cemetery had been allowed to grow up in weeds, but already the weeds are being cut down and the plots replanted. Of course the Japs rifled a lot of the graves, just leaving them open. You see the Chinese bury all of the person's jewels and personal belongings and a large sum of money with their dead, so they will have all they need on the way to wherever they go. Well, we stayed around a while and then came on back and Bill and I wandered around to our little coffee shop and spent the rest of the evening there. It amuses me so, every time we go there they lower the price of coffee, the first time we paid 50 centavos the next time it was 30 centavos, and stayed at that price awhile, and last night it was only 20, same price as in the states. Of course, they know us now, which always seems to make a difference. Well, darling I will close now, and let me hear from you soon. Love Selene (Turn Over) P. S. Please send immediately the four letters of OCS recommendation that I sent home in my papers last summer. Please expedite, I need them right away."

13 May 1945

"Dearest Mother: Well, I had another day off yesterday so no letter yesterday. Today is Mothers Day and I think I will take off this morning and go to church if we're not too busy. I have on a lei of Sambaguita flowers this morning, and they smell so good. Of course they are white, as you are very much alive, but the colored flowers are much too expensive for a little gal on private's pay. We are having the silliest weather today, the sun is shining brightly and the rain is just coming down.

"Yesterday, Jean Ann and Jan and her young man, Ralph Balducci, and Robbie and Clyta Davis and Jimmy Hammel and I met Norma Ongpin, the young lady the kids took to the concert the other night, and her father, Mr. Ongpin, at the front gate at two, and went with them to visit Mr. Ongpin's friend, Mr. Amarsolla (don't quote me as to spelling) who is the greatest living Filipino artist. The first of his things that I saw were at the mansion we visited last week, I told you about it. He does portraits, but his best things are the scenes of the provinces and the Filipino people. His pictures of the provinces are the most beautiful things I have ever seen. The colors and lines are so graceful. Well, to get to the point in a hurry. Would you send me a bank draught for a hundred and fifty dollars for two paintings that he is going to do for me. Jean Ann and I have each ordered two. I know you think this is a terrible extravagance, but somehow, if you buy luxuries, then somehow you just have to make the money for necessities, and it never seems to work the other way around. When you see them, you'll see what I mean. Of course, now comes the problem of getting a crate made, and insurance for getting them home. I don't want to sink that much money into something and then have it ruined. The one painting is a picture of a Filipino in short trousers and a coolie hat plowing behind a water buffalo, it is just about to rain, and you can see it coming across the field. But there is just one last ray of sun that catches the straw hat and stripes across the green of the unplowed part of the field. In the background is the mountain with a cleft in it, where the Filipino people say Noah's Ark landed. The other one is a picture of rice planting, with the people ankle deep in water putting in the little rice plants, and in the background a man playing the guitar and singing. You see the Filipinos plant to music, it makes the work go so much faster. Well, if you would get the money the next time you go to Webster I would appreciate it, but it is not urgent as it will take him about six or eight weeks to finish both of them. The two original paintings were commissioned as a group of six for a wealthy man up in the provinces, but we liked them so well that the artist agreed to get the man to give permission to have copies made, and I don't care whether they are originals or not. After we left the home of the artist we walked way out to the home of another of Mr. Ongpin's friends, who is a famous sculptor and does the most beautiful wood carvings, mostly religious topics. He'd had so many of his masterpieces destroyed by fire in the Santo Tomas Museum in Manila, but he told us that from photographs he is starting all over again to replace them. This is what I call perseverance, starting some twenty-odd years' work all over again. It has been a surprise to me that the Philippines has a culture and style all of its own. Their paintings are of an entirely different style and type from anything I've ever seen, as are the carvings. Of course, there is the Spanish influence, but nothing as somber as so much Spanish art. Well, darling, that just about brings us up to date, so I will close for now. Oh, yes, I almost forgot to tell you. We had a movie night before last explaining the point system for discharge. I am pretty well down the list on points, but for the Signal Corps I think the points will prove to be pretty irrelevant. I don't care, though. I agreed to stay till the shooting was over and I'll stick by my bargain. Love, Selene."

"Dear Mother: I guess you think I'm not going to write anymore. Well, I should give you some warning when long silences are going to occur, because I know. But I didn't think of it. But I have been on the night shift and at that stage of the game I don't do anything but work and try to sleep. It is really terrific but the heat here during the day is enough to knock you out. And to try to sleep through it is almost a physical impossibility, thus nothing gets done. We just moon around trying to sleep and not being able to. Jean Ann is in the dispensary now with a little sick spell. I had a siege of dysentery, but I never missed any work or went to bed with it. I sure did feel terrible, but now that I'm working evenings I'm all OK again. Got a surprise for you as soon as I get something to mail it in. As usual I have a lot of stuff but can't seem to get anything to pack it in to send it home. But I'll get something eventually. Today we had a wonderful time. Paul Kneffley, I think I mentioned him once before, works here in the section with me. And I went out this morning with a picnic in view. We had no idea where we were going, but we started out one of the main thoroughfares. And finally we got out of the Jeep we had ridden in and started up a little lane that wound round and round up a hill where we could see a church. It looked lovely up there, so up we went, went into the church where a nice-looking Spanish priest met us and showed us through the Eglesia de San Juan, which was built in 1602, and the altar and crucifix were brought from Mexico when the church was built. It's a lovely old church with tremendous buttresses and masonry fifteen feet thick in some places. It is situated on a high hill and commands a lovely view. Has a real old-fashioned monastery garden with a wall and fruit trees and rabbit hutches and chickens. It is a monastery of the Dominican Friars and was built by them. You have no idea how picturesque it was with the Friars in their long robes and sandals, and cowls all of white. The front yard of the church was a lovely clipped lawn with a crumbling stone wall covered with vines and bougainvillea. Paul and I were so taken with the whole atmosphere that we asked the priest if he would mind if we stayed awhile. So he invited us to sit under the trees in the front yard, which we did. We had come armed with sketching paper and pencils and crayons from Special Services, so I did a sketch of the front of the church that turned out surprisingly good. I was quite pleased. I am encouraged to the point of trying some other things. I had never done any sketching before, but this seemed the only way to get any pictures. After I finished my picture, we ate our lunch from the mess hall, which consisted of tuna fish, bread, dehydrated lemon juice mixed with our canteen water, and a tremendous Bermuda onion which we sliced and put in with the tuna on the bread. It certainly did taste good. After lunch we decided that we would go visit Nana and Ariel, who are a young couple that Paul and I know. Ariel's father is a well-known lawyer here in town and personal adviser to the president. Also, one of the signers of the constitution. His name is Mr. Perfecto. Does that ring any bells? No? Well, it didn't with me, either. They have a lovely architectural monstrosity on another hill just across a little valley from the church. So Paul and I decided that we would cut cross-country. So down the hill we went by a cute little winding lane across a pasture where some caribou were peacefully grazing, and then across a tiny footbridge where some youngsters were naked in a creek bathing another caribou. Then the little lane wound between stone walls, green with moss and powdery with age. They were covered with flowers in the most unbelievable shades. One vine with golden, waxy looking sort of lilies, and then the usual bougainvillea and tremendous scarlet and pink-and-white hibiscus. Oh, yes, Lantanas grow wild in tremendous hedges all along the roads. And then innumerable other things that I'm not familiar with. It was such fun. When we finally reached the Perfecto place we were really pooped and hot and sunburned. At least our face and hands, although I had on my fatigue hat, which makes pretty good shade. After a short visit we had to leave to get ready for work, so we hiked back to the main road and came on back to town. We were so enthusiastic. I think we will go out again tomorrow. It was a perfect day and I am so glad that I was able to make that sketch. When I have a few I'll send them to you and maybe we can make a scrapbook of pictures and revised letters sometime after the war is over. Well, darling, I haven't answered any questions, but I will. Don't lose patience. I bet I've been working on this letter off and on for the entire shift. That accounts for the variety in paper. By the way, thanks so much for the letters. All five arrived safely and so did the flower seeds. My goodness, honey, you must have gone right down and bought those seeds to get them here in such record-breaking time. I've gotten the melon and marigold seeds thus far. Must close now and go home to bed. Bye for now."

This is June the 5th.

"Dear Mother: Just a short note to let you know that I'm still around. Thank goodness I'm on days again, so maybe you'll get some more letters. Yesterday Paul and I went to church for the first time since Christmas. We went to San Sebastian's, which is a large church just around the corner from us. They had electricity for the first time, Paul told me, so the big pipe organ was working and the music was lovely. I really enjoyed it, that is, as much as you can enjoy a Catholic service. As I say, the music was lovely and the church is magnificent in a very gaudy way, but the whole effect was pleasing. However, I enjoyed watching the people very much. As a leftover from Spanish times all the women wear black lace mantillas to church, and with their light summer dress it is very picturesque. After church we went down to the little roadside cafe, which I believe I have mentioned before, but in case I haven't, it is a cute little place that this nice Filipino family run that we frequent quite regularly. I mentioned earlier in the letter about Nana and Ariel. Well, Nana's brother-in-law runs it and the family, Nana's parents and brother and two sisters, all live upstairs. It is such a cute little place and so immaculately clean. Well, we went down there and cooled off and had coffee and sandwiches and visited with the family. We've been there so much that we know them quite well. In fact, when Nana comes to visit her mother I went over several times in the morning to visit with her. That is just about all there is to do around here, particularly on private's pay. After we finished our visit another friend of Paul's had come in to see Felix, who is the proprietor, and he invited us over to his house, or rather a room, to see his wife and baby. So we walked over there with him. It was just a short walk and it was shady along the small side streets with their high walls and rutted, crooked streets. This chap's name was Raymond, but they call him Moy for some funny reason. Moy is part American or I miss my guess. He was in business before the war but lost everything in the fire—home, business, and all their personal belongings, except just what they could carry away in suitcases. They had a terrible experience. On account of the baby, they had put off leaving the house until the eleventh hour. And the fire was just a few blocks away, so they hastily gathered up what few things they could take and were ready to depart when they missed the baby, who was then just a year old. The fire was getting closer and closer and still no baby. Moy's poor wife was simply wild. The fire was getting so close they couldn't wait any longer so they had to leave anyway. They went to the apartment of some friends who lived in a cement, fireproof building. While they were there the fire was on four sides of them and burning the frame penthouse on the fourth floor. Moy said they were nearly cremated in there, the heat was so terrific. All the time Moy had a strong feeling that the baby was all right. He didn't know why but he did. The next morning, after a night of real hell, down the street, which was now absolutely nothing but smoking ruins, came the Chinese Amah and the baby as clean and pink and white as always. When the Amah realized what would happen she had simply taken the baby and departed. Moy said he doesn't know where she had taken the baby, where she could possibly have taken him, when the entire city was in flames. But he surmises that his little son probably spent the night with some poor Chinese coolie's children in some hovel too poor for the Japs to bother burning. You see, they left the slum districts, not bothering to fire them. Well, you can just imagine the happy reunion. Even as Moy told us tears came to his eyes. Now they are renting a small room about the size of the one I had in Galveston, and have to sleep six in there. Moy and his wife and baby, two Filipino maids who stuck by them during the entire bombing and subsequent fire, and the Chinese Amah for the baby, all living in that one small room. It is pretty awful, but so many families who had lovely homes in the wealthy district are homeless and destitute, because the Japs really went for the mansions in town. However, he is borrowing money at ten-percent-per-month interest and is going to reopen his business and start all over again. You certainly have to hand it to him. Just a young chap 24 years old. He is so thin, and both he and the baby, I believe, are tubercular. It was so hard to get proper food during the occupation. He told us that if it hadn't been for the baby and his wife that he would never think of starting all over again to try and rebuild. We visited them there for a while, and then we took a little pony cart and went to the home of a friend of his who played the piano. They are very poor and I was afraid to sit down, but I was given no choice. That was a very peculiar experience. I have the strongest feeling that they were trying to hide something because this man's wife would hardly let us in the door. She was very inhospitable and that is so unusual for Filipinos. They usually throw wide the door and serve coffee. The husband never did put in an appearance. Moy was terribly embarrassed, so after a very awkward interval Paul and I suddenly remembered that we had to go to work, and made our excuses. I am so curious, but I'll probably never know whether they were collaborators or not. They have so many here and there is no way to tell. Well, I must close and get to work now. Love, Selene."

This is a letter June 8th.

"Dearest Mother: This letter is going to be mostly business and very short. First, I received box number one mailed on the 11th of February containing a jar of cheese, crackers, candy, slip, toilet water, and *Webster News Times*. Everything was in excellent condition even after that length of time. So maybe there is some hope for the other things. The slip arrived just in time, because I was having some trouble making one white slip do with our new white uniforms that we have for dress. You may have seen them downtown, but they're all white with gold buttons and yellow and green braid on the hat. They are shirtwaist dresses, zipper down the front, and a narrow white belt, and long or short sleeves and the little overseas cap. It is hot but it looks cool, so that is all we can ask. The food, as usual, was appreciated by Jean and me at midnight the other night with hot chocolate. There, I knew I had forgotten the other thing. It was the can of cocoa. That is wonderful because I have found that my coffee days are over. In this heat it is upsetting my stomach, along with practically everything else I've been eating. Frankly, at this point, I would give my bottom dollar to be home for the first time since I've been overseas. Jean and I have had recurring attacks of dysentery ever since we got here and nothing seems to help. Neither one of us had been sick enough to go to bed, but it certainly keeps us feeling like the Old Scratch. But I've been trying to do the best I can on the diet that we have. Of course, dysentery isn't what you eat, it's something you catch, and it is rampant here, although I can't see why. Our mess halls are always spotlessly clean and I don't eat out except at the McDonald's, and they have army food, too. As for the cleanliness, it's just like home, only more so. Well, now for the business. First, I want the money for those paintings. First place, it is my money and if I want to buy wooden Indians I'm going to. The second place, I'm no fool and I think very probably know a few more things than you think I do. After all, in spite of what you may think, or the way your letters sound, I do have some brains. So I would appreciate it very much if you would send the money order right away, as I have agreed on a time and would like to stick as close to it as possible. Well, now for another piece. About this divorce. It seems to me that for the first twenty years of my life you did a pretty good job of directing it. And by all calculations I should have been trained to mess it up for myself now if I want to. What you don't seem to realize, Mother, is that things happen in the interim of my letters that I either don't think to tell you or don't want to. I asked you for that information and I wanted if for a particular time. Military expediency made it impossible for me to tell you that. What it was, that Howard's outfit was moving up here very close and I knew that he is here in the city now and is perfectly agreeable to signing the affidavit. And I don't have it. Now he will have to make another trip up later to do it, necessitating more time and trouble and more of his furlough time. If you don't want to handle these things for me it is perfectly all right, because I can handle them directly myself. But if you don't, come out and say so. Now, for another piece of news. You can partly set your mind at ease as for Walter, because he hasn't asked me to marry him, naturally, because I'm not free. And Walter isn't the kind that would ask under such circumstances even if he did have it in his mind. However, I had a date with him last night. Two days ago he called and announced the momentous news that he is stationed in a section about two blocks from where I live. I saw him with my own two eyes, so I knew that this is no wild goose chase. I will say that I'm happier about this than anything that has happened to me since this last time last year when I was with him in Charlottesville. He is the only man that I look up to and to whose opinions I value. If I were free and he were to ask me I would certainly marry him, but I'm not and he's never given the slightest indication that he would, even if I were. But that brings me to another point. I realize how you feel about the racial question. You were brought up that way. OK. Somewhere along the line I've gotten some different ideas, partially because I guess I'm another individual with an entirely different set of genes, or what have you. I don't feel that way about Jews. Another thing, as for the religious angle, all anyone can ever hope to get out of religion is to be a better person and stick in a little bit to make the whole world a better place. By and large the Jews have done as much and more than anyone else. Even Christ himself was a Jew, and our own services are Jewish with a little added in. The Christian ethics are Jewish with a lot of formal stuff thrown in. Since I've been overseas I've made it a point to read the Talmud, also the Old Testament and various Jewish writings. I have really wanted to know why it was that the Hebrew faith and race could endure without organization and without a country for five thousand years. I think I have a vague inkling. Frankly, I would be proud to be married to Walter, not because he is the kind of man that he is. That, too. Nor in spite of his religion. I would be proud of it, and if I were censured in my own group for that I would be surprised and hurt. After all, if a family were to bring up children, the best that God would ask is that they be good people and live by his ordinances. Which, after all, are the same for both Jew and Gentile, and the God is the same, do you suppose he would frown on a Jewish baby and smile on a Gentile? Well, that is only a small part of the way I feel on the subject, but it is a good inkling. Not that I'll ever marry Walter. He will probably never ask me. His wife would have to have a lot more to offer than I'll ever have. I have brains and some sense and can understand a lot of things, but down under I expect I'm just a housewife at heart. But he's the man I would like to have, and anyone else would be second choice. He is perfect in my eyes. Not that he is, but for me he is. He has all the qualities that I want. He's not only fine clear through, but brainy and handsome as well. I didn't realize until I saw him last night just how much I had missed him in the past year. Well, enough on that subject. The main reasons for writing this letter, dear, is certainly not to bawl you out, because if it were it could just wait until I got home and then would be forgotten about anyway. It's just this. Probably I'll be coming home sometime in the next year. I have changed terrifically, like all the other kids that have been in the army, and particularly overseas. We've seen too much and we've taken a terrific amount of guff from everybody. Consequently, we're going to be pretty touchy about people interfering, justly or unjustly, in our affairs. I want very much to give you enough time and warning so that you can get used to the idea. If you could only forget I was your daughter and just treat me as anyone else, the same respect for my opinions, tastes, and peculiarities. I know it must be very difficult to have a daughter with such an entirely different set of tastes and ideas and ways of doing things, but that is the way it is and it can't be helped. If you could only just take the good characteristics and forget about the bad ones. I'd like to be as perfect as much as you would like me to, but I just haven't got it in me. And I really do have quite a few good points. I must or I wouldn't be able to hold my friends the way I do with never a quarrel or disagreement. I never argue with my roommates. We never cross at all, even the girls that I don't care for as much as others. I never quarreled with Lydia or Syd or Jean Ann, so I must have something. I wish more than anything, Mother, that you would think about this a lot before I come home. I'm expecting an awful lot out of that homecoming. Sometimes homesickness over here, with so much destruction and everything so messy and strange, it's like a physical sickness. You'd think that just for one glimpse of home you would give everything in the world. I want it to be perfect in every way, not just the food I want and all the hot water and soap I need, but I want to find that you are the family I've dreamed about. Of course I know you will be all that you were before. I guess I'm expecting a little bit more. I want to be not so much your daughter as your friend. Perhaps like Aunt Jane. You don't try to make her over. You love her, faults and peculiarities and all. We get an awful lot of picking on in the army and I'm sick of it. And if I should marry Walter or someone else overseas, or someone that you don't approve of, it's a lot to ask, I know, but if you would, just for me and for yourself, forget that and forget all the prejudices and love him as another son. For whatever you think my second marriage will or may be, it will not be a mistake. I know that. It will be a success and you and the family would have a lot to do with it. Well, darling, I've spouted off considerably, so I'll wind up. Don't worry about the things I said, but do think about them at length, and talk to Alice and Charlie, too. Love, Selene."

29th of June 1945.

"Dear Folks: Well, here I am making apologies again for not writing, but I just got out of the hospital a couple of days ago and then had a two-day pass to spend with the McDonalds. I went to the hospital this time about as sick as I've ever been with what was supposedly the most dangerous kind of dysentery, and my weight had gone down to 98 pounds, so you can see why I had not written. However, thank heavens, it turned out to be not dysentery at all, but roundworms, of all things. So that is a comparatively simple thing to alter, but I had gotten so weak it took awhile to make a comeback. But now I have color back in my face and eight pounds of my weight back, and all of my own vim, vigor, and vitality. In fact, I feel really good for the first time since I arrived in Manila. It is wonderful to feel like me again. There isn't any news at all except the box you sent to APO 503 last November with the shorts, socks, clothesline, pins, and fountain pen arrived in good condition, none the worse for the long trip over. I was so flabbergasted when I opened it and saw what it was. Needless to say, because while I managed very well without the things, they are still muchly needed, particularly the shower clogs. The panties are exactly what I wanted and the socks, too. You certainly did put in a lot of work on those things. They really are a godsend, and I don't mean maybe. So there is some hope about the other Christmas package. By the way, packages can be sent to civilians here one a week weighing 11 pounds, so if you think of some things you would like to send the McDonalds, whatever you spend take out of my account and they can pay me. But Molly needs underwear and slips and nighties. Both Mrs. Mac and Molly, also stockings. Molly wears size 16 and Mrs. Mac size 14. Molly wears a size 9-1/2 stocking. I won't ask you to send these things, but if you would like to, those are the things they need. Also, things like thread and needles and toiletries, Noxzema face cream for Molly. You can use your own judgment on some of the things. You know the sort of things that they are most apt not to have. Of course, materials for dresses, too, but I know how hard they are to get. Also Singer sewing machine needles. Well, darling, as I say, I'm not asking you to send such things but they would be much appreciated and paid for by them, of course. Walter has been out of town for a couple of weeks now on a liaison job, so I haven't seen him, but he did send me a couple of notes when I was in the hospital to keep my morale up. Yesterday afternoon and the day before Vivian and I had two of the nicest long talks about international business and what was actually going on here in Manila in the business world and political. The business is encouraging, but the politics aren't. However, you would be amazed at all that has been accomplished just since we arrived here two months ago. Molly senior, was telling me about the Escolta, which was the shopping street pre-war and was completely destroyed. The army has cleared it up so clean she said you could eat off the street. That means as soon as building supplies are available all these companies will be able to re-build. I certainly am lucky to have two such brilliant and well-informed men who are interested and sweet about explaining all the intricacies of public affairs to me. Because of both Walter and Vivian I don't miss much. Vivian is that nice English chap that was interned with the McDonalds in Santo Tomas. By the way, he goes back to England probably some time this year. He will stop off in St. Louis to see you and probably stay a couple of days, as he has never been to the States. And when I said something about my family living in the middle west, and our scouting and hiking and so forth, he was terribly interested because he is a Boy Scout still and very much interested in hosteling. So if he does, be sure and show him a good time as I know only you can do. I also have an invitation to their lovely home in Cornwall as soon as I get out of the army and transportation to Europe opens up. I have every intention of taking him up on it. Well, dear, must close now and get to work. By the way, the Macs haven't put in the garden yet because they can't until after the rainy season is over, about October. But they are so delighted with the seeds, particularly the watermelon seeds and the nasturtiums. They are Molly senior's, favorite. Love, Selene."

This is July 2, 1945.

"Dear Mother: I received your letter with the bank draft in it yesterday and muchly appreciated, too. Although that bank teller that told you I could cash the blooming thing nearly goofed me up. Where did he think I was going to cash it? It just goes to show people don't realize the extent of the devastation, because until day before yesterday there were no banks in town and now there is just one that opened yesterday. So I think I'll be able to get it fixed up all right. However, if I don't, I'll have to send it back and you'll have to send me a money

order. I'll let you know as soon as I have a day off and can get downtown to the bank. Thanks again muchly. Then Bill Fornwald is going
to get me a couple of frames built and I'm going to hang the pictures
out at the McDonalds. It is the safest place I know and then when the
insurance companies open up here again I'll get it insured with Lloyds,
and send them home in a crate. About the surprise. I'm still trying to
get something to send it home in, and so you may just have to be
patient for a while. Needless to say, I feel so bad about Lassie. Of
course, it's not a surprise. She lived a long and useful life for a dog
and I don't think we can feel too badly she went so quickly. It isn't as
though she had been run over or poisoned or something. I hope,
though, that you will wait until I get home to get another puppy and
I hope, though, that if you don't wait, you make it a little cocker,
preferably black or rust-colored to match me. Vain creature, aren't I?
Let me see. I believe I mentioned in the earlier section that I received
the package, didn't I? Seems I had something else I wanted to mention. Oh, yes. I know, about the divorce. When the thing finally goes
through is there a paper or something so I can have my service record
changed accordingly? And how long does a divorce in Missouri take
before it is final? Is there a waiting period or what? Well, let me see,
I have done nothing of particular interest in the past few days. Day
shifts don't give me much time to myself. Last night Bill came over to
talk to me a few minutes so I didn't bathe or dress, thinking I would
wait until I was ready to go to bed. So I went to the latrine to wash
my hands and then went on out to the gate still carrying half a soap
dish with a cake of soap in it. Bill arrived all slicked up and wanted to
go out to the McDonalds. I didn't want to, not with all the day's
accumulation of grime still on, but he insisted, so we did. Me still
carrying my little dish of soap. That really did look awfully funny.
Molly senior, got quite a kick out of it. We had all in all a very uproarious evening. It seems as though everybody was just wound up.
Most of it was at my expense. I never took such a ribbing. Even
Colonel Schnoor, Molly's beau and my boss, got in some pretty telling digs. So I thought if he was going to hand it out so could I. So
Molly, Junior, and I started on him about a Red Cross girl that has
camped on his trail. It was such fun. Everyone there was like family.
You know what I mean. It was the sort of ribbing and ragging we
hand out to each other at home. Isn't it funny, if people are the same

kind, it doesn't matter where they come from. Walter and I are going on a picnic tomorrow provided it doesn't rain, although somehow the weather has lost it importance over here, so we'll probably go anyway. Tuesday night has a party scheduled and it promises to be a good one given by some of the fellows who are combat photographers. However, it is a private party with individual invitation. I was quite pleased that Walter and I both received a very cordial one. Well, Angel, I expect that just about winds up the news for now. In re to the packages: the only one I haven't received, is the Christmas package and those old 7996 packages are coming through all the time to the other girls, so I think it will show up eventually. The packages addressed to Manila are beginning to come through, too, so I expect your other ones, too. I will be glad to get them, particularly the shoes. Will close now with a great big kiss to both of you. And remember, if you should decide to get a puppy make it a cocker, please. P.S. I like the cartoon. I pinned it up on my cabinet."

July 6th. Manila.

"Dearest Mommie: I'm alternating at this point between annoyance and amusement at you. I was simply floored at the shoes you sent. I hadn't realized just what shoes you had been talking about when you said old brown ones. I sent those things home last summer thinking Cousin Lily could use them. And when the blooming things trailed me clear to Manila, split and holey sole and run down heel, I could scarcely believe my eyes. Well, darling, maybe I can sell them to the Filipinos for something nice. I'm not really mad, but very amused. That box with the stockings and the ones with my uniform arrived today. I am to the point where I really need skirts, since one of my khaki cotton skirts came back from the laundry yesterday with the zipper cut out of it. How do you like that for thieving to a fine point? I was so mad I think I must have turned purple. I just finished a long letter to Aunt Jane and somewhere along the line I got off on the sketching trip to the church and it went on like topsy. I trust she isn't one of those people who doesn't like long letters. Well, let me see what's new. First and foremost, one of the WAC dogs presented the astonished detachment with a litter of puppies. Jean Ann is going around in a little pink cloud. She heard a good rumor that her hubby is on his way up here. Strictly rumor, of course, but you know how good they can sound. By the way, now that Lydia is home how about having her over to dinner every so often? She always did like to come and she must be simply lost without Gordon, and worried, too. In fact, I worry about him. Navy pilots have about a hundred-to-one chance of coming back. You remember that little flyer I told you about that was killed? He told me the night before that of his entire crew and of the entire team of several planes, he was the only one left. Walter took Jean Ann and me to a lovely party the other night. It was a private affair and we had a swell time. Walter is the kind of a guy who can take two girls out and make neither one feel neglected. Jean Ann and Walter like each other quite well, which, of course, makes me very happy. It was funny sitting there watching them talk. I realized for the first time that they look alike. Isn't that funny? The party was out at a signal outfit, a combat photographer's area, to be exact. It had been a motion picture studio originally and had been destroyed. But they are still using the swimming pool, so after sitting around talking and drinking beer we all went swimming, and it was perfectly heavenly. It was just beginning to rain and the rain was cool and the water was warm, and all quite velvety sort of dark. Gee, it was fun, only I pulled a dilly of a belly-flop and liked to blistered the fronts of my legs. It was the kind of a party where everyone there was very interesting, so no one got drunk from sheer boredom. After the party, too, Walter took us to the McDonalds' where we had a pass to spend the night. We stayed there until noon the next day and then came on home. That is about the full extent of the news so I'll wind it up. Love."

17 July. Manila.

"Darlingest Mommie: I was debating whether to spell that mommie or MOMIE or MOMY, when the teletype goofed it up and put in a 'D'. I just finished a long letter to Charlie for his birthday, only I'm afraid it will be a little late. Somehow the time just slipped up on me quick like. I got the grandest long letter from Lydia the other day. She doesn't write very often, but when she does it's like a breath of apple blossoms. That sounds sort of silly, doesn't it? Well, you know what I mean. I was so delighted that you had had her over to dinner. It meant a lot to her and she even told me what you had to eat, most particularly the Jell-O that has always been such a favorite of hers. Her letters always tell the smallest little details and in the cutest way, pretty much like you do. I know that Gordon must get a

great deal of satisfaction from their correspondence. I have a pro-
found respect for that little gal. Only a navy flyer's wife can know the
agonies of suspense that they go through. I know, and I must admit,
worry. I sure would hate for anything to happen to that husband of
hers. Of course, I suppose it is not the right attitude. After all, I guess
she doesn't love her man any more than anyone else. But anyhow, I
was so sorry to hear about Mrs. Knight, but I know that it must be a
relief to Aunt Jane. Good Heavens, it must be awful to see your mother
fade away like that, and Mrs. Knight certainly must have been well up
in years. It's a funny thing to say, but you can't help but wonder if she
and Mr. Knight have picked up their bickering somewhere on the
other side. They were so devoted it is funny. But someone you know
so well and so long, when they die, you really wonder just where they
have gone and if you really will see them. Or whether heaven is just a
state of mind or what. Sometimes I think that we are awarded with
glimpses of heaven here on earth, as well as glimpses of hell, and I
really often wonder if we are ever entitled to any more than that. I will
always think of last Christmas in New Guinea as being one of the
former. Since I have been overseas and seen so many things it makes
my religion a little shaky in a few spots. I really think for people who
have died in camps like Dachau and Belsen, that there must be a heaven.
I can't think that God would have innocent people suffer so horribly
without some thought of restitution. But on the other hand, for people
like us who live our comfortable little lives without too much thought
of want or worry, and certainly no suffering, physical or otherwise.
This poor letter has had so many interruptions I don't know whether
it has any continuity or not. I had to laugh the other night. I pulled a
boner to end all boners. You know the word masochist, but that is
what it sounds like. Well, someone pulled that out of the hat and
without thinking I said, what is it, another word for masseuse? I thought
I would drop through the floor the minute it was out. Honest, honey,
I haven't done anything of interest in so long that I actually haven't
much to say, thus the lapse into the theological dissertation. A chap
here in the office told a funny story the other night. He lives in Knox-
ville, Tennessee, and one time he attended a little mountain church up
near Gatlinburg. And the minister was ranting and haranguing the
congregation on the virtues of abstinence. And after going on at great
length he wound up with a flourish declaring that if he had it in his

power he would see all the intoxicating beverages in the world poured into the rivers. After that he took a deep breath, beamed on the congregation, asked for a suggestion for the closing hymn. Immediately a hand went up at the rear of the church and an old mountaineer got to his feet with, 'How about singing "Let Us Gather By The River"'? Well, with that I will wind up this little epistle for tonight. By the way, at my suggestion the lad who told me that story is going to send it into *The Reader's Digest* for "Life In These United States." I think it would be good enough. Oh, yes, before I wind up for good, I wanted to say that I think I will either get Mr. Noble to go on with the divorce or get some other lawyer to do it for me, whichever he wants. I realize that Mr. Noble is not a young man anymore and he may not want to bother, so I am going to write to him tonight and thank him for the information and give him the necessary particulars for the petition. However, darling, there is something I wish you would do for me. I won't be there to discuss it with him, so would you read over the petition before he has it drawn up and if there's not enough in it, or if it isn't the sort of thing that should go into such a document, could you make the necessary edits? I feel that you could do it for me, as you know the particulars as well as I do. I realize how you feel about the divorce, but darling, it's something no one can decide but me and I have decided. And I think that Howard wants it, too, regardless of what he told you. Well, anyhow, I know that you are not in favor of it but I hope you will do this for me because, according to the paper, it will be absolutely no less than another year before we get home. And that is for the fellows and girls with critical points. And I only have 34, and the WAC critical score is 44, so you can see where I will be. I fully expect to be overseas at least two years at the very, very least. So after all, it is perfectly possible I might want to marry someone else and I think Howard may possibly already have someone. I got that impression when he was here, so after all, what if it does take a year? I have nothing better to do with the time and I might as well get it over with. I can't see what the Constitution has got to do with it. I can't think the courts in Missouri would grant a divorce that wouldn't hold water in the state, and I don't care about any other state. It can never be contested. After all, I lived all my life in—started to say Texas—rather than Missouri. Well, anyhow, I hope you will do everything you can to cooperate with Mr. Noble or whoever he gets to handle it for me. Love and good night."

July 24, 1945. Manila.

"Dearest Mother: This is going to be a short note because as usual I haven't been doing very much of interest except worrying. Walter came back yesterday after an extended trip down on one of the southern islands, only to announce that he would be going back to his own headquarters, for good, day after tomorrow. So here we go again. But I realize that I have been very lucky to have had him in Manila this long. A couple of nights ago I went out with a boy I met down at Oro Bay. He was a very nice kid but nothing very exceptional or interesting. I ran into him the other day and he had on his first Louie's bars. He had been given a direct commission like Roe had. We went out, but as I said, he's very nice but somewhat of a bore, so I didn't have very much fun. The trouble with me is that I always seem to be a one-man gal. When Walter is around I don't give a darn about going out with anyone else. Oh, yes, did I tell you that Mel Bartell from Base G is up here, too, now? I think I told you about him. He was the one in command of the radio station down there and I did a couple of broadcasts for him. Well, he breezed into town the other day and promptly looked me up. And now Pat Winokur is in town, too, but neither of these two men are going to stay. Mel is waiting for a future assignment and Pat is going home on an emergency furlough. His parents are both very ill. We went out to the McDonald's night before last with Bill Fornwald and Bill Parchman and Ashley Ormsby. Bill Parchman is a combat photographer, and by the way, he was at Panay when Bob Field was killed, and knew him very well. Ashley is a girl in the detachment who goes with Parchman. The four of us went out and saw the Mac family and really had a swell time. As I told you, I hadn't been out to see them very much lately, and I guess they wondered what had happened to me. Bill P. was at Santo Tomas taking pictures, from the top of a tank all during the battle out in the street, for the camp, which the Mac family witnessed from the third floor of the building. Don Lane, who was in Bilibid Prison, just about four blocks away, said that they knew the Yanks had come because when twenty-three-hundred people all together started cheering and screaming wildly you can hear it for some distance. And then later on in the evening, Don said that they heard a big heavy vehicle outside the wall and then an unmistakable voice with a rich southern drawl said, 'Hey, Chuck, where in the hell are you taking this thing?' Then they came right through the wall with a big Sherman tank. Well, I didn't have time to finish the letter the other day so I guess I will continue from where we left off before. Last night I had a date with Walter and we drove in his Jeep along the sea wall. And it made me quite homesick for Galveston, although the wall in Galveston is much prettier and the whole type of neighborhood is different. Then we went back to his quarters and sat in the living room and talked and drank beer with a couple of his house mates. On the way home we hit a tremendous hole in the street, and you know Jeeps have no springs. Jeepers, I am still sore all over from the impact. Walter apologized for not having seen it. And then he drove along in silence for a couple of minutes. Then he turned around and said, 'I never expected to go home via hell, did you?' I thought that was a kind of cute crack, don't you? Yesterday afternoon we had our last date. This is, the last date for the time being. At any rate, we went to his quarters and were batting the breeze and drinking more beer—it sounds like we drank a lot of beer doesn't it—and having a nice quiet afternoon for ourselves when his executive officer bowled in with the news that a Colonel Somebody was up from his Headquarters. So Walter said for him to tell the colonel to go to hell. But on second thought said, 'Tell the Colonel I wasn't here.' But in half an hour the lieutenant was back again with the information that Walter had better get himself over to the office, so it cut our date short. But he said if he knows his section here in Manila he will be up from time to time to straighten out the snarls. This is not precisely what he said, but in view of the fact of censorship and pornographic language in the United States mail, we'll settle for that. The gang in his office will mess things up so badly that he will have to come back, which, judging from the past, shouldn't be too long. I feel encouraged. Oh, yes. I received the first package of the series of three that you sent in May and everything, as usual, was in fine shape. Or did I tell you all this before? Well, I'll tell you again just in case I didn't. The package contained the three white blouses and two skirts, one piece of blue material, and buttons and thread, and more thread and rick-rack and a needle. I was delighted with it. I'm going out to the McDonalds' sometime this week and I will sew up the material on their sewing machine. Well, darling, that is about all that is new, so give everyone my love and keep a big chunk for yourself."

I heard stories about the internees at Santo Tomas in bits and pieces. Some were told to me by Bill Fornwald, who was part of the First Cavalry and who was there. That's how he met the McDonalds.

The internees I knew were Molly McDonald Senior, and Molly Junior, who were mother and daughter. Mrs. McDonald, Molly-O or Molly Senior, had come to the Philippines around 1910. Her husband had been a mining engineer until he died in the '20s. So it was just Molly and her daughter by themselves in Manila. I don't know what they had done as civilians but I gathered they were comfortably fixed but their house and all the furnishings had been lost when the Japanese set fire to Manila.

Northern Manila, Bilibid Prison at Lower Left
Note roadblock on Quezon Boulevard, left center

Triumph in the Philippines, p. 253

The other internees I knew were Vivian Skues and Don Lane. Vivian was from Cornwall in England. He had been Molly Junior's boyfriend before they were taken prisoner. Don was a single man and had been an employee of one of the big department stores in downtown Manila.

Vivian and the two Mollys were imprisoned in Santo Tomas and Don Lane was a few blocks away in the old Spanish prison, Bilibid.

One of the key objects of the Lingayen landing was to get to the internees and prisoners of war at Santo Tomas, Bilibid, Cabanatuan, Los Banos and several other prisons since American intelligence had learned the Japanese were planning to shoot all the male prisoners, internees and the prisoners of war.

In the initial landing, the First Cavalry broke away from the rest of the troops and came flying right down Highway 3 through Japanese-held territory. Highway 3 was the main highway from Lingayen straight to Manila from the north. They came so fast that the Japanese were too surprised to engage them in combat. Part of the outfit, I think it was the Rangers, broke away and went to Cabanatuan to liberate the prisoners there, and the First Cavalry went directly to Santo Tomas.

Release of Internees from Santo Tomas
Triumph in the Philippines, p. 251

All along Highway 3 there were spies. The Filipinos had devised a clever way to send messages. There would be a house and in the house there would be watchers. Someone inside the house would put a sign up in a window for just a split second and it was the job of the watcher in the next house to pass it on.

There was a house just outside the big stone wall around Santo Tomas where a watcher was receiving messages about the progress of the Americans as they headed toward Santo Tomas. This watcher would flash a kilometer sign to the people on the inside. As the troops got closer and closer and closer the word was passed around so that when the soldiers arrived at the gate they were expected on the inside.

A battle broke out in the street in front of Santo Tomas. Bill Parchman was taking pictures of the battle while the two Mollys and Vivian were watching from the third floor of the Santo Tomas building. The Japanese were also fighting from the other side of the river. Tragically the fifteen-year-old daughter of Molly-O's best friend was killed by one of the artillery shells from the south side of the Pasig River.

The American soldiers entered by driving their tanks right through the front gates. At that point, part of the group proceeded to the Bilibid Prison and liberated the prisoners there.

During the occupation there was a Japanese colonel at Santo Tomas who was a nasty, I mean a nasty, SOB. The American internees hated him and vowed vengeance if they could ever lay hands on him.

When the dust settled the morning after their liberation, the American prisoners looked for the hated Japanese colonel. But the American forces, knowing the hatred the prisoners had for him, had quietly spirited him away. They then informed the prisoners that the Japanese colonel was really a Japanese-American and was an American spy. In the end those people owed their lives to him.

August the 8th.

"Dearest Mother: This is going to be very short because I don't have your letter here by me to answer and I just want to let you know that I'm still in circulation. I'm on the evening shift now and don't have much time to write. Besides that, I've been in a sort of a low frame of mind lately and it's very hard to write when I feel like that. There's no particular reason except that I'm just being homesick and

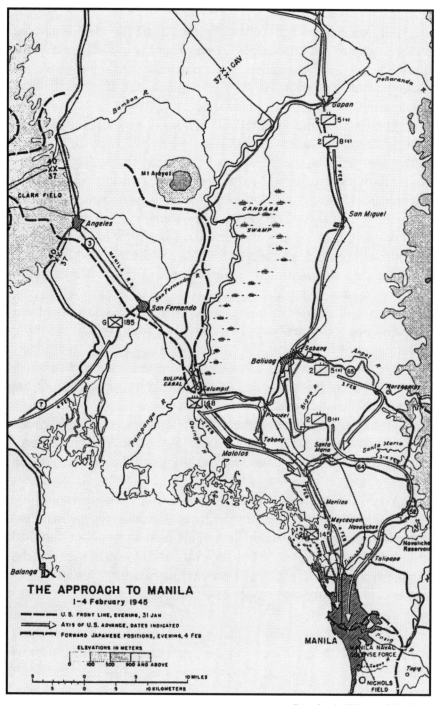

THE APPROACH TO MANILA
1-4 February 1945

― ― ― U.S. FRONT LINE, EVENING, 31 JAN

⟹ AXIS OF U.S. ADVANCE, DATES INDICATED

▬▬▬ FORWARD JAPANESE POSITIONS, EVENING, 4 FEB

ELEVATIONS IN METERS

| 0 | 100 | 500 | 900 AND ABOVE |

0   10 MILES

0   10 KILOMETERS

Triumph in the Philippines, folio of maps

disgusted generally with the setup with Filipino politics, both in and out of the army, et cetera. Of course, one sore spot is the lack of ratings. Kids that came overseas with us as privates are now master sergeants and here are we still privates. Of course, I'm not alone in that. No one in our outfit has gotten ratings. Somewhere along the line they forgot to assign us, so that is the trouble. By the way, did the article about the War Manpower Commission come out in the States? It came out in *The Daily Pacific,* our daily paper, that the War Manpower Commission had stated that it deemed it advisable to put ex-officers in all executive positions after the war in private industry. What do you think of that? Fine people we have in our government. Somebody must have a commission who never had anything before and be afraid of losing what little he has now. Well, enough of that. I haven't done much of anything of interest lately. Went out to the McDonalds' the other day, last week I guess it was, and wore the things you sent me. Made quite a hit with Bill. Poor guy, he couldn't take his eyes off me. There are so many sad things right now in my mind that sort of knocked me for a loop. But just yet I don't feel much like writing about it. I guess I will sometime, though. It is just that I have met a young Jewish girl not too much older than I am who is dying of cancer in the hospital. The first time that she and her husband have known any peace in 12 years. They are from Vienna and after 12 years of wandering the wide world over she has at last succumbed to the brutal treatment and starvation and will never live to see another spring. She is such a jolly, good-natured person. Her husband, Peter, is such a lovable chap and they are such good sports and show so much spunk, and it just makes me want to cry every time I see them. Well, honey, I'm in such a lousy mood that I better give you all my love and sign off. I'll try to do better next time. Love, Selene."

When the atom bomb was dropped on Japan it was the 6th of August 1945, according to our calendar. Of course, it was the 5th of August in the United States. When we got the news we were simply stunned. We understood very well the moral implications.

Some of us knew about splitting the atom. That had been around for quite a while. But the fact that we had made a bomb and had dropped it gave us very serious pause to reflect.

However, what we knew firsthand and did not have to be told, was that this would probably end the war immediately and would mean all those lists of men scheduled to be part of the invasion of Japan—my husband, Jean Ann's husband, just about all the men we knew were on orders—would not be going. What we also knew was that we would have been on orders to join them very shortly thereafter.

I remember one of the girls went to the *Bible* to the Book of Revelation to try to give a religious context to this. Most of us really couldn't quite see it. Did it change the world? Yes, it certainly did. I think we all foresaw the pitfalls and the dangers. What we never saw was what the development of the atom bomb would mean for medicine and for other things. I, myself, probably owe the fact that I'm still alive to the discoveries made in developing the atom bomb.

We did question the second bomb. In all the years since then I've had moral misgivings about it. But I do not look upon it as the immortal Armageddon. I do believe it would have been worse, far worse, had we had to fight for Japan. The Japanese would have defended their own islands in the very same way they did Manila. The loses of both Japanese and Allied forces would have been horrendous. I believe it would have wiped Japan off the face of the earth.

I have been upset over the Smithsonian's reinterpretation of history and their wholesale swallowing of "The Greater East Asia Co-Prosperity Sphere" line used by the Japanese to rationalize their actions in the Second World War.

August 15, 1945. Manila.

"Dearest Mother: Well, first and foremost, I will thank you for the bras that put in their appearance in the mail today. You never told me that you had mailed these off. Many thanks muchly for the bras. You didn't tell me you had sent them just in an envelope. In answer to your last letter, as for Baguio, the town itself was completely destroyed. But I understand from the kids who have been up there that the outskirts of town are intact and some of the lovely homes are still standing. Of course, the Filipinos did a pretty good job of looting everything but the studding out of most of those places. As for Camp John Hay, I never heard anyone say. Everything in the walled city was completely demolished with the exception of the big St. Augustine Church. I believe that is the one that, for some reason or another, was not damaged very much. Other than that, it was leveled to a building. The greatest loss of all, I understand, was the old Santo Tomas University which is now, or was, the Santo Tomas Museum. The New

Santo Tomas University, the one where the McDonalds' were interned, is a little away from the heart of the city but still downtown. Mr. and Mrs. McDonald came out to the Philippines 30 years ago from California. He was a mining man. I understand that he died about 1928, or thereabouts. Molly Junior, was born down on Cibu, I believe it was. She has never been to the States. Isn't that funny? I wasn't sure of Vivian's name when I first met him. I misunderstood it. You know how that is when you are introduced to someone. Now for the list of Christmas things you asked me for. Well, first and foremost, toothbrushes and tooth powder, and good shoe polish, brown, of course. Then food. I don't need to tell you how to pack it, but be careful because Christmas packages get rougher treatment than generally accorded the mail, and there will be many more this year with the influx of troops from Europe. Well, and then I want some lipstick, any good brand of dark, vivid red. Let Lydia get that for you. She knows about what I like. And then some nail polish, preferably Revlon. It seems to hold up better and I don't have to put it on so often. And then too, the bottle lasts a lot longer than any other brand. Revlon lipstick is what I like, too. Oh, yes, then I would like some of that new perfume that comes in a solid. It is like those little balls of pomade from Paris that you used to have. They are wonderful over here and there is no danger of breaking. Oh, yes, some short shoestrings. I have had to wrap my shoe laces around my ankles and they are nearly shot. Our PX has plenty of such things as cookies and cheap candy, but nothing useful like deodorant and Tampax. Please send me some. See if you can send it first class, a package at a time. I am desperately in need of it. Really, really desperate. And then you can send me any of the other little thing you know I like, like colored socks, pretty panties, or sachet bags. By the way, coming back to nail polish, make it a good red-red. We can wear anything in the way of nail polish that we like and we make up for the drabness of our uniforms with nail polish and socks. Most of the kids wear red socks. It looks cute with slacks. Well, I can't think of anything else. But Lydia could get you some of these little things without any trouble and she knows pretty well what I like. Of course, it goes without saying that the fruit cake last year was definitely in order, and a little dry sherry poured over it wouldn't be so bad, either. Washcloths. This letter is growing to monstrous proportions but it seems that I have slipped up on my letter writing lately. I have had some rather interesting things happen lately, but would rather not put them in the letter. You know, censorship and all that sort of thing. Don't worry, I won't forget them, so you can hear all about them when I get home. Tonight I have a date with Bob Howell, that nice chap I met on the boat coming over and went out with him in Hollandia a few times when I was down there. He's such a nice guy. I wish more than anything that Alice could meet him. He is just the kind of a guy that she would like. He is tall and quiet with a cute, dry sense of humor, particularly when he tells about his sisters and the babies. It seems that he is always getting hooked to look after them. He comes from a good-size family in upstate New York. Well, anyway, to top it all off, he is simply devastatingly good-looking with deep blue eyes, and six-feet-two. I only wish that Sis was a WAC. By the way, speaking of men, do you suppose Alice would like to correspond with Bill Fornwald. He doesn't have a girlfriend and over here they are at a premium and he writes awfully cute letters. I can vouch for that. He's awfully nice but the girls aren't much impressed because he's quite bald. But they don't know a cute guy when they see one. But he would appreciate it much.

"Well, somewhere along the line I didn't finish this letter, and several days and a lot of history has elapsed. Right now we are on the midnight shift again and are waiting anxiously President Truman's announcement. I can scarcely believe that the war may possibly be over in the next day or so. It's just unbelievable. I would ordinarily have a lot of other interesting things to write about but somehow I can't even remember much what I've been doing for the past few days. We had two false alarms and Manila went wild and got drunk, but somehow that doesn't appeal to me. I must admit frankly that this is the first time I felt like going off in a corner by myself and having a real good cry. Silly, isn't it? Well, darling, I'm going to wind this up and I guess by the time you will receive this it will be over one way or the other. Hope so."

V-J Day, Manila

August 18. V-J Day.

"Dearest Mother: While it doesn't seem possible, but it is, the war is over. Of course we had four days of celebrating before the actual confirmation by President Truman. The first night was last Friday when we heard that surrender terms had been accepted by the Japanese with limitations. I was out at the Pryors' for dinner with Colonel Hasenbush, and while we heard the news over the radio it didn't really soak in. And we were very much surprised to go home in the Jeep and find the entire city of Manila gone completely wild. The troops were down from the hills and tearing down Rizal Avenue in trucks and such a racket you've never heard. I had the hell scared out of me when somebody threw a sizable firecracker in the Jeep at my feet, but I got it out before it went off."

That was not a firecracker. Somebody pulled the pin on a hand grenade and tossed it in the Jeep. I tossed it back out. I don't know what happened to it because so much was going on I just didn't see whether it went off or not.

"Well, of course that was premature. Then Saturday, or rather Sunday morning at 1:00 a.m., the kids over here at the Signal Center let out a yell that could be heard clear over in our area. So we all piled out of bed for the second celebration. Gee, it was exciting! I pulled on my clothes over my pajamas and dashed over to the Signal Center to get any late news flashes. And that was when our country had answered

167

V-J Day, August 14, 1945

the Japanese proposals. Gosh! All the outfits in the Manila area had gone completely berserk. The sky was filled with pencils of light from the searchlight battalions. It was so pretty. And all the boats in the harbor opened up on their whistles. It was very exciting. All the whistles began to blow and the bells from San Sebastian's began to toll. That was when our flesh began to creep. Well, after things quieted down a little we went back to bed again, but whistles blew continually all night. Then began the waiting. Finally, Tuesday afternoon we got the news. We finally got the news that Japan had accepted. That was terrific. Jean and I dashed around the corner to OWI," (That was Office of War Information) "for a paper and a confirmation of the rumor, and sure enough, it was so. The Filipinos were all crowded around the gate crying for papers. They put out a red-letter extra and I have saved the copy I managed to get. We went back to our tent and sat down on our beds and looked at each other and the tears were streaming down our faces. It was just too good to be true. After almost four years of war for us, and 13 years for the Chinese, and 8 years for the British, it was all over at last. And you can't tell me the Japanese aren't glad, too. Well, now is the question of now what? For us I don't know a thing, although rumor has it that a lot of us with Civil Services experience will be asked to go to Japan, or we may just be sent. No one seems to know anything about what they are going to do with the WACs yet. We are conspicuously absent from the news. Other rumors have it those who will volunteer for duty in Japan will be given a discharge and will go as civilians. I understand that that is what they did in Germany. But it is all rumor, so as yet no one knows. But one thing, it will be a long, long time before I get home. At any rate, I haven't been in the army long enough to accumulate very many points, although I have two combat stars, which gives me ten points, which helps considerably. I certainly didn't earn the darn things, but I'm mighty glad to have them for all of that. What is puzzling me at this moment is the whereabouts of Herman Agostini. I haven't heard from him in months and I have written several letters. In fact, I write him almost as often as I do you. I don't know whether he is home. He's old enough to get out on age. I wish that you would write and see what you can get back in the way of an answer. The mail, now that the war is over, is terribly messed up. We haven't had a stateside mail since last Friday and no promise of any for some time to come. And I don't know how long it will take to get my letters to you. Well, honey, I still can't believe it is all over, but I guess you can when you see the men pouring through Union Station on their way home. That will be a happy day when I arrive at Jefferson Barracks for my discharge and can come home from the war on the streetcar. Seems funny that your daughter should serve a short hitch at the barracks when Charlie was there under such vastly different circumstances.

Well, we'll call it a day, and heaven knows when I will hear from you or what news my next letter will bear. Good night and all my love. Selene."

29 August.

"Dearest Mother: Well, here I am again. I know you think I am a meanie for not writing but at this point I'm sure you understand why it is so hard to write. Censorship regulations are still very much in effect, so I can't tell you as many things as I would like to. Of course I realize that a great deal of our restlessness and homesickness is a very natural feeling of anticlimax now that the war is over and we are all so anxious to get home. It seems as though we never will. As yet they haven't lowered the points and I am eleven short of the critical quota. So it doesn't look so good for me. Of course, other than that we have had to go into skirts and stockings are so miserably uncomfortable. And skirts look so baggy after slacks. And our tent leaks like a sieve and every time it rains every stitch we own, and all of our books, even belongings in our footlockers, get wet. And the chow is horrible and our mail hasn't been coming in regularly, so all in all you can see why we are unhappy. And of course the job is so boring that we almost go crazy. And then, too, now that the war is over the brass hats have nothing better to do than heckle the underdogs to make life just a little bit more miserable. All in all it is a jillion small things. A jillion in a day to make life just a little more like hell. Of course, there is one bright star on the horizon. Walter is back in Manila. For a few days only, that is true. But it sure makes a difference having him at all, although the poor chap feels just about like I do and indeed we do make a miserable couple. He's been suffering the tortures of the damned with a bad sinus attack with all the rain and dust. And then too in a few weeks he will be going up to Tokyo with the Allied Military Government Team, and he dreads that. I can't say as I blame him. I'm just hoping against hope that they don't send us there. I have had enough of the army and I want to get out. After all, I'm certainly not getting any younger and if I plan on going to college I'd better get started. Another thing, too, I see no point in having the WAC now that the war is over. I wanted to stay in until it was all over, but now that it is finished I'm in a great hurry to call it a day. Even all the fruit salad I have accumulated garnished with battle stars doesn't interest me anymore. Nor, by the way, the one little stripe the army saw fit to bestow upon this humble servant last week. Of course, the only reason they did is that after six months overseas and a year in the army it becomes automatic. So, I will at least have the army's deep appreciation for a job well done. Of course, I may sound a bit bitter and cynical, but don't think for one minute that I'm not. Well, there is another bright spot on the horizon and if it weren't for that I'm sure we'd all go completely stark raving mad. And that is our friends. I thank God every day for the fact that I wound up with Jean Ann and Clyta and Jan Douglas and Jimmy Hammel for roommates. They are nice and lots of fun. We have made a stove out of tin cans, the sawdust out of our beer ration and gasoline. We have been fixing coffee and toast in the evenings to pass the time. It is very pleasant because the fire keeps the mosquitoes away, but after we get in bed, unless we watch our nets very carefully, we're just about carried away. Well, honey, I know this letter isn't much, but I'm hoping that some kind senator will take pity on us, dispense with the WAC, and we can all come home. Love, Selene."

Also 29 August.

"Dearest Angel Pie: I got your letter in the afternoon mail yesterday and it certainly did come at just the right time. I wrote mother such an unhappy letter, but when yours came and we had fresh potatoes for supper, and then after supper I found that the fairies had stuck an old, beat-up 25 gilder bill in my sewing bag without my ever knowing about it, I found myself in a much better frame of mind all the way around. Of course, there's nothing like finding money that you didn't know you had. It really is funny. In the first place I'm the only one of our little family that ever has money, because I don't buy my cigarette rations and liquor, so I always have that. My only luxury is my laundry, and I don't consider as such. Well, very much against my better judgment I lent a girl $20. Of course I will get it back, but not before payday. Well, the entire family is flat broke, and so we were all going to have to do our laundry, all the skirts and shirts and everything. Needless to say, that wasn't a very happy prospect. So when I was using my sewing things to mend some undies last night I just happened to notice a piece of money folded up in the bag. When I opened it I was amazed to find that it was 25 gilders. A gilder, if you will remember, is the denomination of money that we used in the Netherlands East Indies at Hollandia and a gilder is worth fifty-three cents. So that is about $13. Happy day! So the entire family sent their laundry this morning and we are all feeling vastly happier. Also, we just scrounged a 100-watt bulb from supply in place of the 25-watt bulb that we swiped last month. So now we will have someplace to read. We aren't issued bulbs, so we have to swipe them. I have become the best little bulb snatcher you ever saw. I had a date with Walter last night and I had a perfect time. We went over to his quarters and I believe I told you before he lives with other Government Affairs Officers. Well, he still lives there and we sat around the big table in the living room and drank beer and ate cheese and crackers from a K-Ration. Their generator is on the blink so we had a candle in a beer bottle. You have no idea how cozy it was, just the two of us there, the rain falling gently on the roof and the smell of flowers drifting in from the garden below. All of his house mates had gone to the picture show, so that's why we had the house to ourselves. We talked about Camp Wallace days and sang and talked about home and sang some more. Later, when the rest of the fellows came home they joined us and then we had a real party. I don't know when I've enjoyed myself as much as that in a long time. While I'm still sleepy from the beer this morning, I have that nice, pleasant feeling that you always have the morning after a pleasant evening. I haven't much else of interest, except that this morning I picked up our paper, *The Daily Pacific,* to find staring me in the face on the second page, pictures of the steamboat *Admiral* and the showboat *Goldenrod.* I had let out a whoop that brought everybody in the office flying over to see what I was so excited about. Oh, I knew that I had something funny to tell you. The other day on our way back from the mess hall Jean Ann and I passed a Filipino with a stick across his shoulders with a basket hung on each end. The basket was of heavy wicker-work with a top on it. We kept hearing these peculiar noises and we gave each other and the baskets some very puzzled looks before we caught up with him and got close to see through the wicker into the baskets and discovered that they contained four little pigs each. Never a dull moment. Well darling, I'm afraid that it will be a long time before I get home so don't get your hopes up. But you never can tell. I will close now and be a good girl. By the way, I have never received the pictures of the baby that you said you sent. Love, Selene."

PART FOUR

It's All Over

After V-J Day, Manila

This is 31 August.

"Dearest Mother: I got your letter of the 23rd today and that is record-breaking time. That's just a week ago today. It was such a nice letter and I positively drooled at the thermometer reading 59. Lucky you. We are absolutely dripping all the time over here. It never gets any cooler, although now that we live in the tents, it is fairly cool at night. But when we have to sleep in the daytime that is absolutely impossible. We can never sleep later than ten o'clock in the morning. Of course, you can't even sit in the tent it is so terrific. Just like an oven. Walter was so horrified when I told him that when I worked on the midnight shift I didn't get any sleep but every other night. You see, since we have been in Manila they have made one concession to us that we didn't have at Base George, and that is we have to work only every other night. So one week on the midnight shift we work three nights and the next time it comes around we work four nights. The only time we write letters is on the shift at work as we never have enough to do. And then along about 3:00 in the morning you begin to feel depressed and oh, so low. You have no idea how it gets so hot and clammy. Of course, if it weren't for the fact that we do get some sleep every other night on that shift, I don't know how the girls would hold up at all. And then too, the shifts are only a week long. All in all, though, it is pretty rough because even when I sleep at night I can't get more than about five hours' sleep at any one time because when we work the evening shift from 5:00 to midnight we have to get up just the same time, at 6:00, for breakfast. And then it is so noisy you couldn't sleep anyhow. So I will be glad to get home with a decent job with some civilized hours. Right now I'm on the day shift. It lasts a week, of course. There is one thing about working the midnight shift, and that is I have plenty of time to go swimming and do the things I want to do. Otherwise I would never have a chance to do anything. I don't have the McDonalds' address yet but I will get it as soon as possible. But if I don't get it in time, would you send their things to me and then I could give it to them. I haven't been out in a heck of a long time, but they have started to clamp down on hitchhiking and that is the only way we ever had of getting anyplace. That makes me so mad because we all hitchhiked at the start of the game here when there were Jap snipers all over the place and troops down from the front and all sorts of things. But now when it is perfectly safe they won't let us do it. That is the army for you. I miss hitching rides because we always met the most interesting people that way. It was perfectly all right because the uniforms guarantee against anything out of the way happening, and then GIs give us a lot of cat-calls and so forth, but they would never do anything to hurt a WAC. And just let anyone else try it. We have to laugh. You have no idea how inordinately proud we have become over here of our American men. They give us an awful lot of trouble, but they are such swell guys by and large. I have yet to see the toughest, roughest old soldier who could resist a baby, no matter whose. When I was in the hospital the last time they had some little Japanese children that the 38th Division had found beside the road up on northern Luzon. And they picked them up and sent them down to the hospital to be taken care of. And it didn't make any difference to the guys in the hospital that they were Jap babies. Those were the most petted and indulged little kids you ever saw, and they really weren't a bit cute. Poor little things. One or two of them later died of starvation. They were too far gone when our men found them to save. Did you ever see a baby starving to death? It is horrible. They are just little skeletons like the ones you've seen the pictures of. The skin hangs on them in loose folds. I went to the hospital the other day to see one of the girls. I was so amused to hear the Jap kids greet the new day with a very American version of God Bless America. I can't help but wonder now how their parents would have felt had they been there to hear them, but those kids were getting the best of everything, and plenty of loving and petting, too. Maybe that is what the Americans have in their homes that other people lack that make the difference. Gee, honey, I will be so glad to get home where it smells nice and is clean. Every meal we have to walk about five blocks to mess and it is terrible. I don't think I have missed once on any trip seeing some grown man open his trousers and use the gutter. It is so sickening. And did I tell you that little boys here don't wear any trousers until they are old enough to go to school? I don't mind that too much. After all, they are so little. But one of the girls said the other day that presenting the facts of life to these children would present no problems, they are right there before their eyes all the time. I haven't much news except that Jean Ann's Walter came down today, much to her surprise and delight, so she took the afternoon off to be with him. I wish you could see him. What a swell guy! I'm almost as fond of him as I am of Jean Ann herself. He reminds me so much of Charlie. I guess that's the reason. I have a date with Walter tonight and I have to hurry home this afternoon to press my off-duty dress and wash my hair. I don't know what we will do, but there never is much choice so I guess we will spend the evening in his living room batting the breeze as usual. By the way, would you know how I write all your letters? I bet you could never guess. As you can see, they have been written on a teletype, but I cut a tape like the one I have enclosed and then run it through a thing called a TD and it comes out on the paper. It is much quicker than to type it out. I can cut a tape like the one I have enclosed and then I run it through. It comes out at 80 words a minute that way and I run it through the TD as I type. I can type faster than the machine works. That is probably clear as mud, but just for fun I have enclosed a little story on the tape and an alphabet to figure it out with. Hope you like it. I guess you thought it funny that I mentioned in my letter to Lydia about the letters that you had sent me. Well, honey, you may or may not remember that I mentioned something of the sort down at Base G and I guess you forgot about it, but I thought maybe coming from Lydia it would make more of an impression. But I must say that your letters, with the exception of about four of them altogether, have been just swell, particularly the ones in the last week. To come home from a nasty day at the office when a thousand and one things go wrong, and then there waiting on the bed is a swell letter from home, it makes things look so different. And you do write such swell letters. Keep them coming. By the way, tell Alice that when using the pronoun 'I', to use 'me' when the object of a verb. Well Darling, will close now. Love, Selene."

Let me make some comments on that letter. When we got to Manila we were moved into a building on the Far Eastern University Campus. The building right behind it was the mess hall, which had been a Japanese torture chamber.

Later we were moved out of that building to accommodate more headquarters offices. The occupants of the tents on campus were moved out and we moved in.

After the war was over buildings were built for us on land that had been cleared of rubble. It was a very unattractive place to live because it was just leveled rubble. That's all. No earth, no green, no shade, no anything. However, it was a nice enough building except there were twenty-four women living in it. The buildings were close together and the metal roofs made it frightfully hot as no breeze could get in. The worst part was that we were five blocks away from all of our meals, five blocks away from the orderly room, and five blocks away from work.

That meant we had to go back to having escorts to get to work and return home on the night shifts. Things hadn't been that great in the tents but at least we were close to everything and it was reasonably attractive with some shade.

It changed the whole atmosphere. Things really did turn very sour after the war ended, and as you can tell from my letter, morale was poor.

10th of September 1945.

"Dearest Mother: Well, we had some more news about coming home. Don't get your hopes up because I certainly don't want you all to be disappointed. But we had a message through tonight to the effect that men with 70 points or more would be discharged by October 1st, and that takes in Howard. And that means that as soon as his orders are out I can get my orders and get myself out of here as fast as I can. That is as it stands tonight. In any case, don't send any Christmas or birthday presents. Needless to say, we all are so excited that I promptly picked all of my beautiful manicure off. We are really wound up tonight. This is the first good news that we have had concerning getting home, and I can scarcely believe that it is possible for anything that good to happen to us. We have had such a consistently lousy deal ever since we got in the army. No rating or anything. That would mean that Jean Ann and I probably would come home about the same time, and if we have anything to say about it we will come together. I know how you feel about the divorce business, but it looks as though we will both be home to handle it in the orthodox manner, so I have one more favor to ask of you. I got a very nice letter from Mr. Noble in the mail day before yesterday asking what he should do about things now that the war is over and the possibility of us coming home imminent. Well, honey, would you mind giving him a ring on the phone as soon as you get this and tell him just what I've told you? Tell him to do whatever he thinks best, that as soon as I know any more I will let him know and you, too. Keep all of this under your hat until I can tell you something different, and don't, please, darling, get your hopes up because you know the faculty the army has for changing its mind, and really this all sounds too good to be true. Somehow I can't think it would work this way. I haven't done much of anything of interest lately. Walter has been in the hospital for over a week now and I've spent every afternoon and evening with him. He has the same old sinus trouble that he's had ever since I've known him. He's getting along very well now so I expect he will be out very shortly. I was interrupted, but I guess that is all that is important, so we'll close for now with lots of love and kisses for everyone. Love."

11 September.

"Dearest Mother: Well, nothing more about the points has been heard since I wrote you day before yesterday on the subject, so I don't know whether things will work out that way or not. But knowing the army I'm afraid I doubt it, but we will see. My, you should have been in the mess hall today. They've been flying the girls up from Oro Bay yesterday, and today and all the rest of the Monmouth gang has been arriving all last night and today, and the rest will be up tomorrow. What a happy reunion. You never heard so much yelling and screaming in all your life as there was today as each new truck-load of girls arrived from the airport. It has been nearly a year since we saw them last, although we've kept up with them pretty well through letters from the whole gang. God help the officers now that the whole crowd is together again. Walter is still in the hospital, although I think he will probably get out in a day or two. Of course, that will be a very mixed blessing because he has to board a ship for Tokyo as soon as he gets out of the hospital and I won't see him again for heaven knows when. Not until we get back to the States at any rate. And the United States is a pretty big territory, but the future will tell. I guess if fate stepped in and arranged things for us to be together such a long time in Manila, certainly something will come along. Gee, it will be lonesome without him, though. It is amazing how dead things have become since the war's end. Doesn't seem possible that so much could be stopped so quickly. Oh, by the way, I got the first of the boxes of Tampax today and just nicely timed, too. By the way, did you notice these letters are no longer censored? It is so funny, during the year that I knew all my letters were being read I thought of a dozen nasty things I would loved to have said, but now that they are sealed and only you read them, I can't think of a single thing that wouldn't pass the censors. Of course, things have changed considerably and things that seemed terribly important at the time have been relegated to history and will be related as such when I get home. And so it goes. Gee, I haven't done anything of interest in such a long time. I have positively nothing to write about. I spent a very quiet afternoon sewing today. This is the first day that I haven't been out to see Walter, but in the afternoons he has to take treatment for his sinus and I can't see him anyway even if I do go out. However, tomorrow morning I am going to try my luck on making the visiting hours to suit myself and see if I get thrown out. Hope not. Although I have been pitched out of better places than the 80th General Hospital since my advent into the army. Well, I'm rambling on like an old wreck, so will wind up for now and tell Alice I hope that something better works out than going back to nursing. I know it will be a big disappointment to her, although I will say that I was wondering how she would get along at Ashenbrenner's. They have never had a good reputation as to their business dealings, and that usually indicates that the relationships with their employees leaves a lot to be desired. And if Sid Senior is anything like Sid Junior this is understandable. I always thought he was a little nasty snip. Well, bye for now. Love, Selene."

This is 17 September, 1945.

"Dearest Mother: Well, Angel, how are you this morning? Nothing much new in the way of come-home news to report, except that is was announced that as of October 1st the critical score for WACs will be reduced to 36 from the 41 it is now. That will put me right in there with my 40 points, so it looks as though I may be home in time for Christmas. So start saving sugar. Well, Walter is still in the hospital, although he was quite a bit better yesterday afternoon when we went out. Jean Ann and I have tomorrow off and we expect to hitchhike up to San Jose to see her Walter who is in a field hospital up there with a mild attack of malaria. San Jose is about 90 miles from here and quite near the little town of San Fernando, which is where we went when we first came here to Manila. You remember, of course, then I couldn't tell you where we went. By the way, the opportunity I've been looking for has finally presented itself. We are planning a trip to Baguio. A doctor at the hospital, who I have gone out with once or twice, has been transferred up there to help open up a new Leave Center at Camp John Hay, which is to be open the 10th of next month. So he said yesterday on a trip down here that he could put us up in the nurses' quarters up there, and so I think we will go up some time next week when we can get time off. Because we just possibly might not still be here the 10th of next month and that is one of the places I particularly wanted to see. It is very difficult making arrangement for such trips because we have to find places to stay and, of course, the only means of transportation is left thumb. Another place I want to visit before I leave is Corregidor. I've made several attempts to get over there, but something always comes up to spoil it and I wouldn't dare show my face at home without visiting that spot. Well, that is about all the news. Oh, for goodness sakes, I almost forgot a most important piece of news. I got a letter yesterday from Van and it was datelined somewhere in the Pacific and he said that probably he would be here before the letter got here, but I don't know yet. I went to the port command yesterday, but it wasn't on the board yet, so I have a friend watching the call board for me to let me know when his ship arrives in the harbor. Terribly excited about seeing him. Van has always been one of my favorite friends. Seems funny that I should run into so many of my old friends over here so far away from Camp Wallace. Poor Van, though, from his letter he is expecting something quite different from what is actually here. He's used to seeing ruin and destruction in Europe, which is nothing to compare to this. After all, the only places you can get good food and good liquor here are in the mess hall and the officers clubs. However, I think I can do pretty well and show him a good time. As I say, though, nothing to compare with the stuff they could get in Europe. From the sounds of the letter, though, he isn't half as interested in the city as he is in seeing me. Although I am very, very thin, I haven't changed much. Well, dear, I will close now and write you again day after tomorrow and tell you about our trip to San Jose. It should be quite interesting."

The next day we took off hitchhiking. When we didn't find Walter at San Jose we continued on to the central highlands of Luzon Island, up the Cagayan Valley.

It was a cold, rainy and muddy day in the mountains as we hitchhiked from one place to the next asking about Walter Bowman. Around noon we got out of a Jeep we had caught a ride in and were about to enter a building when a convoy of American trucks carrying Japanese prisoners of war pulled up to the junction near us. We watched as the prisoners were getting out of the truck. They were in appalling condition. They were ragged, dirty and starving.

When you take prisoners of war under the Geneva Convention the actual administration of authority over them is exercised through their own officers. A Japanese officer was standing by the back of the truck as the prisoners were climbing down. One of the enlisted men did not move fast enough to suit the officer. He grabbed him and began beating him as he fell. The officer kept slapping and when he was on the ground he kicked him hard.

Jean and I, who were standing only 10 or 15 feet away, looked at each other in disbelief. She said, "Treacy that man is dead." That officer had kicked a dying man. I know the Americans found this difficult to deal with and certainly this American did.

We went in to have lunch with the local outfit. The guys were always glad to see us. Unfortunately we had to return to Manila before we could find Walter. Later we learned his illness was minor and that he would not be sent to a station hospital.

I have more to say about the Japanese. Officers looked all right, not great, but they were not starving and were fully clothed. The enlisted prisoners were skeletal and were in rags.

The officers often had their families with them so the American troops found Japanese women and children who had been left behind in the mountains. In one of my letters I write about the condition of the Japanese babies found in the Cagayan Valley. When I was in the hospital with the intestinal parasites in the summer of '45 I shared a shower with Japanese women who had been brought down from the Cagayan Valley with some of the children.

I stood in the shower staring at these naked women in shocked disbelief at their physical condition. They were so skeletal you could see every bone in their bodies. The breast tissue was entirely gone. The breasts were like two little flaps of skin, the same with the buttock. Even the pubic hair was scant. Why didn't these men send the women and children home, I don't know.

In later years I heard that the Japanese men on Saipan threw the women and children over the cliffs to avoid capture by the Americans. You would have thought they could have thought of something else to do with them.

25 September 1945.

"Dearest Mother: I had to laugh at you reading that letter on the street car. Didn't you cause some curiosity hauling out a thing like that in public? I'll admit my letters aren't very pretty, but can you see me writing that much in longhand? I can't. First about Christmas and birthday present. I hope that you haven't sent them because I am reasonably sure that if I am not home by that time I will be well on my way. By the by, today I made T-5, which is another form of Corporal. High time, isn't it? I will probably get one month's pay for all the time sweating out this miserable setup. Of course, right now I'm on the midnight shift and things look pretty grim. And I'm rather soured on life, because when we went over to eat at midnight the coffee looked like the Mississippi at flood stage and tasted just about the same. And the bread was in two-inch hunks and nothing but peanut butter to put on it. We are supposed to call that a meal, because according to army regulations, personnel working from midnight on are supposed to get a meal in the middle of the night to make up for the one they don't get at noon. Well, needless to say, I wouldn't feed a self-respecting pig the stuff they shove at us and actually expect us to eat it. Frankly, I am damn sick of going to work hungry. And about the magazine subscriptions, the *Time* has always come through but I have not always received the *Reader's Digest.* I will be home before any of the magazines could reach me, anyway. I'm glad that you liked the little story about the parrot. I thought it was pretty funny, too. I can just see that old parrot with a lecherous look in his eye. They're evil-looking birds, anyway. Well, Angel, I haven't done much of anything outstanding lately, outside of a big washing tonight. I'm so tired and feel like the wrath of God, so I'd better sign off. I just wanted to let you know that I was still around. That letter of the 13th was so good! I read the part about my letter out loud to the kids and they got quite a kick out of it. Good night, honey. Love, Selene."

I sent several letters and they all got to her but some didn't survive. As a matter of fact, several letters were lost after the war and I think it may be that we gave them to people to read and simply didn't get them back. I think the letter about the trip up in the Cagayan Valley must have been one of those letters.

27th of September.

"Dearest Mother: This is going to be a short one for now. Well, if nothing comes up between now, 2:00 a.m. and 7:00, I will be flying up to Baguio by eight o'clock. I'm very excited. I almost thought this afternoon it was all going to fall through. Jean Ann isn't going and so I have to go by myself. But a gang from the hospital is going, so I will have company and a chaperone or what have you. I was afraid that he wasn't going to be able to make it and I wouldn't risk going by myself. After all, there are limits to what fool stunts even I will pull off. Right now things look pretty messed up for the kids getting home on the September quota, so heaven only knows what will become of us poor, low-score people. But I still expect to be on my way by Christmas. Rumor has it that all WACs will be out of the Southwest Pacific by the first of the year. I hope that is right. There would certainly be no excuse for anything otherwise. I guess you notice that I've finally gotten a rating. Not much, but better than telling everybody that after eighteen months I was only a PFC. And that is a gift from Congress for long and faithful service. I had a very sad piece of news today that has sort of knocked the props out from under me. Van lost his mother in May. He thought he would see me and be able to tell me in person, but we missed each other so he wrote it to me in a letter. I wondered why none of my letters to her had been answered. I feel so badly about that. She was one swell person, and for poor Dr. Van Woert to lose both wife and mother on the same day must have been almost too much. Well, dear, nothing new, so we'll wind up for tonight. Just a note to tell you that I'm still alive and kicking, but sometimes I wonder how or why."

One day about this time I was standing in the ticket line at a theatre downtown when all of a sudden I felt a light-touch feeling on my hair. My hair was long and to meet army regulations I rolled a handkerchief up and tied it around my head with a bow in the front. My hair was tucked in all the way around. That way it was off my collar which met regulations.

I turned around to see a tiny Negrito woman behind me softly patting the roll of hair on my neck. She was all smiles with a fascinated look on her face. She was patting my hair to see what it felt like. A lot of these people had never seen red hair. I ran into this a lot in both the Philippines and New Guinea.

This is October the 21st. Manila.

"Dearest Mother: Well, long time, no write. It isn't because I didn't have anything to write about, but I had a deal on the fire, so to speak, and didn't want to say anything until I knew if I had something definite to report. And I do, so I guess I will tell you. It seemed that the Associated Press needed some people over here pretty badly and I applied with another girl from this office, Margaret Rose. Then when the wire went through to New York for authorization, no women, and that was the end of that. I didn't particularly want to stay over simply for the sake of staying over, but the chance of getting in as a foreign correspondent with no experience or further ado was too good a chance to miss, and I took it. Well, that was the end of that. We were hoping to get to Shanghai. I figured that if in six months things looked as though they were going to settle down, and living conditions were such that I could get an apartment or a house, I was going to get you to come over. Oh, well, it was a lovely idea. I have another offer from a paper in Honolulu, but I'm going to think that one over after I get home and can see things in civilian perspective. If you want to go to Honolulu we can think about it, but I promised myself that I'm not going out of the States again for any long periods of time again without you. Of course I know that if I want to go abroad again that you will always be glad to come along. That is an unalterable premise, that you're always game for anything. I've often thought and said that I wish you could be here. Not that I would wish the hardships off on you, but we've had some of the most fun. And you would have gotten such a big kick out of all the hitchhiking around. Well, to get back to the subject at hand. If something else outstanding turns up in the way of a writing job, I'm afraid that I will be forced to take it. But don't worry, it will have to be something as good as the Associated Press one would have been for me to consider staying in the Orient. But rest assured, if I should, you will have your name put on the first available passenger list coming over, and Alice, too, if she's interested. You know, in a way I hate the prospect of leaving the Orient now with so much going on. I would like to stick around and see just what is going to happen. I'm afraid that England is going to have some real trouble on her hands. You know the Dutch and French colonial policy has left a great deal to be desired, and if she has to defend theirs along with her own, there is going to be a lot of rough stuff over here. And she will, because in this part of the world the imperial policy was not popular. I wrote a letter from New Guinea criticizing the Dutch policy in New Guinea and the letter got handed back to me by the censor. But the natives in New Guinea hated the Dutch much worse than the Japs, and the fuzzy-wuzzy angels made fine reading, but wasn't always the case. The natives did a great deal in the way of spy work, *et cetera*, for the Japs.

"Just as an example, we saw a native boy about nineteen years old in one native village. He was a very bright, intelligent looking chap and could speak a little English. They called him Number One Boy. He had scars all over his arms at regular intervals, and when we asked what they were, we were informed they were cigarette burns. And we naturally surmised that the Japs had done it and said as much—and were told that the Dutch had done it—that every time one of the men was late that was the punishment. They had a system that you were quite familiar with: Commissary Store. They paid the natives eleven dollars a month, or thereabouts, and charged them eleven dollars for a pair of cotton khaki pants or some other necessary item. And of course the poor native could never have quite enough money to make ends meet. And they were required to work for the Dutch and required to wear pants and required to buy them from the Commissary Store. So you see just what they were up against. Comparatively little effort has ever been put in to rid the country of malaria and other tropical disease, or give the natives medical attention—some, of course, it was sound business practice to do so. But they had malaria so terribly and beriberi and all the other indigenous tropical disease, yaws, and so forth. For natives the idyllic life of the South Seas isn't idyllic at all, but disease-ridden and poverty-stricken and bowed down with superstition. So if the Dutch are that way in New Guinea, I see no reason to think they are very different elsewhere. I don't know what the British have done. I haven't been long enough in British territory to find out. I give them the benefit of the doubt. Vivian Skues and I have had some very heated arguments about British foreign policy. Theoretically his points sound fine, but I'm afraid that I have seen too many imperial politics to be very much impressed. The situation in India looks pretty bad and everyone knows that the Mohammedans and Hindus can't seem to see eye-to-eye. But you know yourself that if it were to Britain's advantage to have them see eye-to-eye, something would have been done a long time ago. After all, America has pretty well had the same situation in the Philippines, and on the surface, at least, settled it to everyone's satisfaction. But frequently it is to her advantage to play both ends against the middle. Well, so it goes. If I'm a little verbose tonight it is because its the midnight shift and I have nothing else to do. By the way, you asked me if I could tell you just what has gone on, things I couldn't get past the censor. I will be home soon and I can tell you much better than writing. And believe me, there are many things that time has not softened. By the way, a year ago today was the landing on Leyte, and the beginning of the end of the Japanese empire. By the way, Ross is here in Manila."

Let me comment here. Ross Brooks was a friend of mine from my high school days.

"And we went out the other night and had such a good time. He hasn't changed a bit. It just seems like old times. I was pretty sad to learn of the death of so many of the chaps that I used to see out there at Creve Coeur Lake sailing had been killed and were buried around the world. It is hard to believe that it has been seven years ago last summer that we made those trips out there on the streetcar. Ross is stationed on Corregidor. I'm expecting to make a trip out there real soon, as soon as I can get a day off. This past week has been pretty busy. I spent quite a bit of time down at the Associated Press. Even if I didn't get the job, I certainly met some swell people and heard some interesting tales from their war correspondents down there. Also, the USO team that stayed with us in Baguio is in Manila, so I've been out two evenings visiting with them and batting the breeze. I ran into Molly McDonald Junior in the building the other day and find much to my surprise that she is working right here in the same building. Sometime I will tell you why Jean and I quit going out there, but in all justice to everyone that will wait, too. I've seen Vivian twice downtown, and met him for lunch one day, and he is still waiting for his replacement to get transportation up from Sidney before he can go home. But he is planning on stopping over in St. Louis and maybe I will be there then. I hope so. It would be more fun. As for when we are leaving things look very discouraging. They didn't give a damn how they sent the WACs over, but they are sort of touchy about how they send them home. And they have girls sitting around the Disposition Center from the August quota. And the gang was relieved from evening the 12th and are still sitting in the area because the Disposition Center is too crowded for them. So there you have it. The chances of our getting home by Christmas look pretty slim but I am still hoping. I will probably spend Christmas someplace on the high seas. Naturally you can guess the temper of the WACs as a whole about now. Discipline has absolutely gone out of the window. The officers don't give a damn what the kids do and would be afraid to do anything if they did. It is pretty disgusting to see the holy mess things are in. Jean Ann put in a request for discharge two weeks ago and they lost it. They wouldn't let her take it through channels herself, and so now she has to get in contact with Walter's outfit and start all over again. Not only did they lose the durn papers, but they have taken the attitude, 'Well, isn't that just tough, sister? What are you going to do about it?' Well, everyone's tempers are a little edgy these days, so I guess I better sign off. By the way, the McDonalds' address"—and I give it—"same as mine. Well, say a little prayer for me that I will get home by Christmas and in time to get in on the midterm at some college. All my love, Selene."

I talked earlier about going to Baguio. Baguio was the summer capital of the Philippines, and was 200 miles or so north of Manila on Luzon, in the mountains. It was a gorgeous place. Unfortunately, the letter I wrote to Mother about Baguio was one of the letters lost after the war.

Anyway, I said in one of my letters in late September that "If all goes well I'll leave tomorrow morning for Baguio." Well, all went well and I did leave. I went with the major from the hospital. We went to the airport and hitched a ride to Lingayen. Lingayen was where the original landing on Luzon had taken place. They came ashore there and then came down Highway 3, towards Manila.

We flew as far as Lingayen and from there I was on my own. I hitched a ride part way up the mountain then hitched another ride in a truck and went as far as the truck went. I remember standing on the road all by myself. Nobody was around. I was totally alone. I thought, "Great Scott, suppose nobody comes? Am I going to be able to walk the rest of the way to Baguio?"

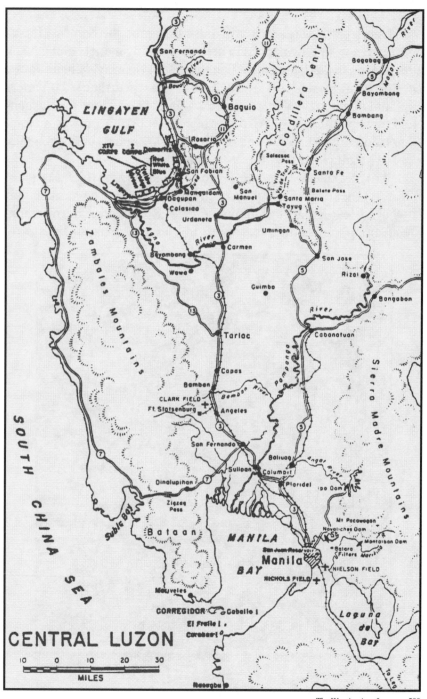

CENTRAL LUZON

10 0 10 20 30

MILES

I started walking. I had my musette bag on the harness. It was not very heavy and I was used to it. I was walking merrily along when a Jeep came by and gave me a ride the rest of the way. When I found Dr. Robinson, he was still on duty. I didn't stay in the nurses' quarters as planned, but in the general's guest house. There were several generals there while I was. Also sharing the guest house was a small USO troop. I got to know one of the guys pretty well and when they were in Manila later they looked me up.

We had General MacArthur's former chef and the food was good! It was another case of army chow in the hands of a true master. This is where I learned all the things you could do with a fresh lemon. Fresh lemon, with a little seasoning on a lamb chop is superb.

Road to Baguio, Philippines

Triumph in the Philippines, p. 469

The downtown part of Baguio was totally destroyed. The Japanese had done to Baguio pretty much what they did to Manila. But the houses in the surrounding hills were too widely spaced for the Japanese to have gone around destroying them one by one as they did up and down the streets of Manila so the countryside was lovely.

It reminded me of northern California, wonderfully cool and misty in the morning. The difference between Baguio and California, of course, was that there were orchids. In the garden of the guest house there were orchids in wooden baskets hanging from all the trees. I was fascinated.

Dr. Robinson made house calls among the Igorots who were the native people in that area of Luzon and had been pro-American. You could not say the same for all the other indigenous people. There were areas where the collaboration between Filipinos and Japanese had been serious. The Igorots were quite primitive, but very bright— they had been the ones who kept the power plant operative. When the Japanese came they disabled the plant and simply disappeared into the mountains. No Igorot that I ever heard of was caught or taken prisoner by the Japanese.

But when the Americans were back in Baguio, just as mysteriously as the power had gone off, it came back on. Whatever they had done to the power plant, the Japanese never figured out and I don't think the Americans ever understood either. The Igorots had a high rate of tuberculosis. I don't know why, but it was rampant. Dr. Robinson, who was a gentle man, a great guy and a very good doctor treated the Igorots in their remote homes.

One day he said, "Treacy, do you want to go?" I answered, "Sure." So we got into his Jeep and he asked me to drive, which I thought was great. I hadn't driven anything since I'd left the States. I drove until he pointed to a spot on the road and said, "Stop here." I looked around and there was nothing. I said, "Here?" He said, "Yeah." He had a grin on his face from ear to ear.

"Come on, I'll show you." He led us on an absolutely invisible path down the hill. At the base of the hill was the Bued River. It was a raging white water torrent, pouring into the Gulf of Lingayen. He said, "We're going to cross here," as he pointed to a two rope bridge with wooden slats between, but no handrails, strung across the river. Dr. Robinson was not a young man. He was probably in his late forties. He walked right across as if it were nothing. I thought, "Treacy, old girl, if he can do it you sure can." So I did exactly what he did. I just took a deep breath and walked straight across, didn't look down, didn't stop. If I had stopped, I'd been dead.

We went to a little house of poured concrete. It had two rooms and virtually no furniture. Inside I was invited to sit on the floor in what was the living room. There were several people sitting around dressed in native garb. The Igorot women and some children wore brightly colored clothes that reminded me very much of Navajo Indians.

Dr. Robinson treated his patient and we left. I said my prayers, held my breath and went flying across the bridge again.

In Baguio, Saturday was market day. The market was off limits for GIs, and that included me. However, generals could go wherever they wanted. One of them asked me, "Would you like to go to the market?" "Yes," I answered.

"Look. I'm going to tell you why it's off limits for GIs, and if you think you can't handle this don't go." It was the dog market. Igorots raise dogs for food. "You will see people buying dogs and carrying them off yelping and howling and they will eat them." I said, "Well,"— I swallowed hard—"yeah, I still want to go. Yes, I can handle it." The market was large enough that I didn't see where they were selling dogs, however, I could see across the crowd to where it might be.

What I did see was a young Igorot girl, probably about eighteen, dressed in native dress so much like the patterns I had seen in the Southwest worn by the Navajo. She had a little pig for sale. That little pig had been scrubbed to within an inch of its life. She had him in a covered basket but while she was taking him out to hand him to someone, the pig got away. Quick as a wink that little pig scooted right between my feet. I clamped my ankles together and caught him between my field boots. You never heard such squealing. That was one unhappy pig. I reached down and picked up that squirming, struggling, furious little pig, and handed it to the girl. We exchanged glances and it was one of those incidents of perfect communication. We both burst out laughing. We stood there with the pig between us laughing our hearts out. That was one of the high points of my adventures in the Philippines. Sometimes if something is funny, it's funny the world around.

While I was in Baguio I suddenly spiked a high fever. Dr. Robinson came to the guest house to look me over and said, "You have strep throat, a real beaut." This was my first experience with penicillin and I've never forgotten it. People tend not to remember that fifty years ago when penicillin was first available it was a thick, viscous substance that had to be refrigerated. It took a big needle to make it work and you got it in the hip. I tell you, that hurt! Dr. Robinson called my CO down in Manila to tell him I wouldn't be back at the end of my three-day pass. I was there about six days in all.

When I was well enough to return home, Dr. Robinson was not pleased at my simply going to the road outside Baguio and hitching a ride to Lingayen where I planned to catch a flight to Manila. So he drove me down to the airport in the Jeep. Again he asked me to drive. This trip I discovered why he was so anxious for me to drive, the clutch wasn't working worth a darn and he didn't want to fool with it. He wasn't a very mechanical guy for a doctor. There were times going down that mountain when we were out of gear and simply went flying down the road and hoping we wouldn't meet anyone. How we got down safely I've never known and I assume he got back to Baguio all right because I continued to receive letters.

At the airport I wasn't having much luck hitching a ride south. Finally I found a plane heading north into the mountains to a place called Bagabag. Even though it was the wrong direction, I asked for a ride. The crew asked if I was a nurse. They couldn't tell from my uniform because none of us wore insignia, even the officers didn't wear their bars.

"No, I'm not a nurse, I'm a WAC."

"Well, can you take a pulse and blood pressure and temperatures?"

"Yeah. Sure I can do that." I'd had first aid.

"Well, look, we're going up to Bagabag to pick up a load of Igorot TB patients and take them down to the hospital in Manila and could use some help."

I answered, "Sure, I can do that," and jumped into the C-47 as it was taking off. Onboard there was just me and a couple of guys. The floor of the plane was a piece of plywood. There was nothing else in the plane, not even seats. On the floor in the back of the plane was a Coleman stove where the crew sat cooking breakfast as we flew over the mountains of Luzon.

These mountains were certainly not the Himalayas, but they were high for the rest of sea level Philippines. We circled around until finally they said, "The landing strip is down there."

I looked out and said, "Down where?"

They pointed and replied, "There." What they pointed to was no landing strip. It was a meadow of tall, yellow, sun-bleached grass about two feet high. We landed and had lunch with the small American unit there, then took off with a full plane load of Igorot TB patients.

Those poor patients. I felt so sorry for them. They were all wrapped up in blankets and the most I could do was hand them cups of water and keep them tucked up in their blankets, but they were miserably cold. Holy mackerel, it was cold up there! Upon landing in Manila they were taken away in ambulances and I never knew where they went. But they probably went to Santo Tomas Hospital.

The Igorot's hadn't engaged in direct combat for the Americans, but, boy, did they harass the Japanese. They were headhunters who had reverted to type during the Japanese occupation. They got out their bolo knives and kept them sharp. The rumor was that they did take Japanese heads if they could catch them.

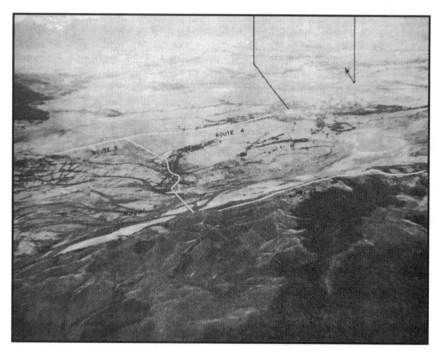

Bagabag, Philippines

Triumph in the Philippines, p. 464

Return to the United States

26 October 1945.

"My Darlingest Angel Pie: Well, as of today my army career is finished. We received orders and were relieved of duty today and it looks as though Jean Ann and I will be coming home together, I hope. Our orders came as a complete surprise. We never expected them so soon. In fact, we were told the other day that it would be doubtful if we got home in time for Christmas. And now it looks as though we will be in the States for Thanksgiving and my birthday. Needless to say, we are wild with excitement and I started going through my stuff tonight giving away things that the kids who are staying can use. The two playsuits that I made and my yellow housecoat went to Nada Smatlick who came overseas with us and has been one of our favorite partners in crime off and on ever since Oglethorpe. She needs them and I've gotten plenty of wear out of them. And then, too, it is sort of a WAC custom to give things away. I have the most conglomerate collection of other people's clothes you ever saw. We started putting our ribbons and stuff that goes on our uniform together, too. I have the Philippine Liberation Ribbon and the Southwest Pacific Theatre Ribbon, and the little red job for being a good kid, or rather not getting caught at being anything else. I have two battle stars, too. Thank heavens for those. That is ten much-needed points. Without them I would be putting in quite a few more months over here. And then my Corporal Stripes and the two little Gold Overseas Bars. About the uniforms at home; don't worry about them. They are mine now. In all the rush and mess of all the moves we have made, and everything I have lost, about three sets of clothes, and then the mess, those things are no longer charged to me and I will be issued new ones tomorrow to wear home. I'm planning to make a suit and an odd jacket out of those two I have at home. That lovely material, dyed chocolate brown, would last forever, and I have no compunction whatever about keeping them or the coat. By the way, did I ever tell you that the flannelette pajamas were for you? I guess I couldn't because of the censor. Well, as of now they are, so get them out and wear them. They will feel good on a cold night, and you always did like those kind. We are rabidly looking through old issues of *Mademoiselle* and *Vogue* that by some mischance found their way over here. I don't think much of the clothes and think I will make do with what I have for this season, with maybe a few additions. I see no reason for rushing around spending money just because I will have three hundred bucks, or three hundred dollars mustering-out pay. Of course, I'm wondering about my black suit. If you need it that's OK, and Alice may keep the black Chesterfield coat. I have no doubt but that she needs it. And I will have the field coat. I hope it will be ready by the time I get home. This is a terrible letter. I'm using a borrowed typewriter perched on my knees, and the whole thing reflects our surprise and exhausted state of mind. We can't believe that we are actually all but on our way. Of course you understand that we don't leave tomorrow or anything like that. In fact, it may be a couple of weeks. But at least we are on orders to the States, which is something. Well, I could go on in this mad vein indefinitely, but it is sort of silly, so I will close. One thing, one of the girls has very kindly offered to send cables to our families the day the ship leaves so you will have a vague idea about when to expect a call from San Francisco. Jeepers! Even thinking of that big ol' ship steaming into San Francisco Harbor and seeing the Golden Gate Bridge again, and then the train trip across the country, gives me cold chills. I could almost throw the typewriter over my head and dance the Highland Fling. Honey, fourteen months away from the good ol' USA is one hell of a long time. Bye for now. No doubt I will be able to write a more coherent letter tomorrow or the next day when the first shock of surprise wears off. Of course the usual rumors are rampant, having us leave Monday, *et cetera*. But when you quit hearing from me and receive that cable, then start the ice cream freezer rolling and kill the big red rooster; your wandering progeny is on her way home. Love, Selene"

Well, that was the last letter. The only correspondence between then and the time I arrived back in St. Louis were four telegrams.

It was twelve days between the time I wrote that letter and the time we sailed out of Manila Harbor. I went around and told everyone good-bye, all my Filipino friends, the men who were not leaving this soon, and I made one last trip to the McDonalds. I don't remember very much about our last days in Manila. I guess the excitement of going home just wiped them out of my memory.

In 1950 Nada Smatlick and I became neighbors in New York. She had come back on a later shipment than me because she was one of the Signal Corps WACs who had been in Base B and didn't have the campaign stars I did. She said that the months after my group left, the Message Center was in a state of collapse.

In reading Mattie Treadwell's book about the Southwest Pacific Area WACs, the day before I wrote my last letter she cites a cable written by Colonel Boyce, who was the Director of the Women's Army Corps sent by the Army Chief of Staff to investigate the dreadful situation of the WACs. The cable stated, "I recommend all enlisted women in this theatre be enroute USA for discharge or reassignment not later than 1 January, 1946." She goes on to say that she "was disturbed by the poor health of members still on duty, most were underweight, and all were highly fatigued." Well, that was an understatement. The book goes on to say, "A final problem was presented. The shipment of the women to the United States." Colonel Boyce, while still in the theatre, found the first large group already boarding the *Evangeline* for return. The ship appeared unsuitable, vermin-ridden, ill-ventilated, with men obliged to walk to mess through the WACs' sleeping quarters. The women's physical condition left much to be desired. They had no woolen clothing such as was issued to men for a comparable voyage, the original clothing in which they arrived having long since deteriorated in distant warehouses. However, Colonel Boyce was unwilling to stop the shipment in view of the crowded state and poor housing, the scarcity of ships of any sort, and the women's eagerness to get home. She radioed her office that she was "extremely disturbed at the condition of the women and feared that they will make a very poor impression upon their communities unless their general condition can be improved upon their arrival."

Well, I have a couple of comments on that. From my last two letters you can tell that we knew pretty much what was going on even though we didn't know the details. I think the reason we were on orders so quickly without any warning—usually there were rumors—was that Colonel Boyce's cable to the War Department had results. When I said the army was getting very fussy about the ships they sent the women home on, the ship that we got certainly showed that. Also the fact that we were being issued new, wool uniforms. We were not issued coats at that time. However, we were landing in November and it really wasn't going to be that cold. I suppose if we'd needed coats we would have gotten them in San Francisco.

We were astonished to board the big naval transport ship, *The General John Pope*, to find that we were displacing field-grade officers for their quarters on the top deck with lovely staterooms. There were four to a room but it was very comfortable, with lovely bathrooms, showers, and hot water. These were the first hot showers we had had in fourteen months—since we had left Camp Stoneman. We were served three meals a day in the Officer's Mess with china, silverware, linen tablecloths and linen napkins. We had sheets and white, fluffy navy towels. Oh, boy, such luxury! We reveled in it. We also had a lounge which we shared with the officers. It was beautiful and comfortable and you could go out on the deck and walk up and down. It was a glorious trip.

It really is funny when I think about the exchange of cables that must have gone between Colonel Boyce and the War Department. Somebody must have scooped us up to make a gesture by putting us on *The General John Pope*. We were a fairly small group of women. There were nurses, WACs, and some civilians—a kind of mixed bag.

There were about five thousand troops, most of them enlisted men, below in regular troop quarters. Unlike regular passenger liners, this ship had been designed as a troop transport. The men were crowded, but were much more comfortable than the men had been on the other ships where they were simply down in the hold. Traveling in the hold is awful because holds are not designed for people, they are designed for cargo and so have absolutely zero ventilation, as I can attest.

We sailed north out of Manila and stopped at Yokohama where we picked up more passengers, some very interesting ones. Some were the nurses who had been on Corregidor and had been imprisoned in Tokyo. We also picked up some male prisoners and one very interesting prisoner of war, a young sergeant who had married the daughter of the Turkish ambassador.

Their story was most romantic. She had been on the street when the American prisoners from the Bataan Death March had been paraded through downtown Tokyo. She spotted a young American sergeant in the line and was able to give him a note to say who she was. Somehow she found out who he was, maybe he had been able to whisper his name. By virtue of being the daughter of the neutral Turkish ambassador, she was able to see him and be seen by him. She spoke perfect English but they were not allowed to talk, however, they did exchange notes. She smuggled in food and medicine to keep him alive.

After the war she and her father, the ambassador, were there to meet him when he was released. They simply took charge of him. The day before we picked them up they had been married and so she was able to go home with him. The captain, bless his heart, gave up his quarters to them so that they, for the first time, were alone together. We didn't see very much of her. But when we did, what a nice person. Of course we WACs were dazzled at the story and at her bravery.

There was also the daughter of the Swiss ambassador traveling with us.

One morning while in port I saw Mt. Fujiyama rising up through a cloud cover and was very excited. The closest I ever got to Japan was the dock at Yokohama. From there we headed for the Aleutian Islands.

One night not too far from the Aleutians we hit a Northern Pacific winter storm. Was it a beaut! We kept hearing the ship's bell. The ship would heave and the bell would ring, and the ship would heave again and the bell would ring again. Well, the captain's quarters were just down the passageway from us. He had finally had enough, and so he had the ship come about so someone could go out to tie the bell down. When that great ship came about in the high wind, dishes crashed. You could hear them. We were up on the top deck and could hear everything that went on. We swore up and down every dish in the place was broken. It was one almighty crash! At breakfast the next morning we were amazed to find we were eating off dishes. They must have had a nearly inexhaustible supply. That same maneuver to tie the bell down knocked nearly everybody out of bed and the next morning there were a lot of black-and-blue people.

There were two highlights of my military career. One of them was Christmas Eve 1944 and the other was landing in San Francisco. The ship was fast. We sailed on the 8th of November and landed in San Francisco on the 22nd of November. It was Thanksgiving Day morning. We came into the roads offshore about eleven o'clock the night before.

Nobody went to bed that night. We knew we were landing the next day and it was going to be Thanksgiving. Everyone was pressing uniforms and making sure we had all of our fruit salad on and the brass polished before lying down to rest. Finally we heard the engines stop and the anchor chain dropping, that wonderful sound that sounds like nothing else, the clank, clank, clank, clank. The tension on the ship was palpable.

About four in the morning we heard the engines start up again and heard the anchor being raised as we prepared to head into San Francisco Bay. All of us were already up and dressed and so we ran to the top deck. Jean and I and some of the other Signal Corps WACs traveling with us went to the prow of the ship to watch the dark shoreline turn into the beautiful necklace of lights that was the Golden Gate Bridge. Just as we steamed under the bridge the sun came up behind San Francisco and we were home.

Jean and I turned around to look behind us and the entire superstructure of the ship was a mass of young soldiers. I think every one of the 5,000 troops was up there hanging on somewhere. As we steamed under the bridge such a roar went up it's a wonder it didn't take it right off the cables.

In the harbor we were met by fire boats with colored sprays, a ferry with a band on it and all kinds of people who had come out in little boats and individual yachts on that glorious Thanksgiving morning to escort us home.

The first to be unloaded were the women, the nurses from Corregidor, the WACs, and the other army and navy nurses. As we walked down the gangplank the troops on board cheered us. All the thanks I would ever need was the gratitude and the appreciation of my fellow soldiers.

The dock was a mob scene. Newspaper photographers were there and parents who knew their kids were on that ship, and parents who had come just to greet anyone's kid. There was a bus waiting and we were whisked off to Camp Stoneman where we had an emotional Thanksgiving dinner. We had an awful time eating, but, oh, boy, did we appreciate it! I still have the menu from that meal. After dinner I sent Mother a telegram and then we just wandered around and looked at those beautiful California hills.

I don't remember very much about our stay at Camp Stoneman. I remember Jean and me going into San Francisco for one weekend and staying at a hotel where I got a good look at myself in a mirror for the first time since basic training. Mirrors were nonexistent in New Guinea and Manila and the mirrors in the staterooms aboard *The General John Pope* weren't very big and the light wasn't good. I burst into tears at how awful I looked.

We Southwest Pacific WACs all came back looking pretty bad. Our worst problem was atabrine, which caused our skin to be lemon yellow. We were terribly thin due to poor diet and lack of fresh foods. I had two white wings in my hair and I could rub my teeth together and powder them off.

Another day we went into Oakland and went into a supermarket. It was absolutely wonderful. The manager saw us come in and there we were, two Southwest Pacific WACs with all our ribbons. He said, "What would you like?" He was about to give us the store. All we wanted was lettuce. Jean took the head and pulled it apart and we luxuriated in munching it. We had had virtually nothing fresh for fourteen months. That head of lettuce was heavenly. We wandered up and down the aisles luxuriating in everything, things we hadn't seen for so long and had missed and thought of the people back in Manila who had nothing.

We went through a physical but I remember very little about it. As I said in one of the telegrams to Mother, we were held up at Stoneman for five or six days before a group of thirteen or fourteen of us was sent to Fort Des Moines, Iowa, to be discharged. We came back on the Old Northern Pacific route. I'd never gone that way. All of my trips out west had been on the way that we went out, the Missouri-Pacific, the D&RGW, and whatever else it was, Western Pacific and Southern Pacific.

About halfway across the country, Captain Bleaker, who was our escort officer, came to me in the car and said, "Treacy, you're not supposed to be on this train."

Looking up I asked, "Well, ma'am, do you want me to get off at the next stop?"

She continued, "I don't have your service record."

I was floored. What the hell was she telling me this for? It was her responsibility to carry my service records. Believe me, if we had carried our own I'd have had it. She had gotten on the train without checking records against people and here we were halfway across the country when she discovers she has a WAC with no service record. There was nothing to be done about it at that point, but I was furious, absolutely furious.

Jean Ann was on the train with me and we said good-bye when I got off at Fort Des Moines, Iowa. She went on to Fort Dix, New Jersey.

We arrived in Des Moines in the middle of the night and, of course, were fed, we were back in the States. When you travel you get fed. So here we were at 4:00 in the morning, or some ridiculous time, having breakfast. I crawled into bed in an upper bunk. It was dark and I hadn't seen any of my new surroundings.

The next morning when the lights came on I looked across and was astonished to see a black girl in the bunk opposite me. I must have looked startled because this lovely girl looked over and burst out laughing. She said, "Ma'am. We've been integrated."

For purposes of discharge, the WACs did integrate but we had never been integrated before and the army didn't officially integrate for another couple of years.

She had been there several days and was waiting to get discharged. She had been secretary to the commanding general of Fort Huachuca, Arizona, which she told me was an all-black post. Of course, in those days they called it Negro. She showed me around and I enjoyed her thoroughly. For me, a southerner, this was a totally new experience. But you know, to be in quarters with a black WAC, after all I'd been through, was pretty small potatoes, even for a southerner.

I remember very little about Fort Des Moines except the WACs from the Southwest Pacific were treated strangely by other WACs who were being discharged from state-side duty. We were the only overseas WACs being discharged at this time because all of the European WACs were already out. Here we were, with campaign ribbons and battle stars while our fellow WACs had good-conduct medals. We must have looked pretty fierce. We were all so thin and yellow and grim. I've seen pictures of myself in the year following my discharge and I had a somber look. There is no two ways about it, my expression had changed. So its no wonder people were a little afraid of us.

One morning a group of us who had come on the train together were in the mess line together. We'd gotten our food together, we'd eaten together and we got up to leave together. Someone from our group had taken oatmeal, which turned out to be burned. Burned oatmeal is not edible. The mess sergeant who was standing by the line where we were dumping our trays together started to give this WAC a hard time about not eating her oatmeal. Together, those of us from the Southwest Pacific surrounded the sergeant and silently stood there. We didn't say a word but we must have been threatening as hell because the mess sergeant said to this hapless WAC, "Oh, go on." When we got outside we looked at each other and collectively realized we had just pulled a very new kind of rank.

Well, everyone on my orders had been discharged and sent on their way and old Treacy waited. And I waited. And I waited. I knew perfectly well what had happened. It was that lost service record.

The morning of the sixth of December I decided I'd had enough. I walked to the orderly room in perfect uniform and saluted smartly. Politely I said, "Ma'am, tomorrow is my birthday, and if you want to find me"—I had written my name and address on a piece of paper and I put it on the desk very politely and said, "here's where I will be. I'm going back to quarters and pack." I saluted, did an about face, and walked out.

I had scarcely walked in the door of the barracks before a sergeant came in on my heels and said, "Come back to the orderly room." I went back to the orderly room where they proceeded to put together the discharge record I have to this day. I don't know if my service record ever showed up but I went through all the procedures and was released that day with a plane ticket from Des Moines, Iowa, to St. Louis, Missouri. I sent a final telegram to my mother and caught my first civilian flight into Lambert Field.

I arrived in St. Louis at 11:50 the night of the sixth of December. By the time I arrived at my mother's house it was early morning of my birthday. I had taken a taxi and was so excited I handed the driver a twenty dollar bill and headed for the house. He came running after me and said, "Hey, wait a minute. You've forgotten your change."

The porch light was on and I was absolutely astonished to see on the door, inside the window, the white star on the red and blue background indicating this house had someone in service. It was the first sign of recognition I had received from my mother regarding my soldiering. The house was full of chrysanthemums. I was welcomed home.

Return to Civilian Life

In order to understand the origins of the difficulties service women met when returning to civilian life after the Second World War, it is helpful to consider the demographic background.

In 1940 the population of the United States was in the neighborhood of 160 million people. Of that number, one in ten was in uniform during the war. Of those only 2.3 percent were women, or roughly 350,000.

The need for more persons in uniform was desperate, but that need ran right up against two strongly held views of the American people, one was an intense aversion to women in uniform and the other was an equally strong aversion to conscripting all able-bodied persons for war work.

The British had had to do it. The elderly in Great Britain were out at night as aircraft spotters. However, there was one significant difference between Great Britain and the United States. The enemy was right there, and the people were willing to do what it took to safeguard their own territory.

Hawaii, Alaska, and the Philippines were the principal USA territories that had been attacked by the Japanese. To most Americans those places seemed remote. But virtually all Americans were one hundred percent behind the war effort after the bombing of Pearl Harbor. Still there were limits to what they would give up in the way of strongly held views.

But in order to fight a world-wide war, it was essential to get women into uniform, and so the WAAC was formed. Within a year the WAAC was plagued by rumors and slander against the women in uniform. It was so serious it resulted in investigations at the highest levels. Mattie Treadwell devotes an entire chapter in her book to the Slander Campaign.

At first it was thought the slander campaign was an Axis plot to restrict the country's ability to recruit women to replace men for service in combat. However, as a result of the most thorough of investigations it was found that the Axis didn't need to raise a finger, the American people did the job all by themselves.

Rumors originated everywhere, and most people were willing to believe them and to repeat them. Such things as, the WACs are recruited to serve the officers overseas. A shipload of five thousand pregnant WACs just returned from North Africa to Fort Devens, Massachusetts. (There were never five thousand WACs in North Africa!)

Those rumors in all their virulence were still being repeated and believed when the women returned home. While overseas, particularly in the early days, we had been spared the worst, but after the war in Europe ended and troops came from there to the United States, they brought the rumors with them.

This was more of a problem for the War Department than it was for individual WACs. The slander campaign resulted in the Women's Army Corps having a hard time recruiting. Many women who probably should have been in the army weren't because they did not want to buck the tide of disapproval on the part of men.

My June 9th letter reflects some of that. Obviously my mother must have repeated something of the sort to me making me apprehensive upon my return home.

No one in the family confronted me directly about this slander, but there was a coolness between us that kept us from discussing any part of my service. Years later my brother admitted that he had heard and had believed the worst about the women in uniform.

Because my family and I did not discuss these rumors, my mother went to her grave in 1973 never having heard anything about my war service other than what I had written to her in my letters. She never wanted to hear anything more about it, and she set the tone for the rest of the family.

My sister, Alice, died in 1968, and the same applied to her. My brother, Charlie, after the death of his wife in 1987, on a visit to my home in New Jersey, said to me, "Sis, can you ever forgive me?" He wanted to hear everything and we must have talked nonstop for several days.

Finally, he said to me, "Selene, I am so proud of you. I never knew."

I replied, "No, Charlie, you didn't, and you lost your baby sister for forty-five years." Happily, in the remaining four years of his life we regained everything we had as children: the jokes, the confidences and the companionship by telephone.

On the professional level, my return to civilian life was shielded by my two years as a GI student at Washington University between 1946 and 1948, where the veterans had virtually taken over the campus.

However, when my GI Bill ran out, and I needed to find a job, I found it was virtually impossible. There were two factors operating: one being a female veteran and the other was the secrecy of my work. I had nothing on the record to show for my service.

So, when, in the spring of 1948 I moved to New York and was told to my face, "We don't hire ex-WACs," I took that part of my army service off my resume. I simply put down "Clerk Typist, 1941–1945, U.S. Army" and that was the way it stood for the rest of my professional life.

Epilogue

Service in the Southwest Pacific Area was known as the toughest assignment for women in the entire Second World War. According to Mattie Treadwell, the Pacific Theatre Headquarters first asked for WACs the same day I joined the army, February 11, 1944. The first WACs arrived in Sydney, Australia, in May, four months later. To move troops halfway around the world, particularly female troops, to an area where there have been no female troops, takes a lot longer to do a decent job planning than four months. In other overseas theatres there had been a year between the time the WACs were requested and the time they actually went. This is true of both North Africa and the European Theatre.

The entire span of time WACs were in the Southwest Pacific Area was from May 1944 until January 1946 when the last ones left from Manila on *The West Point* in January 1946. The entire history of the Women's Army Corps in the South Pacific is less than two years.

Unlike North Africa, Europe, and the other theatres where women were, the Southwest Pacific Area was spread from Australia to the Philippines, including the intervening islands creating a horrendous supply problem for all groups from beginning to end. There were small units of men stuck on small islands. I well know this because my husband was in one tiny place in the Philippines. They got supplies only when a little boat stopped by and dropped them. With just 5,500 women in an absolute sea of men, supplies for women got lost in the shuffle.

Those of us in the Signal Corps were sending all the messages back and forth and understood this perfectly. Consequently, we were able to handle the supply problems well.

The bitterness and anger that we often felt, as reflected in my letters, was directed against the individuals at the local level who did things that made our lives pure hell. We tolerated poor supplies, poor food, long periods without mail, long hours and hard work, heat, humidity and filth. Those were things nobody could do anything about.

For myself, I never forgot that I volunteered. I was old enough, sophisticated enough and well read enough to know that war is hell and I fully expected it to be and it was. But gratuitous interruptions of sleep, inadequately prepared food, senseless regulations such as no more hitchhiking in Manila or requiring skirts when we didn't have the proper underwear; those were the things that were very hard to take and they were the things that engendered rebellion.

It is clear from my letters that I was pretty philosophical about the things that no one could help. The things that could be helped, we tended to help ourselves through improvisation and sponging off our male friends.

Actually, conditions may have been harder for the officers than for the enlisted women. There were so few of them and they had virtually no support. They were responsible for the enlisted women and there was very little they could do for us.

I complained and griped about the small stuff. I was no different from anyone else and I certainly was no paragon of virtue on that score but by and large I was glad I was there. I never for one instant was sorry that I had joined but most importantly I felt I was making a measurable difference in winning the war along with all the others.

However, after V-J Day, the bottom fell out of morale, including mine. It was a result of the war ending so much sooner than anyone expected. We were geared up to go into Japan and then we didn't. No one was prepared for what to do with the WACs. Our discipline and morale reflected this.

Another important aspect, and I can only speak for myself on this, of my adaptation to the army was that I was very much a woman of my time. I did not question the differences in treatment between men and women except on obvious things. I say in one of my letters that I was so angry that men had been given decent clothes, six to eight sets of khaki shirts and pants and we had been given none. That I thought was pretty discriminatory, but when I applied for the job with the Associated Press and they wouldn't hire women, I didn't consider that they necessarily should have. At that time, I thought this was entirely within their prerogative. This belief saved me a lot of heartbreak.

Women had always been treated differently. My treatment in the army was so much more liberating than anything I had previously experienced that, comparatively speaking, I thought the army was pretty great. Given the context of the time, I still do. Our treatment by the Signal Corps was unfailingly professional and dignified and made working with the Signal Corps a joy. I don't think I would have done as well in the army had I been in another service where we were not treated as professional women.

I wrote once about the men causing us problems, explaining that they whistled and made catcalls. But at no time in my experience, either as a civilian in the army or in my service career, did I ever experience anything remotely like what happened to the women at Tailhook. I think the times for us were different. There was always a degree of decorum, and even the roughest soldier didn't treat his female colleagues that way. It was unthinkable. Yes, they whistled or yelled, but we were used to it; we laughed it off, and went on our way. It was not anything that we took personally, or that we thought was anything more than mildly insulting. We had other things more important to think about and so it just rolled off.

My army experience sent me home with a strong sense of accomplishment. I knew both from my training experience and what I was able to accomplish in my work experience that I could do anything I wanted to do in the way of education or training. As a cryptographer I was an essential component to winning the war and it gave me a sense of self-esteem and an inner core of strength I would never have gained otherwise.

When we came home, meaning all veterans of the Second World War, we had won the war. We were proud of it. We were proud of how we had won. The millions of returning young people not only had a sense of accomplishment, they also shared a very clear dream.

They wanted to come home and start a family; statistics tell us that is exactly what we did. We started families with a vengeance.

Remember, we were the generation that had grown up during the Depression, and so there was a backlog of unmet civilian needs, the like of which this country had never seen. We came home by the millions needing housing, washing machines, cars, diapers, and everything else. The country got off to a roaring start fulfilling those needs.

Most of us in one way or another over the years did realize our shared wartime dream. The little house on the hill, the white-picket fence, the three children in the yard, the dog, and the mother in the kitchen. Even we women who had been soldiers didn't question that dream.

This dream comes through very clearly in my letters; however, I was not interested in being married at that point. I was more interested in getting an education, something that I never would have done had it not been for the army.

When I married a second time in 1954, I reverted back to this post-war dream. I put my career plans on hold and sailed into having children, keeping house, and all that was our dream.

In our rush to fulfill this dream we didn't pay close enough attention to the downside of the war experience for individual soldiers. We arrogantly expected soldiers who had experienced the worst hell man can imagine to, without missing a step, pick up this dream.

Most of us simply walked away from war. In a letter to my mother I talked about what was going to happen and it seems to me I was prescient on that one. We did not, and this includes me, talk about our experiences. Our attitude was, "it's over, forget about it, go ahead and live your life." For thousands of veterans this didn't work and their needs were not dealt with by either the Veterans Administration or society as a whole. As a result, there are still World War II veterans who suffer from post-traumatic stress disorder.

How does this compare with the returning Vietnam veterans. They didn't come home in a wave of euphoria created by winning the war. Instead, they returned as a despised minority. Over the intervening twenty years, little by little, we have dealt with some of the Vietnam veteran issues. We are acting more quickly with the problems of the Desert Storm veterans. Are we doing it adequately? Probably not. But at least we recognize the problems are there.

This was never done with returning World War II veterans. We never recognized there were problems. Everything was considered peachy keen and you were expected to fit right back into civilian life. I can tell you, it didn't work that way.

I personally never had the conversations I so longed for with my family. In a sense I shared their same attitude because I never forced the issue. My mother said, "It's over with. It's in the past." She never understood the changes that had taken place within me. I had been gone four years but mother never recognized this and neither did the rest of my family.

For other veterans it was exactly the same. My family was not very much different from everyone else. And I wasn't much different from other veterans. We met our financial obligations and material needs as a generation but did not meet our psychological needs at all.

Howard and I divorced in 1946. About 1955 we had a legal problem that needed solution and my lawyer located him. Other than that, I never knew what happened to him.

My last contact with Jean was in the early '80s when I asked her and Walter to write letters for me describing my health problems in the South Pacific to support my application to the Veterans Administration for service connection for those problems.

The only other person I had contact with was Dallas Townsend. I kept track of him until the 70s. He continued as a newscaster for CBS radio and when he retired in the 80s there was a program about him on TV. When he died in the mid-90s that program was re-run.

Other than that I have had no connection with any of the other Signal Corps WACs. I think the reason for this is that, unlike the men, it was not in the best interest of women veterans to maintain an identity as a veteran and so we simply forgot about being veterans.

Even though I applied for veterans' health benefits in the early 80s, I didn't take up my veteran identity until the mid-80s when I was granted compensation for my service-connected health problems. I then became a member of the Disabled American Veterans.

But I didn't feel the pride of being a veteran until I was handed a sheet of paper by another female veteran at the VA Hospital in Durham, North Carolina, telling about the women's memorial in Arlington, Virginia. The memorial has changed everything for me. Since that time I have gotten the disabled veteran's license plate to which I am entitled and display proudly. I have made speeches about my experience and spent a wonderful week as an honored guest at

Fort Gordon, Georgia, which is now the headquarters for the Signal Corps.

That week went a long way toward undoing the anger and bitterness I found buried under fifty years of silence about my experience. Since then I have dusted off my miniature medals, and wear them with great satisfaction on appropriate occasions.

With the writing of this book to answer my son's question, I have gone full circle to the pride and joy I felt that Thanksgiving morning in 1945 when I sailed into San Francisco Bay.

Justification

To those who ask, "Why did you join the WAC?"

I am a WAC,
One of thousands.
We like the sound of the Four Freedoms,
(But we heard the incessant chatter of Machine guns,
And the ominous sound of strange names.
Guadalcanal, Bougainville,
Coral Sea, and the Soloman Islands.

Then the country called,

And we came—

We came overseas too.
Sure—Sweat has a stench
So do blood and plaster casts.
It rains like hell here.
And fox holes fill up quick.

But the country called,

And we came—

Yes, we like high heels, soft lights and a Scotch and Soda
But the pulsing rhythms of the Conga became the sounds
    of distant cannons.
The muffled sound of footsteps on the carpet
Were the faint soft sounds of a Jap shifting his position,
And the tap of our shoes, the click of shells.

And then the country called,

And we came—

So to those who question,
You had a good job
Why did you join?
The tropics is no place for women,
Didn't you know?
Sure we knew, that and a whole lot more.
But I have seen the white crosses at Buna.

And I am proud

That when my country called

I came—

Selene H. Treacy
May 1945

To Harold

What was it like, my friend,
To die,
For your country?
You with the hair
Like Kansas wheat in the sun.
Was the water cold,
Closing forever
Over your gallant head?
Was there no warning?
Didn't you know—
When you buzzed the base,
And gaily flapped your wings
So I would know
That it was you.

Yes,
I like to think
That you knew.
That the nose of your flying boat
Was not turned out to sea,—
But to some celestial
Landing Strip.
And that when the war is finished,
And my soldiering is done,

I will find you there,
Forever young.

Easter 1945
Selene H. Treacy

Night

Out of the East glides the Night,
Shod in velvet, gray and white,
Clad in robes of rose and blue,
Trimmed in deepest midnight hue.
At her heels the milky way
Pursues the saffron shades of day.

Then with her court, the gleaming stars,
Heralded by the glittering Mars –
She moves in state across the sky,
Receives a crown, the moon on high.
Now on her head is a royal mark,
For she is Empress of the Dark.

Selene H. Treacy,
On board SS *Maui*,
At sea, April 19, 1945

To Army Public Address System

How I hate that damned P.A.
Disturbing my thoughts in that insolent way,
Like an omnipotent being
Hades born,
Sent to plague us night and morn.

Written in stark desperation on board
the SS *Maui*, Selene H. Treacy, April 1945

On Passing Palau at 7:00 AM

The sea lies in calm undulations,
The sun, not yet risen
Tints the eastern sky pale lemon—
High above the ship

Describing an exuberant arc
Wings a bird.
Whence come this tiny celestial creature,
Wheeling so joyously
In the gray morning sky?
Who charts his course
Across the infinite span of heaven?
What motivates his homeward flight
As evening dims the light of day?

Aye, it is the same benevolent hand
That guides our footsteps through
Chaos and carnage and bleak despair,
Then flings across the sky
The glorious mantle of morning
To sustain our hopes
With its beauty and grandeur.
It is he who plots the paths
Of Man and Beast
Of Creatures of the Sea
And the stars in the sky.
He is the Master at the helm,
The Divine Skipper of the Universe.

Selene H. Treacy
At sea, SS *Maui*,
April 20, 1945

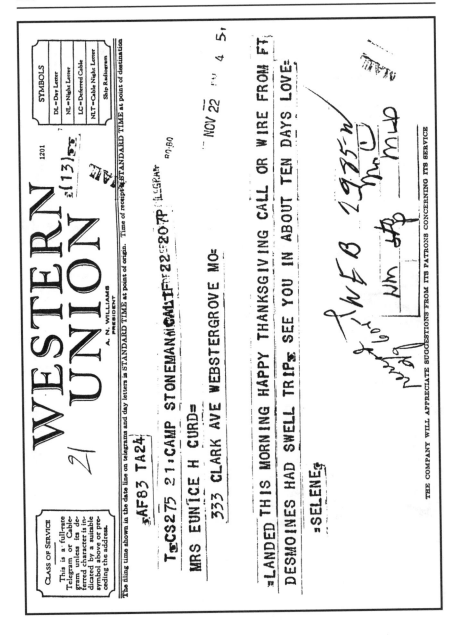

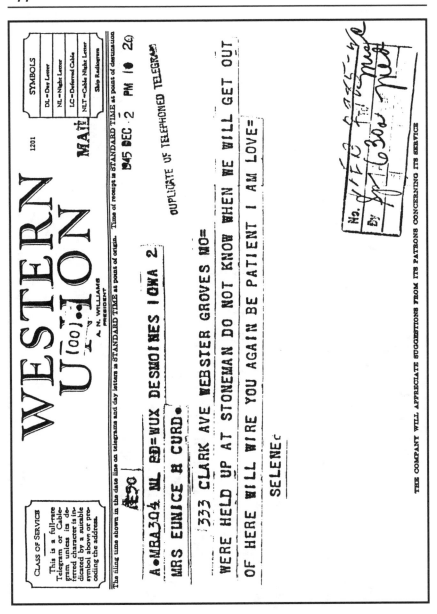

WESTERN UNION

A. N. WILLIAMS
PRESIDENT

CLASS OF SERVICE

This is a full-rate Telegram or Cablegram unless its deferred character is indicated by a suitable symbol above or preceding the address.

1201

SYMBOLS

DL = Day Letter
NL = Night Letter
LC = Deferred Cable
NLT = Cable Night Letter
Ship Radiogram

The filing time shown in the date line on telegrams and day letters is STANDARD TIME at point of origin. Time of receipt is STANDARD TIME at point of destination

1945 DEC 2 PM 10 20

A·MBA304 NL RD=WUX DESMOINES IOWA 2

DUPLICATE OF TELEPHONED TELEGRAM

MRS EUNICE H CURD·

333 CLARK AVE WEBSTER GROVES MO=

WERE HELD UP AT STONEMAN DO NOT KNOW WHEN WE WILL GET OUT

OF HERE WILL WIRE YOU AGAIN BE PATIENT I AM LOVE=

SELENE·

MAIL

THE COMPANY WILL APPRECIATE SUGGESTIONS FROM ITS PATRONS CONCERNING ITS SERVICE

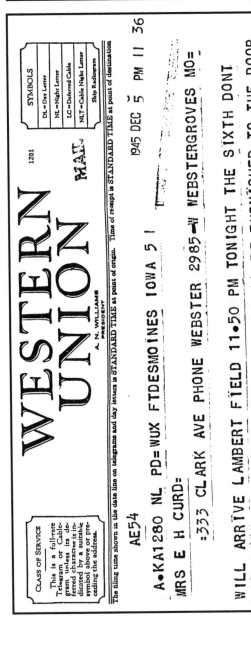

Appendix C—Military Documents

USASOS SIGNAL CENTER
APO 707

11 January 1945

SUBJECT: Recommendation for Appointment as Warrant Officer

TO: Whom It May Concern

1. Private Selene H. Treacy, A-810828, is at present assigned to this signal center, and has worked as a message center clerk under my direct supervision for the past two months.

2. EW, who is also a cryptographic technician, has at all times impressed me as being capable, conscientious, and eager to perform her duties in the best way possible.

3. It is understood that, prior to enlisting in the Army, EW occupied a responsible administrative position at Camp Wallace, Texas.

4. Recommend that Private Treacy be considered for appointment as Warrant Officer, JG, in the field of either signal communications or administration.

DALLAS S. TOWNSEND, JR.
1st Lt, Sig C

SEE INSTRUCTIONS ON BACK

APPLICATION FOR APPOINTMENT AS WARRANT OFFICER

...BASE..G.,..APO..565...........
(Place)

...11..JANUARY..1945...........
(Date)

FROM............TREACY............SELENE............H............A-810828............
(Last name)   (First name)   (Middle name)   (Army Serial No.)

PRESENT ADDRESS...5222ND..WAC..S.U.,..APO..565,..C/O..PM..SAN..FRANCISCO,..CALIF...
(See par. 7 of instructions)

LEGAL RESIDENCE.....333..CLARK..AVENUE,..WEBSTER..GROVES,..MISSOURI...........
(Number and Street)   (City)   (County)   (State)

To: The...COMMANDING..GENERAL,..BASE..G,..APO..565,...........
(See par. 4 of instructions)

I hereby make application for appointment as...WARRANT OFFICER (JUNIOR GRADE)
TECHNICIAN (CRYPTOGRAPHIC)............(See par. 5 of instructions)
...ADMINISTRATIVE(CLERICAL-GENERAL)..ADMINISTRATIVE (SUPPLY)...........

In connection with the application I submit the following information, as called for herein, together with inclosures as required by pertinent Army Regulations and as indicated in paragraph 3 of instructions on page 4 of this form:

1. Are you at present or have you ever been a member of any of the following? Army of the United States, Regular Army, Officers' Reserve Corps, National Guard, Enlisted Reserve Corps, Navy, Marine Corps, Coast Guard?......YES............If so; state which, giving dates of service, organization, and grade.
(Yes or no)

WAC..FEBRUARY..1944..TO..PRESENT..SIGNAL..CORPS..PVT...........
(See par. 6 of instructions)

2. In what town, country, and State (or foreign country) were you born?......NATCHEZ,...........
MISSISSIPPI...........

3. On what date were you born?............DECEMBER............7............1921............
(Month)   (Day)   (Year)

4. Are you a citizen of the United States?......YES...........
(Give date and submit proof in case of naturalization)

5. Are you white, colored, oriental, or Indian?............WHITE...........

6. Are you single, married, divorced, or a widower?............MARRIED...........

W. D., A. G. O. Form No. 61
August 19, 1942

(7)

385TH MEDICAL SERVICE DETACHMENT
UNITED STATES ARMY SERVICES OF SUPPLY

APO 565
12 January 1945
702.6   NMK/mm

Subject: Physical examination

To   : Whom it may concern

1. The following named enlisted woman, Pvt Selene H Treacy, A-810828, was this date given a preliminary physical examination and was found physically fit to qualify for a Warrant Officer appointment.

2. Upon receipt of Laboratory and X-ray reports, complete WD AGO Form No 63 (Report of Physical Examination) will be forwarded.

NOAH M KOENIGSBERG
Captain M. C.
Commanding

WAC SERVICE UNIT
HEADQUARTERS USASOS

APO 707
13 January 1945

SUBJECT: Warrant Officer Recommendation

TO   : Commanding General, United States Service of Supply

1. It is recommended that Pvt Selene H. Treacy, A-810828, be considered for appointment as Warrant Officer.

2. Pvt Treacy was a member of my detachment from 7 November through 15 December 1944. During the time I found her to be very cooperative, honest and industrious. She was a good soldier and amendable to discipline and orders.

3. It is my opinion that as a Warrant Officer she would be most efficient and dependable.

ROSEMARY M. GUILD
1st Lt., WAC
Comdg

WAC DETACHMENT
Base "G", APO 565

26 January 1945

TO: Pvt Selene H. Treacy

    1. Attached hereto is your application which failed to meet the requirements of the Board of Officers.

    2. It is suggested that you retain this application and, if you so desire, resubmit at a later date.

FRANCES A HARDISTY
1st Lt., WAC
Commanding

HEADQUARTERS CAMP WALLACE
OFFICE OF THE TRANSPORTATION OFFICER

In reply refer to:

TC 230.

WNM/gld
Camp Wallace, Texas.
28 January 1944.

To Whom It May Concern:

Mrs. Selene H. Treacy was employed at Camp Wallace, as a Civil Service employee, from 1 May 1942 to 1 November 1943.

Other than for the first six (6) months, she was employed in the Passenger and Troop Movement Section of this office, and her work was under my personal supervision for that period of some fifteen (15) months.

Mrs. Treacy was a very efficient and faithful employee, and her duties involved a high degree of technical knowledge and detail handling. Her work was mainly on her own initiative and the responsibilities with which she was charged were always very efficiently performed.

Upon request of the Gulf, Colorado and Santa Fe Railway Company, Galveston, for assistance and recommendation in locating an employee capable of handling railroad passenger tariffs and tickets, Mrs. Treacy was recommended for the position to enable her to progress, and it is understood that her services with them have been very satisfactory. The severance of her services here, therefore, was due only to her efficiency, and the confidence which was placed in her.

For duty in United States Government service, or in civilian enterprise, she is heartily recommended. In the event of enlistment in the Women's Army Corps, it is believed that she is definitely Officer material, and would prove an asset to public service.

Yours very truly,

W. N. McKINNEY
Major, Transpn. Corps,
Transportation Officer

Bibliography

———. *Papuan Campaign: The Buna-Sanananda Operation, 16 November 1942–23 January 1943*, Center of Military History, United States Army, Washington D.C., 1990.

Dod, Karl C. *United States Army in World War II, The Technical Services, The Corps of Engineers: The War Against Japan*, Center of Military History, United States Army, Washington, D.C., 1987.

Fowle, Barry W., general editor. *Builders and Fighters: U.S. Army Engineers in World War II*, Office of History, United States Army Corps of Engineers, Fort Belvoir, Virginia, 1992.

Holm, Major General Jeanne, USAF (Ret.). *Women in the Military*, an Unfinished Revolution, Presidio, Norato, California, 1982. (Revised.)

Smith, Robert Ross. *United States Army in World War II, The War in the Pacific, Triumph in the Philippines*, Center of Military History, United States Army, Washington D.C., 1993.

Thompson, George Raynor, Dixie R. Harris, Pauline M. Oakes, and Dulany Terrett. *United States Army in World War II, The Technical Services, The Signal Corps: The Test, (December 1941 to July 1943)*, Office of the Chief of Military History, Department of the Army, Washington, D.C., 1957.

Thompson, George Raynor, and Dixie R. Harris. *United States Army in World War II, The Technical Services, The Signal Corps: The Outcome (Mid-1943 through 1945)*, Office of the Chief of Military History, United States Army, Washington, D.C., 1966.

Treadwell, Mattie E. *United States Army in World War II, Special Studies, The Women's Army Corps*, Center of Military History, United States Army, Washington, D.C., 1991.

Weise, Selene H. C., Ph.D. Letters and telegrams to her family, and miscellaneous military correspondence and orders. The Archives, Women in the Military Service for America Memorial.

Index

229